RETURN TICKET

RETURN TICKET

One hundred and one stories
of long-term unemployed people
who successfully made the
journey back to work

edited by
HARTLEY BOOTH MP

assistant editor
MARK MALLON

Supported by an all-party group of MPs
and sponsored by over thirty companies
and Her Majesty's government

Lennard Publishing

Published by Lennard Publishing
a division of Lennard Associates Limited
Mackerye End
Harpenden
Herts AL5 5DR

© 1994 St Luke's Trust

ISBN 1 85291 123 9

All rights reserved. No part of this publication may be reproduced, stored in a retrieval system, or transmitted, in any form or by any means, without the prior permission in writing of the publisher, nor be otherwise circulated in any form of binding or cover other than that in which it is published without a similar condition including this condition being imposed on the subsequent purchaser.

A catalogue entry is available from the British Library

Cover design by Cooper Wilson
Editors: Caroline North, Kate Truman, Mark Stephenson, William Hodge

Printed and bound in Great Britain by
Butler & Tanner Limited, Frome and London

CONTENTS

Introduction by Hartley Booth   7

The Case Studies
List of case studies   10
Key to geographical locations   14
Index of jobs and activities   16
Self-employed (starting successful businesses)   18
In Employment (winning new jobs)   74
Special Needs   110

The Directory
Contents list   123
Organisations that can help   124

A glossary of abbreviations   207

WHERE TO START

1. Look through the lists and index on pages 10-17 to find the story of a person closest in location and/or situation to you.
2. Check the Directory for the contact details of any of the agencies that helped the case studies in part one and which can help you.
3. Don't forget the banks (see page 124).
4. Take heart and take new determination.

ACKNOWLEDGEMENTS

The editor acknowledges with thanks the financial contribution of the following companies towards the research, development and distribution for this project:

ARCO Chemical Europe, Inc.	Lloyds Bank plc
Barclays Bank plc	Marks and Spencer plc
Berwin Leighton	Midland Bank plc
Blue Circle Industries plc	National Westminster Bank plc
The Boots Company plc	North London Training & Enterprise Council
British Urban Regeneration Association	
BT	Norwich Union Insurance Group
Cadbury Schweppes plc	Pentland Group plc
Carlton Television Limited	Prince's Youth Business Trust
East Midlands Electricity plc	J Sainsbury plc
Eastern Electricity plc	Shell UK Limited
Ford Motor Company Limited	SmithKline Beecham
Forte plc	South West Water plc
GrandMet Trust	Tesco plc
Healthcall Group plc	Training and Employment Agency (NI)
John Laing plc	TSB Group plc
KPMG Peat Marwick	WH Smith Group plc

Support for this project has also stretched across the political spectrum with MPs from all three major parties having played a key role in its development. Particular thanks go to the Chairman of the Employment Select Committee, Greville Janner QC MP, Glenda Jackson CBE MP, Sebastian Coe OBE MP, Harry Greenway MP, Nick Harvey MP, Ernie Ross MP.

Thanks are due to successive Secretaries of State for Employment, Gillian Shephard MP, David Hunt MBE MP and Michael Portillo MP; the Secretary of State for Wales John Redwood MP, Scottish Office Minister Allan Stewart MP and Northern Ireland Minister Tim Smith MP; all of whom have lent their time and/or support to this project.

Finally, last but not least, thanks go to the team of researchers and writers who chased, visited, phone and followed up every lead to find the right examples to put in the book. Most important has been the skill, patience and tenacity of Mark Mallon, who has spent a year as assistant editor and joint fund-raiser for the venture.

This book is a 'not for profit' undertaking and all royalties are being donated to charity.

INTRODUCTION

Return Ticket is for the long-term unemployed. The writers have talked to hundreds who have returned to employment from lengthy periods on the dole. A hundred examples have been chosen to show how climbing out of the unemployment rut has been achieved. Some learned new skills. Many successfully created their own job with their own business. The stories of how it happened are told simply and shortly, demonstrating how people won their way out of one of the worst of all misfortunes.

It is an important account because it is not just one more reference book but a set of true narratives through which it is impossible not to feel encouraged. The aim of the book is not only to be a practical help to people who find themselves currently unemployed; but it is also designed to be an antidote to the despair and sense of rejection which far too often lead people to forget that they all have something to offer the rest of us, that they have talents, that there are skills to acquire and, above all, that there are opportunities to find.

There is something here for all groups, ages and geographical areas in the UK. Pages 14 and 15 show where every contributor lives. Examples are drawn from England, Wales, Scotland, and Northern Ireland, male and female. Nearly ten per cent have special needs. Various ethnic groups also contribute success stories. Indeed, the account which sparked the project was by a woman from the Caribbean.

This first tale was reported to the Prime Minister when I worked in the Civil Service in 10 Downing Street and for me it was unforgettable. I met the lady in the Full Employ office in Bristol. She was beset with difficulties. She was a single parent, she felt her race was not exactly the the choice of every employer and her education was minimal. So at 29 she had been unemployed almost continuously since leaving school. Yet she had the dream that she could start her own business. She realised that almost her only skill was an ability to clean and she felt she could clean and polish any office as well as anyone.

What could she do about it? She was fortunate in finding Full Employ. They drafted her business plan with her and guided her through the red tape nightmare that faces all would-be business start-up schemes. I met her nine months after she began her venture. She pointed out of the window at two sizeable office blocks and told me how she had won the contract to clean them. She was now employing three others and was going from strength to strength. If she could do it, so could others.

In this book, long-term unemployment does not always last as long as in that lady's experience. We use the same criterion as the Department of Social Security for defining 'long-term' – in excess of six months. However, success in business is taken to be longer than nine months. In this book the businesses must have been successfully in existence for a minimum of a year.

The acknowledgement and thanks to the dozens who helped produce this book are set out on the page before this introduction. While the work and support for this book has been very generous and diverse, the inspiration for it has come from people who have proved what they have within them.

In reputedly the worst council estate in Glasgow – and probably in Scotland – in the mid-80s, it was said that there was 98 per cent unemployment and that the situation was so bad that if anyone gave the name of the estate as their address in a job application the job was mysteriously no longer available.

A group of eight or so individuals decided that they would approach Glasgow District Council to see whether they could win a commission to protect the estate against vandalism and crime. The council agreed and gave them a contract. In effect they became a security firm for the council estate. Others came forward from the estate telling the council 'we can paint', 'we can repair', 'we can do building jobs' on the estate and each time the council agreed and installed a secretary to service these small start-up businesses in one of the vacant flats on the estate. Dozens of small businesses started to operate and began to offer services to neighbouring council estates and residential property. Again, the picture there provided hope for everyone. And it is the message of encouragement for all unemployed people that I wanted to describe in this book through real examples.

Included are examples of typical problems experienced by job seekers. So if readers think they are too old to be re-employed, glance at Tony on page 92 who is 58 or John on page 102 who is 57 years old. Unemployed nine years? See what John Elliott did on page 36. There was Carol, page 76, who came back to employment after 15 years as a Mum; Diane, page 89, is a single parent; George, page 96, and Dan, page 79, were previously convicted prisoners; Kate, page 43, had the typical problem of being overqualified. Also not unusual was the depression experienced by Violet, page 81, and the lack of motivation of Michael, page 92. Many were members of minority groups such as Ibrahim, page 68. Several were illiterate or dyslexic, see Noah, page 78.

Persistence pays off. Bob Scullion and Allan Rice, page 61, battled with town planners and Rueben, page 77, wrote 518 job applications. Annie used minimal start-up costs, page 50. Most used a major agency such as a TEC. The tale is one of effort alongside the help listed in the Directory which begins on page 121.

Banks can provide invaluable help, see page 124. Dozens of people in this collection of evidence sought and gained the help of the Prince's Youth Business Trust. Each account can only hint at the help and advice they received. The most important statement in this book is more than the help; it is that readers should have confidence in themselves. 'You can do it'.

A job or business may end or may fail. No answer to unemployment is necessarily the permanent solution. But this book is one important 'return ticket' to employment.

THE CASE STUDIES

SELF-EMPLOYED

PRAKESH RAM BANGA (51): Bus operator 18
SARAH BARKER (29): Shoemaker 18
CLAIRE BEARD (27): Contract furnishing 20
JUDITH BECKETT (38): Garden improvements 20
VICTORIA BLIGHT (26): Stained-glass artist 21
JOSEPH BRENNAN: Fish processing 23
IAN CARTLEDGE (32) AND DOUGLAS HEBENTON (28): Display signs 25
CHARLES CHALLENGER: Shipping and export agent 26
PETER COADY: Inventor 27
GARRETT CONNELLY (44): Potter 29
DEBORAH CORNWELL(33): Health therapist 30
MOHAMMED (32) AND RAZA (30) DATOO: Car care 31
KAREN DIESNER (32): Knitting business 32
SUSI EARNSHAW (38): Theatrical agent 33
WALTER ECKLES (56): Pub landlord 33
JOHN ELLIOTT (44): Toy-maker 35
MICHAEL ELLIOTT (44): Forklift instructor 36
SYLVIA (43) AND IAON (47) EVANS: Brewery 37
JOSEPH FERGUS: Computer consultant 38
ROGER FISHER (28): Gift boxes 39
MALCOLM FLACK (48): Fish-and-chip shop 40
TREVOR FORD (31): Illustrator 42
KATE GEMMELL(43): Soft furnishings 43
TREVOR GIBBON (41): Weighing-machine services 44
JEREMY GILL: Children's nursery 45
STEPHEN ILLIDGE (24): Firework displays 46

ANDREW JACKSON (27): Laundry service 47
MARK JAMES: Writer, bricklayer and lecturer 48
LOUISA LYLE: Sun-bed hire 48
SARAH MABBUTT (28): Designer 49
ANNIE MANLY (39): Personal taxation services 50
TASHA MARDON (27): Disc jockey 51
RICHARD MARSHALL (50): Wine merchant 52
VALERIE McALISTER: Bookseller 53
GARY McEWAN (26): HGV instructor 55
HUGH McMAHON (44): Sandwich bar 56
GLEN AND GARY MILLER (27): Folk group 56
ANNE MORRIS: Industrial cleaning service 58
ADAM AND JASON PERRY (23): Mobile recording unit 59
DONALD RIDDELL (22): Auto repairs 60
CHRIS SAUL: Doughnut maker 61
BOB SCULLION AND ALLAN RICE: Diving centre 61
HILARY SHEDEL (29): Photographer 62
RACHAEL SPEERS (26): Plants for hire 64
PANAGIOTIS AND MARI STAVROS: Greek taverna 65
DAVID SWAN (33): Bicycle shop 67
IBRAHIM SYED (25): Import and retail 68
MARTIN THOMAS (25): Wind and surf shop 68
ANGELA WATSON (44): Dog beautician 70
GEOFF WITHERSPOON (46): Plumber 71
MARK (32) AND GRAHAM (30) WRAY: Industrial cleaning supplies 72
DAVID WYATT (28): Bus services 73

IN EMPLOYMENT

JOSEPH ATWERE (23): Burger King award winner 74
CRAIG BERESFORD: Delivery driver 75
CAROL: Receptionist/typist 76
REUBEN CLARKE (49): Hospital deputy training manager 77
NOAH COOPER (40): Road-sweeper 78
DAN (47): Careers adviser 79
ANDREW ERSKINE (21): Trainee production manager 80
DAVE FRANCE (49): Computer support 81
VIOLET GLEESON (37): Local health authority worker 81
MARLENE HENDERSON (23): Administrator 82
ANNE JAMES (52): Wildfowl Trust warden 82
ROBERT JAMES: Outreach support worker and job club leader 83
IFAN JONES: Information technology tutor 85
DAVID KNOTT: Warehouseman 86
DAVID LINDSAY (30): Sales assistant 87
LINDA MACDONALD: Employment training 87
STUART MACKAY (43): Butcher 88
DIANE MAXWELL (28): Office worker 89
SHONA McCARTHY: Projects officer 89
MICHAEL: Computer operator 92
TONY MORRIS (58): Leisure administrator 92
JOHN MUNRO (30): Porter 93
CHRIS PEMBERTON (48): Residential social worker 94
PHILIP: Book-keeper 95
DAVID ROBERTS (58): Vehicle accessories 95
GEORGE ROBOTHAM (23): Computer adviser 96

NEIL RORISON (43): Warehouseman 98
MANJIT SIDHU (25): Personal tax assistant 99
MELADO STEVENS (28): Sales assistant 100
PHILIP STROUD (43): Computer administrator 100
LISA TAYLOR (20): Pub trainee 101
JOHN TURNER (57): Horticultural instructor 102
DEREK TYSON (50): Hygiene manager 103
ALAN VENNING (37): Assistant steward 104
ROBERT WATSON (23): Butcher 105
JEAN WILKINSON (50): Bookseller 106
WINIFRED WILKINSON (39): Computer lecturer 107
JOHN WRIGHT: Computer programmer 108
HARRY YATES (52): Forklift driver 109

SPECIAL NEEDS

CLIVE BULMER (49): Employment training 110
HEATHER CLARK (32): Journalist 00
PHILIP DOWNS (38): Disability consultant 00
COLIN JULIAN: Local council administrative assistant 00
EDDIE NOLAN (48): Domestic assistant 00
DAVID PORTER: Computer design 00
STEVE (34): Unit manager at a training centre 00
KEVIN WILKIN (38): Fitter/machinist 00
FRED WILLIAMS: Centre co-ordinator 119
FAY YOUNG (29): Administrative assistant 120

KEY TO GEOGRAPHICAL LOCATIONS

SELF-EMPLOYED

No.	Name (age)	Page
1.	Prakesh Ram Banga (51)	18
2.	Sarah Barker (29)	18
3.	Claire Beard (27)	20
4.	Judith Beckett (38)	20
5.	Victoria Blight (26)	21
6.	Joseph Brennan	23
7.	Ian Cartledge (32) & Douglas Hebenton (28)	25
8.	Charles Challenger	26
9.	Peter Coady	27
10.	Garrett Connelly (44)	29
11.	Deborah Cornwell (33)	30
12.	Mohammed (32) & Raza (30) Datoo	31
13.	Karen Diesner (32)	32
14.	Susi Earnshaw (38)	33
15.	Walter Eckles (56)	33
16.	John Elliott (44)	35
17.	Michael Elliott (44)	36
18.	Sylvia (43) & Iaon (47) Evans	37
19.	Joseph Fergus	38
20.	Roger Fisher (28)	39
21.	Malcolm Flack (48)	40
22.	Trevor Ford (31)	42
23.	Kate Gemmell (43)	43
24.	Trevor Gibbon (41)	44
25.	Jeremy Gill	45
26.	Stephen Illidge (24)	46
27.	Andrew Jackson (27)	47
28.	Mark James	48
29.	Luisa Lyle	48
30.	Sarah Mabbutt (28)	49
31.	Annie Manly (39)	50
32.	Tasha Mardon (27)	51
33.	Richard Marshall (50)	52
34.	Valerie McAlister	53
35.	Gary McEwan (26)	55
36.	Hugh McMahon (44)	56
37.	Glen & Gary Miller (27)	56
38.	Anne Morris	58
39.	Adam & Jason Perry (23)	59
40.	Donald Riddell (22)	60
41.	Chris Saul	61
42.	Bob Scullium & Allan Rice	61
43.	Hilary Shedel (29)	62
44.	Rachael Speers (26)	64
45.	Panagiotis & Mari Stavros	65
46.	David Swan (33)	67
47.	Ibrahim Syed (25)	68
48.	Martin Thomas (25)	68
49.	Angela Watson (44)	70
50.	Geoff Witherspoon	71
51.	Mark (32) & Graham (30) Wray	72
52.	David Wyatt (28)	73

IN EMPLOYMENT

No.	Name (age)	Page
53.	Joseph Atwere (23)	74
54.	Craig Beresford	75
55.	Carol	76
56.	Reuben Clarke (49)	77
57.	Noah Cooper (40)	78
58.	Dan (47)	79
59.	Andrew Erskine (21)	80
60.	Dave France (49)	81
61.	Violet Gleeson (37)	81
62.	Marlene Henderson (23)	82
63.	Anne James (52)	82
64.	Robert James	83
65.	Ifan Jones	85
66.	David Knott	86
67.	David Lindsay (30)	87
68.	Linda Macdonald	87
69.	Stuart Mackay (43)	88
70.	Diane Maxwell (28)	89
71.	Shona McCarthy	89
72.	Michael	92
73.	Tony Morris (58)	92
74.	John Munro (30)	93
75.	Chris Pemberton (48)	94
76.	Philip	95
77.	David Roberts (58)	95
78.	George Robotham (23)	96
79.	Neil Rorison (43)	98
80.	Manjit Sidhu (25)	99
81.	Melado Stevens (28)	100
82.	Philip Stroud	100
83.	Lisa Taylor (20)	101
84.	John Turner (57)	102
85.	Derek Tyson (50)	103
86.	Alan Venning (37)	104
87.	Robert Watson (23)	105
88.	Jean Wilkinson (50)	106
89.	Winifred Wilkinson (39)	107
90.	John Wright	108
91.	Harry Yates (52)	109

SPECIAL NEEDS

No.	Name (age)	Page
92.	Clive Bulmer (49)	110
93.	Heather Clark (32)	111
94.	Philip Downs (38)	112
95.	Colin Julian	113
96.	Eddie Nolan (48)	114
97.	David Porter	115
98.	Steve (34)	116
99.	Kevin Wilkin (38)	117
100.	Fred Williams	119
101.	Fay Young (29)	120

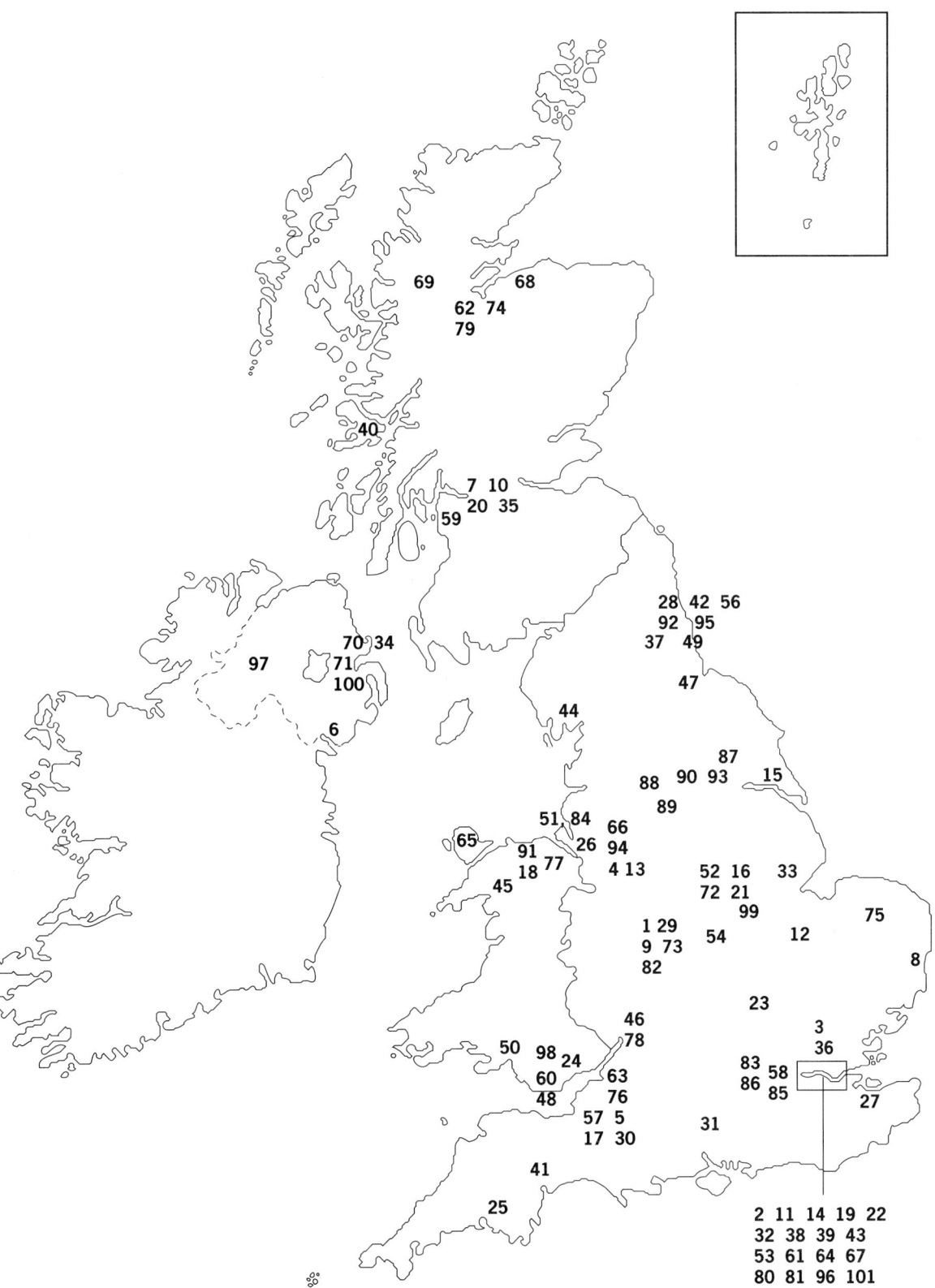

INDEX OF JOBS AND ACTIVITIES

Accountancy - book-keeping 95
Accountancy - tax services 50, 99
Administrative assistant
   housing 120
   local council 113
Administrator 78
Agent
   shipping and export 26
   theatrical 33
Art
   illustrating 42
   pottery 29
   stained-glass 21

Bicycle shop 67
Book-keeper 95
Bookseller 53, 106
Brewery 37
Bricklaying 48
Bus operator 18, 73
Butcher 88, 105

Car repairs 31, 60
Careers adviser 79
Catering
   assistant steward 104
   bakery hygiene manager 103
   doughnut making 61
   fast food 74
   fish and chip shop 40
   Greek taverna 65
   public house 33
   sandwich bar 56
Chemical products 27
Chidcare, nursery 45
Cinema, see film
Computers
   administration 100
   adviser 96
   consultant 38
   design and DTP 115
   lecturer 107
   operator 92
   programmer 108
   support services 81
   technician 96
   training 110

Consultant
   business 38, 95
   careers 79
   computer 38, 81, 96
   disability support 112
   tax 50, 99
Craft
   curtain and cushion making 43
   firework making 46
   gift box manufacturing 39
   shoemaking 18
   toy-making 35

Design
   furnishing 20
   gift boxes 39
   graphic desin 49
   knitwear 31
Disability consultant 112
Disability self-help centre co-ordinator 119
Disc jockey 51
Display signs manufacturer 25
Distribution, see warehousing
Diving centre 61
Dog beautician 70
Domestic assistant 114
Doughnut-maker 61
Drinks, see licensed trade
Driver
   deliveries 75
   forklift 109

Employment training 87, 110
Engineering, radio frequency equipment 117
Entertainment
   disc jockey 51
   firework displays 46
   folk music 56
   popular music 59

Film, projects manager 90
Firework displays organiser 46
Fish processing 23
Fish-and-chip shop 40
Fishing - manufacture of bait 27

Fitter/machinist 117
Folk music 56
Food
   bakery hygiene manager 103
   butcher 88, 105
   doughnut-maker 61
   fish and chip shop 40
   fish processing 23
   hamburgers 74
   sandwich bar 56
Footwear 18
Forklift driver 109
Forklift instructor 36
Furnishing 20

Gardening
   garden improvements 20
   horticultural instructor 102
   plants for hire 64
Gift boxes 39
Greek taverna 65

Health service
   hospital porter 93
   hospital training manager 77
   local health authority worker 81
Health therapy 30
Horticultural instructor 102
Horticulture, see gardening
Hospital porter 93
Hospital training manager 77
Hygiene manager 103

Illustrator 42
Importer and retailer 68
Industrial cleaning services 58
Industrial cleaning supplies 72
Information technology tutor 85
Instructor
   forklift 36
   HGV 55
   horticulture 102
Inventor 27

Job club leader 82
Journalist 111

THE CASE STUDIES

Knitting 31

Laundry service 47
Lecturer, see teaching
Leisure administrator 92
Licensed trade
 assistant steward 104
Licensed trade
 brewing 37
 pub landlord 33
 pub trainee 101
 wine merchant 52
Local council
 administrative assistant 113
 road-sweeping 78
Local health authority worker 81

Manufacturing
 chemical products 27
 display signs 25
 gift boxes 39
 shoes 18
 toys 35
Massage 30
Mechanic
 motor 60
 weighing machines 44
 cars 31, 60
Music business
 folk group 56
 disc jockey 51
 mobile recording unit 59

Nursery, children's 45

Office worker, ferry company 89

Pets, dog beautician 70
Photographer 62
Picture-framing, production
 manager 79
Plants for hire 64
Plumber 71
Porter, hospital 93
Pottery 29
Production manager, picture
 framing 79
Programmer, see computers
Pub trainee 101
Pub landlord 33

Receptionist 76
Recording studio 59
Residential social worker 94

Restaurant
 Burger King 74
 Greek taverna 65
Retail
 bicycle shop 67
 bookselling 53, 106
 butcher 88, 105
 cosmetics 100
 diving centre 61
 fish and chip shop 40
 imported Indian goods 68
 sandwich bar 56
 wind and surf shop 68
Road-sweeper 78

Sales assistant 87, 100
Sandwich bar 56
Services
 bus transport 73
 diving supplies 61
 dog beautician 70
 industrial cleaning 58
 laundry 47
 massage 30
 picture-framing 79
 plants for hire 64
 plumbing 71
 sun-bed hire 48
 tax consultancy 50, 99
 weighing machines 44
Sewing 43
Shipping, export agent 26
Shoemaking 18
Showbusiness
 disc jockey 51
 folk music 56
 popular music 59
 theatrical agent 33
Social work 94
Soft furnishings 43
Sport
 leisure administrator 92
 windsurfing and sailboarding 68
Sun-bed hire 48

Tax consultant 50, 99
Teaching
 computer skills 107, 110
 employment training 87
 information technology 85
Theatrical agent 33
Toy-maker 35
Training, unit manager 116

Training manager, hospital 77
Transport
 bicycles 67
 bus services 18, 73
 HGV instructor 55
Travel 18
Typist 76

Unit manager at a training centre 116

Vehicle accessories 95
Vehicle repairs 31

Warden, Wildfowl Trust 82
Warehouseman 86, 98
Warehousing
 forklift driver 109
 forklift instructor 36
Weighing-machine services 44
Wholesale, industrial cleaning
 supplies 72
Wind and surf shop 68
Wine merchant 52
Writer 48

Self-employed

(in alphabetical order)

Stopping Along the Way

PRAKESH RAM BANGA (51): *Bus operator*

When Mr Banga was made redundant at 50 from a leading West Midlands Bus Company where he was a senior inspector, he decided to explore the possibilities of self-employment. His research resulted in his investing in two buses and launching his own company, taking routes within the local vicinity.

With the help of Wolverhampton Training and Enterprise Council, Mr Banga took advantage of the counselling and business skills seminars and began trading with help from the Enterprise Allowance Grant and equity from his redundancy settlement.

Banga Travels was launched on 24 May 1993. Mr Banga's commitment and considerable knowledge of the business have helped him to overcome many obstacles, not least of which was the fierce competition from other operators. This culminated in a parking ban for his buses at certain times and stops along the route. Happily, Mr Banga's enthusiasm and determination have seen his business expand to overcome these difficulties and he now has a fleet of seven buses and a turnover in excess of £100,00 per year. Wolverhampton TEC are pleased to have been able to support Mr Banga and continue to service his needs when requested.

Best Foot Forward

SARAH BARKER (29): *Shoemaker*

Christmas is the most important date in Sarah Barker's calendar. She spends virtually all year preparing for it and earns the majority of her livelihood from it. Gift-hunters in Hong Kong, New York and shops around England buy her products in their thousands at this time of year. Sarah herself is to be found at a market stall in Covent Garden selling her hand-made slippers, experiencing customer appreciation at first hand. This is how she started four years ago and it is from this base that her company, now employing nine staff, has grown.

It was from seeing consumer reaction to her products that she became certain that a market existed for her brightly coloured footwear. Felt boots in greens, reds and yellows with tassels and bells would traditionally be associated with harlequins but at Christmas her slippers make the perfect gift. They come in all sizes but those for children naturally comprise the majority of her turnover.

Sarah obviously enjoys the playful nature of her product but this does not obscure a thorough and competitive appreciation of the business environment in which she operates. Her workshop in a small business development in London houses modern equipment and staff work to strict daily quotas on their particular tasks. Although what is produced lends itself to fairy tale images, its methods of production belong firmly in the modern commercial world.

Sarah studied shoe design at college in Hackney but then went on to work for a retail company, purchasing merchandise. After she was made redundant by the company she was unemployed for over six months. During this period she fostered ideas of establishing her own business drawing on the skills she had learned at college. Soon realising that manufacturing conventional shoes would prove too costly, she came up with the idea of entering the novelty market with lower capital investment and production costs.

She was assisted in compiling her business plan, forecasting initial cash flows and developing her marketing strategy by advisers at her TEC. 'I had very extensive help in all the relevant areas,' she says. 'At first much of it seemed like common sense but it was vital to realise exactly what I was doing and where I was going.'

The group exercises at the TEC where she met others in her position taking the first steps in private enterprise were essential in building the confidence required to strike out alone. 'Suddenly I realised that there were others in my position and that mine was in fact a very sound proposal.'

The early years have not been easy, but the £10,000 loaned to her by her father has been paid off and now, having established a specialised market, Sarah is confident of being able to develop her position. Her year is taken up with creating new designs and constant production for her stall at Covent Garden and is often heartened by the positive feedback she receives. Sales would suggest that the appreciation of her product in other cities is the same.

Sofa so Good!

CLAIRE BEARD (27): *Contract furnishing*

Claire Beard left college after five years with an MA in design, which included both furniture and interiors. She worked for two years as a contract furnisher for the Government Crown Suppliers, which then closed down, leaving her unemployed for two months before she found work with a former colleague. Six months later, her contract expired, and she spent a further six months searching for a job.

Eventually, a friend told her about the Chelmsford Enterprise Scheme but, due to the lack of information available from the local unemployment office, it was three months before Claire managed to approach the organisation and arrange an interview. When she did so, she was accepted for a six-week business training course, during which she received £10 a week on top of her unemployment benefit.

Two days a week were spent learning book-keeping, including estimating cash flows and making profit projections, while she spent the other three working on her plan for a contract furnishing business. Estimating expenses such as telephone and petrol costs was difficult for someone who had never previously considered such figures, but she says with hindsight that 'you'd be surprised how close you actually are'. She successfully submitted her business plan to the Chelmsford Enterprise Scheme for assessment, which entitled her to receive Enterprise Allowance benefit of £40 a week for six months.

Her annual turnover rose, within two years, to around £20,000 and her success led to her being offered a well paid position with another company which she subsequently accepted.

Claire now says that, during unemployment, 'I had a very low self-esteem, especially because many of us were made redundant from the same employer. I wouldn't have chosen to be self-employed,' she says, 'but now I'm glad I made the effort.'

A Buzy Lizzie

JUDITH BECKETT (38): *Garden improvements*

Judith Beckett was 36 and married with a small son when she was made redundant.

'I had to work out how I was going to spend the rest of my life workwise,' said Judith, adding that 'it wasn't going to be easy with childcare being so difficult'.

Judith started a City and Guilds course in gardening with the intention of working in a garden centre but it became apparent that there was not going to be much money in it and to fit around school hours Judith could only manage a five-hour day.

Starting her own business was the ideal solution for Judith so with the help of the Stockport and High Peak Training and Enterprise Council (TEC) New Business Support Programme she set up her own gardening business, Buzy Lizzie. Judith has not looked back since.

Since starting her business, Judith had to advertise only for the initial weeks; most work has come in through word of mouth.

'It's not like being an employee, it's more like being a friend. Collecting the money isn't my prime motivation.'

In the first year of trading Busy Lizzie made a small net profit which enabled Judith to invest in a car and tools for the business. By this time the business had built up an excellent customer base.

It is hard to believe that Judith still describes herself as 'the least business-like person you will hope to meet!'

Picture This

VICTORIA BLIGHT (26): *Stained-glass artist*

'It was the combination that really made it possible,' said Victoria Blight, who has used many different sources of help to establish herself as an independent stained-glass artist. Since completing her degree in glass design at Stourbridge College in 1990, Victoria has benefited from government training schemes, Enterprise Agencies, the PYBT and her own commitment to developing her ability. She has experienced two periods of unemployment of over six months' duration but now runs a successful business that is rewarding both professionally and artistically.

Despite the specialist nature of her degree, Victoria found great difficulty in finding employment in the field. 'There were so few jobs and so many qualified people,' she explained. Unemployment made her realise that she would have to develop her talents further.

After six months without a job, during which time she had already enrolled in evening classes, Victoria started the Employment Training Programme. She was placed at Lark Hall in Somerset, where she learned stained-glass techniques which in turn led to her first commission. This was a rose window for a church which could not afford to pay a professional fee. It was an ideal opportunity for Victoria to demonstrate her talent while still receiving basic payment on the Employment Training Scheme. Victoria was able to extend her period on the scheme, allowing her to complete the project. 'It was a very good chance to show what I could do. I still get enquiries about it, and have since received another commission on the basis of it.'

Working on her own project gave Victoria a taste of what practising independently was like. However, she still had reservations and on completing her commission and the programme she applied for various design jobs. Once again she found the market very difficult to break into and experienced another period of unemployment of about six months. It was at this point that Victoria decided it was necessary 'to create my own job', as she put it. She approached FAME (Frome and Mendip Enterprise) for advice and undertook a Business Enterprise Programme (BEP) course for four months (one day a week), which led to her compiling a business plan. 'I had to get the plan approved in order to be eligible for the Enterprise Allowance Scheme, but I had all the help and advice I needed for this.'

However, she still needed capital to start up on her own. Despite being advised that it was unlikely that she would be granted help by the PYBT, because of the stiff competition, she decided on her own method of approach. 'I just applied for a market research grant of £200 so that I could go back to them with a fully researched plan that they would be more likely to support.' She registered slides of her work with agencies around the country which are used by architects and undertook research by telephone and mailshots.

Having undertaken this research she returned to the PYBT, which in turn granted her a loan of £1,500. 'There were three parts to my proposal: first teaching, to give me a basic income; secondly trade fairs and then of course large commissions.'

Victoria still works in these three areas, regularly exhibiting her stained-glass jewellery at trade fairs and teaching stained-glass techniques locally. 'The PYBT also supports me at fairs by subsidising the entrance fee. For example, when I exhibited at the NEC in Birmingham I paid only £20 whereas even the smallest stand usually costs £300.' Her larger commissions often come from the agencies with which she registered while conducting her initial research. 'Sometimes I can just get a call out of the blue,' she said. Despite the depression in the building industry she has worked on substantial commissions in London and the West Country.

Victoria attributes her success to the wide variety of support she has received. 'The PYBT and FAME helped me in different ways. It would not have been possible without either of them.'

A Fishy Tale

JOSEPH BRENNAN: *Fish processing*

After leaving school with no formal qualifications Joseph Brennan had a succession of mundane temporary jobs. Unable to find permanent work in his own native West Belfast, where male unemployment can be high, Joseph moved to London to continue his search for employment. Here a number of short-term labouring jobs on building sites were all that materialised and, failing to find a source of a regular income, Joseph decided to return to West Belfast.

Work was difficult to obtain in this area at the time. Unperturbed, Joseph continued in his quest for employment and eventually after some five years was successful in obtaining a job on the government funded Action for Community

Joseph Brennan (centre) in his fish processing factory.

Employment Programme with Turf Lodge Enterprise Scheme. While there project manager, Tommy Hale, discussed Joseph's potential for future employment and introduced him to the possibility of self-employment.

One of Joseph's previous spells of employment had been assisting a fishmonger and he now began to consider the opportunity of pursuing this as a business venture. Mr Hale informed Joseph of the benefits of the ACE Enterprise Scheme (AES), which aims to encourage ACE workers to consider self-employment and which allows approved candidates to develop and try out a business idea while still supported by the ACE Programme.

Joseph undertook a Pre Business Course and Enterprise Training Course with Brookfield Consultancy Service and applied to and was approved for the ACE Enterprise Scheme in June 1990. With the back-up of the Scheme and the guidance offered by Tommy Hale and his colleagues, Joseph researched the viability of offering a door-to-door fresh fish delivery service, initially in West Belfast. Through his time on AES he successfully set up this small business selling a wide variety of fish.

Joseph began to explore ways of expanding his business and discovered a niche in the market for the export of shellfish from Carlingford to England. This opened up further possibilities and he successfully negotiated regular orders with several shellfish dealers in Billingsgate Market.

Such rapid expansion created another problem – the source of funding to purchase plant and equipment and the acquiring of an acceptable factory site. Here the expertise and generosity of LEDU (the NI Small Business Agency) took over. They provided sufficient grants and a purpose built factory in Warrenpoint, Co Down, to allow Brennan Fish Processing, as the business became known, to operate from a European Community approved building and meet with all the standards of European legislation.

The business rapidly developed from a street fish stall to become a fish processing industry specialising in the shelling of prawns, initially to supply the Kilkeel Seafood Industry for export throughout the world. In addition, Brennan's also process premium fish such as plaice, Dover sole and turbot for the local marketplace.

Determination to succeed and a driving ambition to maximise the potential of the local fish industry in export marketplaces has led to Joseph moving in a hectic 18 months from a sole proprietor to that of a key local employer with 23 employees.

This fact is of particular importance to Joseph: 'Having endured the rigours of unemployment and the soul-destroying quest for permanent work I find it most gratifying being able to offer employment opportunities to local people. I aim to further increase the workforce in the near future,' he enthuses.

Signs of the Times

IAN CARTLEDGE (32) AND DOUGLAS HEBENTON (28): *Display signs*

Motherwell men Ian Cartledge and Douglas Hebenton always wanted to see their name in lights. Now they have achieved their ambition through their new company ID Signs.

Signmaker Ian and partner Douglas decided to set up their business in Strathclyde Business Centre, New Stevenston, March 1992 after working for several other signmaking companies. Now the company, which employs four people and has a turnover of around £140,000 a year, plans to build its own customised factory on Righead Industrial Estate in Bellshill.

'We have put in a lot of work since we set up two years ago,' said Ian. 'But it is finally beginning to pay off. We have secured several important customers who have helped to build up our business. Now we are looking forward to seeing the building work start at our new premises.

'I had been made redundant before and after working for someone else again, I decided that I wanted to run my own show. Douglas also felt that he had reached as far as he could possibly go in his job and we decided to start up a business on our own.'

Now ID Signs produce commercial signs for a range of companies including House of Fraser, Scottish Citylink coaches, Compaq and Cummins Engines. The firm has also produced signs for the companies based in the EuroMed Park next to Strathclyde Business Park, including Aortech, Caledonian Medical and Avecor Cardiovascular.

Ian and Douglas were helped to establish their business through Lanarkshire Development Agency's (LDA) Ahead for Business and New Business Grant schemes, administered by Motherwell Enterprise Development Company (MEDCO). The new Business Grant from LDA made sure ID

Douglas Hebenton (left) and Ian Cartledge (centre), founders of ID Signs.

Signs was given enough capital to see it through the first crucial months and the LDA Ahead for Business Scheme gave Ian and Douglas invaluable business advice.

LDA is helping Ian and Douglas with their expansion plans for their new customised factory. Lynn Wilkinson, one of LDA's business development executives said: 'We are delighted that ID Signs has gone from strength to strength since starting up two years ago.

'We are convinced that the firm will continue to grow once it has moved into its new premises.'

Now ID Signs is hoping to take on new staff to cope with its major expansion plans.

Douglas added: 'Without the help of LDA and MEDCO we would never have achieved so much so soon. They gave us valuable help and advice in starting up for ourselves.'

ID Signs will be in its new premises in Righead Industrial Estate by the end of 1994.

Safe Harbour

CHARLES CHALLENGER: *Shipping and export agent*

Charles Challenger spent a year unemployed before setting up his own business, the Challenger Shipping and Export Agency. He had previously spent ten years working in the shipping and export trade but was unable to find work which he felt remunerated him sufficiently for his experience. Having realised that if he was going to continue working the long hours his trade required he would prefer to be self-employed, he decided to consider setting up his own business.

His determination to 'have a go' outweighed any fear of failure: 'Either you can turn up and claim the dole once a fortnight and feel degraded by the system, or you can go out there and have a go at it, even if it doesn't work out.'

Charles' knowledge of his local community enabled him to find a viable market and he decided to concentrate on shipping to the Caribbean. He realised that it was common practice for families in the UK to send boxes of goods out to relatives in their home countries in the Caribbean. There was also a steady flow of people wanting their belongings shipped out as they moved to warmer climates to escape the effects of the recession. Having formulated his basic idea, Charles joined the Enterprise Training Scheme at Suffolk Enterprise Centre. Here he learned 'the hard facts' of owning his own business, and his idealistic hope that self-employment would mean 'owning my own Rolls-Royce and being out of the office every day at 5.30' was soon dispelled. However, the questions he was challenged with, for example 'What makes you think your business will succeed when thousands are failing?', helped him examine his own ideas and to formulate a realistic business plan.

Charles advertised himself entirely by word of mouth, initially by approaching people directly and through family and friends. After this he relied on recommendations from satisfied clients here and in the West Indies, the USA and Guyana, which provided him with an incentive to concentrate on building up a good reputation.

The majority of his clients were exporting their goods in tea-chests and here again, having a close knowledge of his market enabled Charles to provide a more economical product. He purchases the empty metal drums which are used to import liquids such as orange juice and cleans them before selling them to his clients. These provide very hard-wearing containers which withstand the stresses of cargo handling and can also effectively be recycled as containers for storing water: very useful in tropical climates.

The Challenger Shipping and Export Agency has been officially running since July 1992, and Charles anticipates that his turnover for the first year will be somewherre in the region of £70,000. Setting up his own business has allowed him to 'keep my head above water financially', but more important it has also helped to restore his confidence and self-respect while providing a service which benefits his community.

Innovate to Accumulate

PETER COADY: *Inventor*

On leaving school, Peter Coady worked as a technician in a chemical laboratory for several years. When this job came to an end Peter found himself unemployed for six months. However, his knowledge of chemical products was to prove the basis of his new career as an inventor.

Peter counts himself an inventor first, a businessman second. Admitting that he enjoyed playful inventing as a child, his current position as owner and director of a company dedicated to manufacturing and marketing products of his own invention is in many ways a dream come true: 'I get more satisfaction from inventing products than from my millionth sale, but it's good to see some ideas really make it.' For Peter, private enterprise is much more than simply a means of earning a living: it is a way of bringing his personal ideas to life.

However, it is Peter's capacity for invention in actually creating a market for his innovations that marks out his success. By inventing new products, Peter has also had to invent new markets. His unique ideas have been backed by conventional business training and support. 'The fun of inventing is having a go where no one has thought of trying before,' he says.

His company, 'Right Angle', started by producing a specialist chemical bait for fishing which attracted individual breeds of fish. To this he added to a further range of fishing accessories known to anglers as the 'Magmix' range, which is sold throughout the country. Peter is now pursuing a gap in the beauty market with a revolutionary nail-varnish remover, 'Pretty Quick'. 'I was looking for markets open for new ideas and the beauty industry seemed perfect,' he explains.

Advertisements in local newspapers led him to the Birmingham Chamber of Commerce, who recommended him for one of their courses comprising two hourly sessions a week for three months and covering the fundamental techniques of book-keeping, accounting, cash flow management, marketing and forecasting. The grounding this gave Peter provided a firm base from which to attract the financial backing he needed for what might otherwise have seemed simply good ideas. It was while he was drawing up his business plan in early 1988 with the help of the Chamber of Commerce that they suggested he might be eligible for a loan under the government Loan Guarantee Scheme. His business plan was given approval and he was granted a vital £15,000 to help him with start-up costs, for example the purchase of machinery and the expense of locating to new premises at the Rubicon Centre in Lakeside. Peter was also offered a loan.

This determination has shown itself in Peter's exploitation of foreign markets,

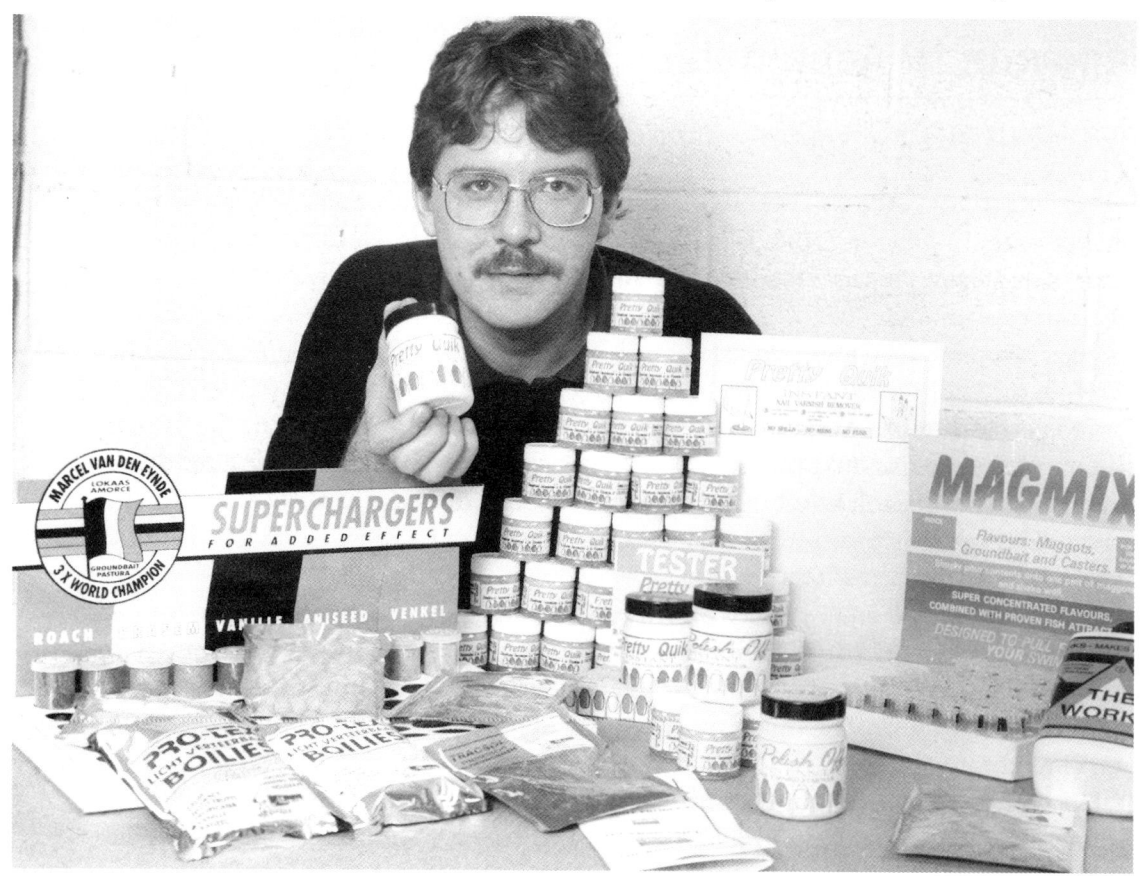

principally European but also Japanese, as today as much as 80 per cent of Peter's turnover is accounted for by exports. He has achieved this position by contacting distributors on the Continent who now market his products to retail outlets. His British sales are similarly managed through distributors. In both cases Peter has had to convince these organisations of the quality and significance of his products. He has 'invented' a market for his inventions, and has achieved the dual satisfaction of gaining his millionth sale and fulfilling his desire to innovate.

Potted History

GARRETT CONNELLY (44): *Potter*

'There just weren't the jobs here in the industry any more.' Garrett Connelly had worked in the potteries of Glasgow since leaving school in 1965. He had experienced redundancy and unemployment before, having been without work for three years in the early 1980s. But when redundancy came again in 1990 at the age of 40, he realised his chances of finding another job were slim. 'At my age I suppose I was really unemployable.' Although a further 18 months' unemployment followed, Garrett prepared to set up his own pottery. 'After my experience and at my age it seemed the only thing to do.'

After he spent six months searching fruitlessly for work the Employment Office suggested he take a business course with IMS Training in Glasgow. This involved a year of weekly sessions covering the basic elements of business administration. Garrett's wife, Mary, accompanied him to the classes as they now hoped to establish their business together. 'I wish I had done this years ago. You might as well have a go; in the end there's nothing to lose,' he said.

At the conclusion of the course the Connellys produced a business plan detailing how they hoped to build on Garrett's experience in making moulds to supply the local pottery industry. On the basis of this they were awarded a grant of £1,000 by the Greater Easterhouse Development Company, one of Glasgow's Development Agencies.

With this award and a small amount of his own capital, Garrett was able to set up a workshop with a small kiln and to start trading at the beginning of 1993. 'It is amazing what you learn. Now I just do the manufacturing, my wife does the marketing.'

From the beginning they have worked in partnership. Mary undertook the marketing and book-keeping, leaving Garrett to concentrate on production. As well as making moulds for use by the neighbouring potteries, Garrett also produces clocks, lamps and ornaments which Mary sells at craft fairs and other outlets. Within a year of establishing themselves, a remarkable 78 per cent of their current turnover of about £2,000 a month represents profit.

However, apart from getting a larger kiln, Garrett is cautious of expansion: 'I have seen at first hand companies in the industry closing once they started to take on too much.' Garrett's third period of unemployment forced him to take a 'gamble', but he believes that 'it is a gamble that has paid off in the long run. It's the best thing I've ever done.'

Get the Massage?

DEBORAH CORNWELL (33): *Health therapist*

Deborah Cornwell worked for a property company until she was made redundant; she then spent 18 months unemployed. She applied unsuccessfully for a number of jobs in her old field before deciding to change tack completely.

Enrolling on a course that gave training for potential health therapists, Deborah gained the necessary qualifications for setting up her own practice. This course of night classes took all her savings, leaving her with practically no capital for her business.

Counsellors at her Enterprise Agency advised her to market her skills at the minimum cost. She did this by sending letters of introduction to a wide variety of companies, and by placing advertisements in health centres. She recalls now how worried she was about the prospect of failure, as this mailshot took the last dregs of her capital. But the inevitable rejections were accompanied by enough enquiries and expressions of interest to enable her to start her practice in autumn 1992.

Her clients now include an investment bank in the City, and the *Economist* magazine. Working in the offices of such companies, Deborah treats sporting injuries and general symptoms of stress; while her other, private, clients include sufferers from conditions such as muscular dystrophy. It is these cases that bring her the most satisfaction. 'I really feel I'm doing something to help,' she says. 'It is so different from my previous job.'

She admits that she occasionally misses her previous salary and security, but she values the chance to pursue her own wishes, which sometimes means putting job satisfaction before financial gain. 'Experiencing unemployment was very difficult and disheartening,' she says now, 'but it changed the course of my life, for which I am now grateful.'

Back on the Road

MOHAMMED (32) AND RAZA (30) DATOO: *Car care*

Mohammed Datoo and his brother Raza had been unemployed for one year and three years respectively when they decided to combine their skills in management and mechanics to set up a vehicle repair business in Peterborough.

The brothers were able to establish their independent garage with grants from the city council and PYBT, which together amounted to £10,000. They also received payments of £40 a week each from the Enterprise Allowance scheme during their first year.

Mohammed attended weekly courses for ten weeks at his local TEC, covering law, accounting, book-keeping and commercial strategy. Without this, he admits that he would have had 'neither the confidence nor the expertise' to succeed. But he is convinced that the real key to their success has been 'a belief in total commitment to customer satisfaction'.

From its beginnings in 1988, Swift Car Care Services has expanded into a business with an annual turnover of £750,000. The company won the 1990 Best Asian Business of the Year Award, as well as the Reader's Digest award in 1992. Mohammed is forceful in his business philosophy: 'I look for opportunities in problems, not problems in opportunities,' he states, and recommends this approach to anyone thinking of setting themselves up in business.

A Pattern for Success

KAREN DIESNER (32): *Knitting business*

Karen Diesner left the workforce in 1987 to start a family. Previously Karen had worked as an executive officer in Customs and Excise at Manchester Airport and a sales correspondent at BASF. Karen vowed that if and when she worked again she would like to be her own boss.

When Karen left work she decided to buy a knitting machine to provide a constructive hobby. She enjoyed this so much that she took a ULCI Diploma course, completing two years later with distinctions in both theory and practice. Karen had an idea for knitting sweaters for chess players offering unique designs for each customer, and was also attracted to the idea of providing private machine knitting tuition.

Karen approached Stockport and High Peak Training and Enterprise Council (TEC) and began the New Business Support Programme. Kittiwake Design was open for business in February 1993.

Karen has a steady stream of customers from the *British Chess Magazine* and believes that she may possibly be the only supplier of custom-designed sweaters for chess enthusiasts in the world. The new project is to design and knit playing card style sweaters for the bridge circle.

On the tuition side, Karen is the only Singer specialist tutor in the north west and her objective is to pass on as much of her experience and knowledge as possible.

Karen was approached by *Knitting Machine News*, a nationwide publication to write for them on a monthly basis as a tutor and her work and designs appeared from June 1994.

Acting Decisively

SUSI EARNSHAW (38): *Theatrical agent*

Susi Earnshaw's first career was in the theatre as an actress. Following that, she worked as a journalist on a local newspaper in North London, leaving after two and a half years to have a baby. When her maternity benefit finished, she spent seven months unemployed, trying to decide what to do next. Being out of office life made her think seriously about setting up her own business. 'I didn't want to be a number any more,' she said.

She approached the North London TEC for advice. The business counsellor assigned to her was impressed by her plan to draw on her previous experience and contacts and set herself up as a theatrical agent. This in turn increased Susi's own confidence, which is, she says, along with a strong initial idea, 'the most important thing'. She developed a business plan, and looked for the necessary finance. Barclays Bank gave her an overdraft of £1,000 against the value of her home, and she also received the Enterprise Allowance of £40 a week. 'Without this,' she says, 'it would simply have been impossible.'

In the beginning much of Susi's income came in the form of children's fees from the theatre school she started but in four years Susi Earnshaw Management has also built up an impressive list of clients who are represented on a commission basis. She provides actors for a variety of projects, ranging from West End musicals and TV commercials to getting her younger clients, whom she particularly enjoys promoting, on to Grange Hill. Her business has, to some extent, taken over her life – one of her son's first words was 'office', and he now appears on her list of clients, while her husband is thinking of joining her in the business.

Room at the Inn

WALTER ECKLES (56): *Pub landlord*

Walter Eckles returned to England in 1992 after 21 years as a flour mill technician manager in South Africa. Coming home after so many years abroad is certainly a daunting prospect, even if you have a job waiting for you. But Walter returned to this

country and had to look for work. He initially spent six months unemployed and, with the added complication that his wife is South African, they both faced difficulties claiming unemployment benefit.

They found they were ineligible for any money from the state and were compelled to live off savings they had brought back from South Africa. It was the Job Centre who informed Walter of the possibilities of enrolling on a course at Hull College, particularly when he mentioned to them that he was interested in running a public house.

When Walter approached the college for an interview, it was obvious to them that he was serious. He was informed that a licensing trade skills course was due to start shortly, and the college was able to squeeze him on to it. The course lasted for three months and involved two days per week of training. At the same time Walter was accumulating practical experience on a placement nearby. These commitments meant that Walter had to cycle an average of four miles a day, but he claims: 'I had a target to achieve, come what may.'

On achieving his British Institute of Innkeepers Certificate, Walter was given the opportunity to act as a replacement landlord while the owner of a pub went on holiday. The local brewery interviewed him and were so impressed by Walter's attitude and knowledge that they offered him a similar temporary relief job in Leeds, over a Bank Holiday weekend.

Walter was subsequently offered a pub to run but before he accepted, another offer was made which appeared to him to have more potential. He explains how it is important to look at a business's strengths and weaknesses. In his case this involved investigating whether the pub had things such as a regular darts team; whether the clientele consisted of regulars or of mainly visitors; and whether there was any serious competition in the immediate area. These were all concerns that Walter had been taught about on his course at Hull College. Taking all this into consideration the first pub he was offered, despite being an attractive building, seemed to cater to daytime trade only whereas the offer he subsequently accepted was what Walter describes as an 'estate pub' with more of a social focus for those living nearby.

After over a year as landlord of the 'Abbey Hotel', Walter's success was recognised by the brewery when they offered him one of their most successful pubs, the 'Bonny Boat', which Walter was delighted to take on.

Walter emphasises that it is the will to succeed that makes the difference. As he says 'People can do anything if they are prepared to work hard for what they want. Age has its difficulties but they can be overcome with determination.'

Child's Play

JOHN ELLIOTT (44): *Toy-maker*

After leaving school, John Elliott had a succession of labouring jobs. When he was working for a hosiery company, he injured his neck and was forced out of work. The company did hold his job open for him for a while, but by the time he was fit enough to return, a year later, it had gone to someone else. John was shocked to discover that finding a new job was almost impossible. 'I was part of a generation which left school and didn't need qualifications to get a job. Now, suddenly, you needed them for even the simplest one,' he says.

He was out of work for nine years, during which time, he says, 'I had periods of very severe depression. Not having any money affects your social life: you become a kind of drop-out because you can't afford to go to the pub. I have a family; and I was having to make decisions about whether to buy the children clothes or food.'

It was this very pressure that led John to set up his business. 'It was Christmas,' he remembers. 'I couldn't afford presents for the family, so I started making toys in the loft, using scraps of wood and second-hand tools.' Relatives were impressed by the quality of the toys, and encouraged him to continue. He mentioned this to his counsellor at the benefit office, who steered him towards a City and Guilds Creative Studies course at the local Technical College.

He attended college one day a week for two years, learning the technical and historical aspects of toy-making and achieving a distinction and two credits to his final exams, as well as passing O and A Level art with good grades. This success encouraged him enormously, and he approached his bank manager with the idea of a small business. He was told to obtain the necessary business skills by attending courses at the Mansfield Town Hall, a service now co-ordinated by Nottingham TEC. 'I went to every single meeting and course that was on offer,' he says, 'even if they seemed the same. Different tutors present things in different ways.'

John managed to compile a viable business plan with the help of the Business Agency (part of Nottingham TEC). He enrolled on the Enterprise Allowance Scheme and rented a workshop, where he started producing toys to sell to retailers and private buyers. 'I make all sorts of toys from puppets to Wendy houses; and in slack periods I also restore antique furniture,' he explains.

John has now relocated to a larger workshop in a converted forge, and specialises in making toys to order. He is delighted with his success: 'I seem to have the self-assurance to turn everything I touch to gold – touch wood,' he says.

An Uplifting Experience

MICHAEL ELLIOTT (44): *Forklift instructor*

Michael Elliott from Bath worked as a forklift driver and warehouseman for 23 years after leaving school. He had only recently been promoted to warehouse manager when he was made redundant.

However, determined not to be instantly depressed by the situation in which he found himself, Michael set about giving his period of unemployment some direction. 'After a while without work I began to think about what I could do with my skills.' During the six months of unemployment that followed Michael began to prepare for self-employment. 'After so long working for others I thought I might give self-employment a shot.' With the recent introduction of government legislation requiring forklift drivers to gain certificates, he decided to dedicate himself to becoming a freelance instructor. 'I had 23 years of experience; I just needed the qualifications.'

Michael funded himself for a ten-day course leading to the qualification he needed to be allowed to instruct forklift drivers. 'I was self-sponsored for this part but it was worth it.'

Once qualified, he approached FAME (Frome and Mendip Enterprise) with his business proposal. FAME recommended he undertake a seven-week course in book-keeping and marketing. Having compiled his business plan he then enrolled in the Somerset Enterprise Support (a version of the Enterprise Allowance) Scheme and started trading in July 1992.

He runs courses for both experienced and untrained operators on their companies' own premises, so, as he says, 'The capital cost was in training rather than equipment.' It means Michael often has to travel considerable distances and stay overnight at the locations where he is working.

After such a long time in employment working for himself has had a great change in his life, but it is a change he relishes: 'As an acquaintance said to me, 'You have to live on the edge – I don't know how you can do it.' Personally, I love it.'

Beer in the Butter Market

SYLVIA (43) AND IAON (47) EVANS: *Brewery*

Sylvia and Iaon Evans have stopped pulling pints behind the bar at the highest pub in Wales to roll out barrels of their own. And the couple have relied on the Enterprise Allowance Scheme plus help and advice from the Business Development Services provided by Training and Enterprise – the North East Wales TEC – to set up one of the country's latest breweries.

The couple decided that a dozen years as licensees was enough and gave up their jobs at the Sportsman's Arms on the Denbigh Moors, which stands 1,600 feet above sea level. Mrs Evans said: 'We wanted to use our knowledge from the catering business in another venture. Tourists often asked for the local brew – but there wasn't one, so we set out to make it.'

To help in the brewing process, 21-year old Patrick Dean has been taken on as a trainee under Skills Training. Qualified as a town planner, he could not get a job due to local government cutbacks across Britain and so swapped careers.

Now Sylvia, Ioan and Patrick are learning their craft together under the guidance of David Smith from York, a qualified brewery chemist, formerly with Sam Smiths of Tadcaster, who is advising them on methods and hygiene. They have converted the Old Butter Market, a listed building in Denbigh which has lain derelict for 20 years, to house two massive stainless steel brewing vessels. Initially they will be turning out ten barrels a week, hopefully increasing to 60 barrels in five years.

Two wholesalers and 80 pubs in North Wales and the north west have agreed to stock the two brews – a premium bitter called Cysur with an alcohol content of

4.2 per cent, and Castell, which is 3.6 per cent. For winter there are plans for a porter, a malt stout drink – once a Victorian favourite, now rapidly growing in popularity again – called Minster's Son.

All the drink advertising and marketing follow-ups, such as drip mats, will be bilingual.

Mrs Evans said: 'Business Development Services Team member Carol Farmer has given us a lot of help and advice on a whole variety of things including funding our training at Sheffield University. It's been reassuring to discuss day-to-day issues with Carol and find out exactly how to deal with them.'

Another Byte of the Apple

JOSEPH FERGUS: *Computer consultant*

Joseph Fergus's background is in computers. He studied at the South Bank University, and then worked as an accounts assistant for a year. On losing that job, he spent eight months unemployed, trying but failing to find work in his chosen field. 'I'd done my training,' he says, 'but just couldn't get the jobs I'd expected.' This led him to consider other options, among them starting his own business dealing with the computerisation of clerical work.

Joseph found help in compiling a business plan from Enterprise Training in Edmonton, North London. 'The pre-start-up process is good,' he asserts. 'It prepares you for what it's likely to be like when you actually get going.' When the proposal was complete, he took it to the Prince's Youth Business Trust to support his request for financial assistance. 'Your plans have to be sound if you want any help at all,' he says.

The PYBT recommended that he should research his market more thoroughly, following which he was awarded a grant of £1,500 and a £2,000 loan. The majority of this went immediately on the purchase of computer hardware and software: since much of his work was to take place at clients' offices, he was able to base himself in the front room of his flat, which reduced his capital outlay substantially.

Computerserve, Joseph's business bureau, has now been in operation for over a year, and he is particularly proud never to have been in the red with his bank. He provides a computer consultancy and training service, running specialist courses on a long-term or a freelance basis. He had not originally intended to specialise in training, but is now thinking of setting up a computer training school. He is, however, well aware of the extra costs involved in finding premises and employing staff.

Joseph attributes his success to his training, the advice he was given, the support of others, and his confidence in himself. 'You've got to believe you can do it, even when things are tough and disheartening, especially in the early months,' he says.

Boxing Clever

ROGER FISHER (28): *Gift boxes*

Roger Fisher, a former interior designer, is exporting a unique Scottish product all over Britain. Roger's company makes hand finished tartan gift boxes in all shapes and sizes for high class stores and hotels throughout the country who are snapping them up.

Since Heather Design Crafts – the only company of its kind in Scotland – started up in Carluke last December, Roger's family business has already won contracts from prestigious companies such as the Hilton Hotel in Glasgow, United Distillers, the Old Course Hotel in St Andrews, John Lewis in Edinburgh and Aberdeen and Baxters of Speyside and many others are set to follow.

Roger, who was unemployed before starting up his business, was assisted by Lanarkshire Development Agency's new Business Grant and the Ahead for Business scheme administered through the Clydesdale Development Company.

The 28-year-old who runs his business with the help of his wife Janice and mum Vi, said: 'The business has really taken off in the first few months. And we expect that it's going to expand rapidly in the first year.

'Production will increase when I take on new staff in the next couple of months and my wife and mum can have a well earned break after their stint as unpaid helpers.'

The company expects to have an annual turnover of around £50,000 to £100,000. But Roger's idea took months of planning before he finally took the plunge into the business world.

'We did months of market research around hotels, high-class stores, small companies, shops and distillers,' said Roger. 'It was really because the response was so favourable from every corner that I decided to go for it.

'Now we are hoping that we can export abroad and get into the foreign marketplace. Already LDA has helped us with brochure and exhibitions support and we are convinced it will pay off. Basically I couldn't have achieved so much in the first few months without the help of LDA and Clydesdale Development Company.'

Heather Design Crafts is run out of new premises in Castlehill Industrial Estate in Carluke, where Roger develops his gift boxes to suit every customer's needs.

Roger added: 'We tailor everything to the customers needs and we can design the boxes to any specification. The boxes are used for food and whisky products plus jewellery and specialised gift items.'

The new Business Grant from LDA made sure Roger was given enough capital to see him through the first crucial months and the LDA Ahead for Business Scheme gave him invaluable business advice.

Lynn Wilkinson, an LDA business development executive, who administers the

New Business Grant, said: 'We are delighted that Heather Design Crafts is doing so well in a short space of time.

'Our New Business Grant Programme is open to anyone who has a good business idea which has a good chance of success.'

Frying High

MALCOLM FLACK (48): *Fish-and-chip shop*

Malcolm Flack had worked in the meat industry since leaving school. Throughout his career he had demonstrated his ability as both a salesman and an administrator, gaining many promotions. In his 40s he became a regional manager for Dewhurst, in charge of many outlets and over 1,000 people. When the company was taken over by new management in 1991 he was obliged to leave his job. At the age of 45, for the first time in his life he was out of a job and out of the area of business he knew so well, in which there were 'few vacant jobs'.

Malcolm was determined to show that 'at the age of 47 you are not too old to change direction'. His idea was to 'stick with my basic knowledge and what I did well. In my job I had been promoted further and further away from what I was really good at, selling and customer care.' Throughout the time he was without a job, over a year, he set about discovering how to establish his own business.

To make the most of his talent and experience, Malcolm's plan was to set up his own butcher's shop. However, when he surveyed his home town of Lutterworth in Leicestershire he found that they were already supplied in this area. 'What they didn't have was good British fast food: in other words, fish and chips.'

Malcolm was convinced that he could make the change. 'I realised that the fish industry was not substantially different from what I knew.' He was sure that he could make a success of a fish-and-chip shop but took the precaution of laborious research and preparation for over eight months before starting up. 'I got myself into a position where I had not committed myself too far to withdraw if it was necessary.'

He took courses with the National Federation of Fish Friers and located a possible site for the shop. 'I used to sit in my car for evenings on end watching the people who passed the site to see if it would be the right spot.' Being unable to raise the capital to purchase the property himself, he found a local businessman who was willing to buy it on the understanding that Malcolm would lease it from him.

Malcolm's final step was to approach Leicestershire TEC, who soon realised that his business plan, research and forecasting were sufficient to qualify him immediately for support from the Enterprise Allowance Scheme. 'The course I was on was aimed at total beginners, whereas I did know what I was doing.'

Malcolm transferred his pension from his previous company into a private scheme using it as security on a loan in order to cover the costs that would initially be involved. The site was then fitted out as a shop with seating for 20, and an open-plan kitchen was designed so that 'nothing was kept secret from the customers'. The shop, Flackie's Plaice, was an immediate success. Malcolm's meticulous planning and commitment to quality began to pay off straight away. 'Turnover was much better than we predicted, as much as £6,000 a week.'

Malcolm relies mainly on 'word of mouth and good quality customer service' to advertise his shop and already has a remarkable degree of customer loyalty, attracting people 'from all around the county'. Malcolm is again able to use at first hand the skills of customer care and salesmanship which had won him his many promotions at Dewhurst. Previously, Malcolm had been 'promoted away from the customer', but now he is building his business by direct customer contact once again.

The work is hard and the commitment required immense but in the last few months Malcolm has opened a high street butcher's shop as well as three franchise butcher's counters in a well known supermarket chain and the fish-and-chip shop now employs 28 people. 'I have virtually no social life any more but I have decided to give it 100 per cent commitment for five years and see where I get.'

The Art of Success

TREVOR FORD (31): *Illustrator*

Trevor Ford was unemployed for a year after losing his job as a copywriter for an advertising agency. Further employment in this field was not forthcoming, so Trevor went back to the skills he had learned at the Maidstone College of Art, and set up as a freelance illustrator. His initial outlay was met with advances he received from his first clients and one advantage of this business was that start-up costs were minimal anyway. 'At first, I worked from home,' he says. 'All I needed were basic materials.'

Trevor's motivation and skill were cemented by the techniques of commercial planning and business strategy that he learned at a course run by his local Enterprise Agency in Barnet. 'I went to every course that was on offer,' he remembers. 'I couldn't have started without that back-up.'

He achieved his initial success by being confident and persistent in writing letters to and cold-calling potential clients. He inevitably received several rejections, but was undaunted. 'It was like water off a duck's back,' he laughs. He went on to receive orders, and has now built up a substantial portfolio, which includes work for Reader's Digest, trade magazines, and the *Mail on Sunday*, who commissioned him after he made a direct approach to the editor.

Working from a studio in the Selby Centre, North London, Trevor now relishes the challenge of being his own boss. 'Sometimes I think it would be nice to be able to leave it all behind, but then I remind myself what it was like working for someone else, and I don't regret a thing. I make a living, and enjoy the way I do it,' he says. He has been invited to join the governors of the Selby Centre to help others who are establishing themselves in business.

Curtain Up

KATE GEMMELL (43): *Soft furnishings*

'I had downgraded my CV many times but I still wasn't getting anywhere. Local companies where frightened by what I had been earning before. It was silly, but I just couldn't get a job.' In 1990, at 39, Kate Gemmell was made redundant from her senior management job with a national fashion retailer. She had been managing a turnover of £220 million. Today she runs her own local business, Curtains and Cushions, making soft furnishing in Buckinghamshire.

Kate continued to make applications for about eight months but without success. 'It wasn't a good time and I couldn't see myself getting anything locally. I felt I had to do something, for both personal and financial reasons.' The option of converting her unemployment benefit into Enterprise Allowance and establishing a small business seemed a 'sensible route to take'. 'I had experience in several fields and thought that either soft furnishings or celebration cakes might possibly work.' To test her immediate market, she placed advertisements in the local press: 'I got quite a few enquiries about soft furnishings and no response for the cakes.'

Believing she had identified a product for her local market Kate approached Milton Keynes TEC to undertake the necessary courses to be admitted on the Enterprise Allowance Scheme. 'Although I had been used to managing a very large budget it was helpful to learn about business on a smaller scale, and to get together with others who were doing the same thing.' Her first step was to contact suppliers and negotiate price rates for the materials she needed. Not yet having trade references, she used personal ones to secure credit.

When it finally came to advertising her service she aimed specifically at the local area. 'I hoped for a lot of local interest.' She placed advertisements in church magazines. 'This was excellent. I was helping myself and the church; the magazines reached the right audience and were very cheap to advertise in.' Kate started trading in August 1990 and is now in her third year of business. Working from home, she employs a full-time seamstress, has her own delivery van bearing the company logo and enjoys running a 'cottage industry'. 'I am well known in the area, which is a good thing, I suppose.'

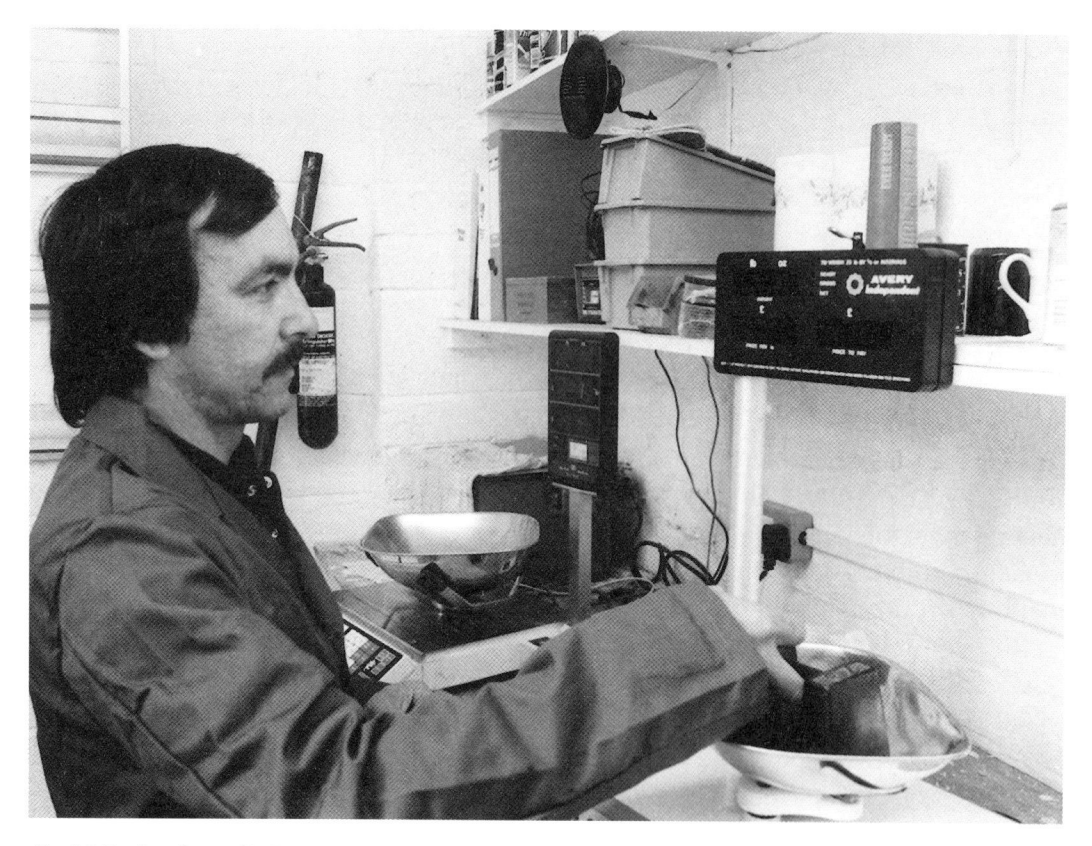

A Weight Off Your Mind

TREVOR GIBBON (41): *Weighing-machine services*

Having worked in the weighing field for some time, Trevor enjoyed his work. He originally gained an apprenticeship with Avery's, where he stayed for four years before leaving to become a junior mechanic with a small company. There he soon became a top mechanic and enjoyed a further career move when he became co-director of a new branch.

Unfortunately, Trevor was made redundant after ten years and subsequently dwelt on the idea of setting up on his own. This idea became more and more attractive during the ten months he was unemployed, as the prospects of finding an appropriate job looked less and less likely.

It was suggested to Trevor by the Job Centre that he apply to Newport and Gwent Enterprise for their allowance. Guided by the organisation itself, he produced a business plan which greatly impressed them, and two weeks later he began a course through the Enterprise Scheme. This course was actually run by Training Management Wales Ltd, and offered valuable lessons in business skills, marketing and finance, as well as informing Trevor and others of exactly what grants were available to them.

Trevor admits that the course could have been more beneficial to him had he attended it at the beginning of his period of unemployment. Nevertheless, he learned a great deal from the seven-week course.

At the end of the course proper, Trevor points out that there was a valuable call-back service available to those seeking any further advice or assistance. This involved weekly half-hour sessions where advisers helped to sort out queries and problems.

Trevor's Enterprise Allowance entitled him initially to £20 per week but after a further review it was decided to award him £40 per week. His receipt of this financial aid lasted from May 1993 until May 1994. It has provided the springboard for his business, which involves the supply, repair and hiring of weighing-machines to both industry and the retail sector. His market, which now includes most of south Wales, is constantly expanding and Trevor is hoping to break into new markets in the new year.

Baby Boom

JEREMY GILL: *Children's nursery*

Jeremy Gill first decided to start up in business when after five years he was forced to leave his gardening job due, as luck would have it, to a form of asthma that made him allergic to grass.

He set up Babycomforts with his wife in November 1987, supplying nappies, baby milk and other babycare products to mothers in the Plymouth area. Aided by a one-day small business seminar, run by Plymouth Job Centre, a successful application to the Enterprise Allowance Scheme and his wife's previous experience as a ledger clerk, the business went very well at first and Jeremy reports a £60,000 turnover at its peak.

When one of the Gills' children fell seriously ill the priorities of the successful husband and wife team were drastically altered. Under pressure from newly formed competing firms and a deteriorating economic climate, Jeremy was forced to start claiming income support from late 1991, and to run the business on a part-time basis only. 'Our new van was repossessed, mortgage rates were rising and at one point we thought we may even lose the house. Things didn't look too good,' he remembers.

When the business finally ceased trading in January 1992 Jeremy began a fruitless search for jobs, even applying for more gardening work. He found his lack of success (and often the lack of replies to his applications), 'soul-destroying', and by September of that year had already started thinking of self-employment again.

At the time his sister was training to become a playgroup nursery nurse and, having already decided to build on their strengths, namely bringing up their three children, Mr and Mrs Gill started looking for premises at which to open a day nursery for the children of working parents.

They attended another seminar on the practicalities of running a small business but found the more humanistic part of the course more helpful: 'They made you ask yourself if you were the right sort of person to be self-employed, and taught me that I had to be a little more assertive, more hard-nosed, and learn to take the good days with the bad,' Jeremy explains. They took their business plan, prepared with the help of Enterprise Plymouth, business advisers, to the Prince's Youth Business Trust, who encouraged them to carry out extensive market research before further advising them on their venture.

The £500 bursary grant and £3,000 loan from the trust enabled them to foot the £2,000 bill for necessary improvements to their Brixton Village premises, and on 4 January 1993 Harlequin's Nursery opened to the public.

The nursery currently cares for 12 children in both its morning and afternoon sessions, employing the help of two qualified nursery nurses (including Jeremy's sister) as well as the Gills themselves, and has an approximate turnover of £450 per week. Aside from co-running the centre and dealing with parents, Mrs Gill is also studying for her Diploma in Playgroup Practice.

'Everything we learned from our last business we've put into practice here. It's nice to be self-sufficient again!' say the Gills.

A Flare for Business

STEPHEN ILLIDGE (24): *Firework displays*

Losing his position as a clerk in an aluminium company meant that Stephen was without a permanent job for two years. He found occasional work as a traffic surveyor but this was unreliable and he experienced long periods of unemployment.

Dissatisfied with this state of affairs he finally contacted his local Enterprise Agency, 'Business Link' in Runcorn, who helped him draw up a business plan which was approved by the Prince's Youth Business Trust. They awarded him a bursary of £1,500 and a loan of £2,000 and suggested he undertake accountancy and marketing courses at NORMIDTEC (North and Mid-Cheshire TEC) in Warrington.

Stephen had always been fascinated by fireworks but had often been disappointed by the displays he had attended. Believing he could do the job better Stephen set up his business 'Pyro-Tech', which now designs, organises and directs spectacular firework displays around the country. His list of clients already includes Granada TV, a number of county councils and a famous international holiday resort.

The first year has not been altogether easy because of the cyclical nature of his business, but Stephen has taken orders for events to be staged over the next four years. Pyro-Tech's orders are currently worth over £220,000 and he is planning to expand by taking on six staff in the coming year.

His Enterprise Agency also suggested he enter the Livewire Competition, where he was one of the ten finalists in the 1993 Business Start-up Awards. As he has to spend 40 to 50 hours planning every minute of each display, Stephen is only too aware that good preparation is vital to success. He similarly detailed preparation devoted to establishing his business and now that he is starting to reap the rewards he is delighted with the support he received.

Pressing Engagements

ANDREW JACKSON (27): *Laundry service*

After a year's unemployment when his job as a salesman finished, Andrew Jackson was inspired by an American idea to form his own laundry service. Having set himself this objective, Andrew raised £1,000 by taking a succession of casual jobs and then enrolling on the Enterprise Allowance Scheme.

Kent TEC sent him on a marketing course run by Laucrom Training in Maidstone. He was 'pleasantly surprised' by the components of the course, which, he says, sharpened common sense assumptions into basic business techniques. Andrew had no previous experience of the laundry business, but realised that there was a gap in the market in his home town of Chatham and the surrounding part of Kent, where he set up Pressing Engagements. He has been proved right: several other similar companies have copied his idea in the region, although most have since ceased to trade. One former competitor even recommends Andrew's company to his ex-customers.

Often working 18 hours a day, Andrew co-ordinates all his company's activities: collection from and delivery to customers; finding staff to work for him, and keeping the books. Three years after he started Andrew now employs 18 people, has a turnover of around £48,000 a year and is about to start franchising out the business as the demand for his service is growing rapidly.

Another Brick in the Wall

MARK JAMES: *Writer, bricklayer and lecturer*

Mark James, of Byker in Newcastle, left school at the age of 15 unable to read or write. He worked as a labourer for many years, until the recession left him without a job and with no apparent prospect of getting one. 'I used to watch younger men going off to work every day, and couldn't believe that I, with no qualifications, would ever find a job again,' he says.

He spent his time watching television and wondering what to do with his life. Then an ad for the Newcastle Education Centre caught his eye, and, realising that he needed some qualifications, he decided to apply for their adult training course. The centre was based in the primary school, which made him feel uncomfortable, but the one-to-one tutoring he received there was invaluable, to the extent that he not only learned to write, but he also discovered a real talent for it.

In 1988, he won the Sid Chaplin Short Story Competition with his book *The Byker Lion*, a humorous account of life in the Byker community. The proceeds have been donated to charity, and Mark's confidence has risen. 'You're never too old to start learning,' he observes. 'The hardest part is picking up the pen.'

Following the course, he retrained in bricklaying at Newcastle College, where he now works as a technician in the bricklaying department, as well as lecturing part-time. 'It's like being born again,' he comments. 'I feel ten years younger.'

Bring Me Sunshine

LOUISA LYLE: *Sun-bed hire*

Louisa Lyle, from Wednesbury, had a variety of jobs, including working in the office at a car auctioneer's and in a building society, when a bad car accident put her out of work. She spent three years in and out of hospital, followed by another two years' unemployment.

As a single mother, Louisa was eager to find work, and on applying for a local Enterprise Allowance, she was told that Sandwell Training Enterprise Council ran courses for people hoping to establish their own businesses.

On enquiring, Louisa was invited to an induction day and she subsequently decided to join the course. In order to qualify for the Sandwell Business Development Loan, Louisa herself had to raise £1,000, which she managed to do.

The training course itself lasted for six weeks and involved two nights per week of actual training, which included accounting, book-keeping, and learning to deal with customers. After the end of the course, Sandwell were extremely helpful in offering further advice. Louisa was also offered a loan by the Sandwell Loan Scheme at a very low rate of interest of five per cent. Louisa also participated in a number of one-day seminars which contributed to her business awareness.

Beginning with seven sun-beds, Louisa advertised in the Yellow Pages and her business boomed. She now has 70 for hire. She has even bought another small company, and her husband has been brought into the company as well.

Louisa's sun-bed hire company is an example of the potential of the small business for successful growth, made possible largely through the hard work and optimism of the initiator. Moreover she claims: 'I am very happy.'

Designs on Success

SARAH MABBUTT (28): *Designer*

Equipped with several O-Levels and an HND in advertising and promotional graphics, Sarah Mabbutt left the Berkshire College of Art and found a job working as a graphic design consultant at Fox and Partners in Bath. Following a disagreement and acting on impulse, Sarah resigned and was left without a job.

After spending six months unemployed, she grew tired of the endless round of unsuccessful interviews and decided that she would be better off working for herself. 'I hadn't a clue what to do,' she admitted, but luckily her benefit office suggested that she should approach FAME (Frome and Mendip Enterprise), who offered her a one-day induction course to explain their Enterprise Allowance Scheme. Thereafter followed six further days (one per week) of training. Sarah was given training in accounting and financial matters, in particular in dealing with banks, and a grounding in fundamental business skills. She learned a lot through this course, which she felt complemented and advanced her HND training, and subsequently compiled a business plan which was approved by Somerset TEC.

Sarah then entered for the Enterprise Allowance Scheme which entitled her to £30 a week and free advice for a year. In fact her progress was monitored for 18 months and she was invited to attend a variety of other one-day seminars, including a short course on taxation and advertising and promotion seminars.

Today, 18 months after Sarah established her own design company from home in Beckington, her success is notable. In her first year in business she made a profit of approximately £17,000 with work including the creation of leaflets and brochures for companies such as Saab and Iveco Ford. Within the next year she aims to enlist the help of a part-time secretary.

Tax Relief

ANNIE MANLY (39): *Personal taxation services*

Annie Manly, from Winchester, worked in accountancy and taxation for several years before setting up her own business. The arrival of children largely necessitated this move away from inflexible working hours, and Annie found it most suitable, as well as challenging, to work for herself.

In little over two years, she has established a reputable taxation service and regularly deals with up to 300 clients. Although she admits that initially the responsibility of running your own company is quite daunting, she says: 'I couldn't work for anybody else now'.

Annie first gained experience in this field working for the Inland Revenue after completing a four-year business studies course at college. She was them employed as a trainee chartered accountant but disliked the auditing involved and subsequently returned to taxation, as an assistant manager. She then worked for an accountancy firm in Winchester for six years before being made redundant in January 1991 due to staff cut-backs.

After the birth of her first child, Annie wanted to go back to work but the most she was able to find was four days' work a week. She contacted a former colleague, who managed to give her some part-time work until she left to have a second baby.

She did not intend to set up a business of her own but many clients were keen to retain her services when they heard that she was due to leave. She began to advertise during her pregnancy and managed to keep approximately 24 clients when she finally departed to set up on her own.

When her second child was old enough to be cared for by a child-minder, Annie turned her attention in earnest towards building up the business. In January 1992 she began to advertise in the local paper and in May was even able to buy the business of a retiring colleague, adding a further 50 to 60 clients to her ever-growing business.

She says that on setting up her business, Annie Manly Personal Taxation Services, she was equipped with only a 20-year-old portable typewriter and a pen, thus dispelling claims that it is initially necessary to buy a great deal of expensive equipment. Annie did all her photocopying at Prontaprint and managed to run the business single-handedly as well as looking after a young family.

During the first year, she estimates that the company swallowed approximately £6,000, but this later proved to have been a sensible investment. Her company now employs up to seven part-time staff on a regular basis as well as several others through a freelance arrangement.

As regards the financial side of things, Annie admits: 'You couldn't do it with nothing to start with, as you need money to keep you going'. For this, Annie made several sacrifices, but as we have seen in other case studies, there are ways of obtaining grants, as well as low-interest loans, for those wishing to set up their own businesses. Annie herself recently took out a loan for £3,000 in order to buy a new computer, as well as a further loan of £7,500 to enable her to move her office to more spacious premises.

Annie is confident about the future and the steady and successful growth of the company and is a fine example of the possibility of establishing a personal and thriving business at the same time as bringing up a family.

Dancing to a Different Tune

TASHA MARDON (27): *Disc jockey*

Tasha Mardon's original career was in catering, but eight months of unemployment forced her to consider other options. Eventually, she attended a women's Business Breakthrough course at the Hackney Business Venture, aiming to set herself up as a DJ.

Having decided on her initial idea, she received help from the Enterprise Training Scheme. This included ideas for market research and information on subjects such as taxation, as well as a free computing and desktop publishing course.

She took the name 'Killer Pussies' from a record cover and, since DJ-ing had been a hobby and she already had her own equipment, immediately set about establishing her business in this male-dominated world by phoning record companies and persuading them to add her to their mailing lists. 'You've got to be persistent,' she advises, 'and never wait for anyone to phone you back.' She sent tapes of her work all over the country, and the offers began to arrive.

As a result of Tasha's persistence, since 1990 Killer Pussies has appeared at the Wag Club in Soho, Sterns in Sussex, and on Kiss FM Radio. Tasha also ran and DJ'd on Easy on the Edge, Europe's only satellite dance music station.

She now works at least one night a weekend, earning on average £100 an hour, and she practises for two hours every day. She believes that you should be prepared, initially at least, to work for free, as each appearance creates publicity. Part of her policy is to play whatever type of music her customers want, and she specifically concentrates on playing music people will know and will enjoy dancing to.

She is glad that she went into business alone: 'This way, I'm the only one who can make a mistake,' she says. 'And it's given my individuality a chance to develop.' And, although it hasn't all been easy, she has found the whole venture extremely rewarding. 'It's a challenge to go out and create something for yourself,' she says, 'rather than being handed it on a plate.'

Sweet Wine

RICHARD MARSHALL (50): *Wine merchant*

Richard Marshall had worked in insurance all his life. After several jobs around the country with Royal Insurance, he had become a managing director of their Estate Agency Division. Yet in 1991, as a result of restructuring within the company, he was made redundant at the age of 47. He was without work for eight months before establishing his own business selling personally labelled wine.

After redundancy Richard launched a two-pronged campaign to get back to work. As well as applying for jobs he started to speculate about the possibility of running his own business. 'I continued to apply for jobs but soon realised that in the climate at the time it would be hard to duplicate the type of position I had had before.' He had the 'galling' experience of being short-listed for several jobs only to fall at the final hurdle, and the prospect of 'taking the plunge' and setting up by himself began to seem more and more appealing.

Richard's research took the form of reading books on the basic strategy of business start-up and attending exhibitions by other small entrepreneurs at the NEC in Birmingham and Olympia in London. He took the view that the product was secondary to the techniques used to market it. 'I came to realise that you shouldn't be daunted. The most important thing in any new business is selling and marketing the product. After a life-time in insurance I knew that I could do that.'

Richard's next step was to find a product. 'I looked at areas where I felt my experience and skills must be appropriate,' he explained. These included travel agencies and print-shop franchises, but these, he felt, were, 'essentially green-field exercises that had already been exploited. The simple rule of enterprise is that you need something different, unique.' It was at one of the exhibitions he regularly attended during this period that he came across the product he was looking for: a specialist method of merchandising wine, printing promotional material and company logos directly on to the bottle.

With his product, marketing skills and a business plan he approached Lincolnshire Enterprise Agency, who approved him for the Enterprise Allowance Scheme after their induction course.

Richard works from home, marketing his product to companies for use in their own promotional activities. The printing work for the labels and advertising material is sub-contracted, as is the design work: his role is essentially one of agent. 'The capital costs in buying plant would have been prohibitive,' he explains. 'The product can speak for itself.' The size of his contracts varies from a few to as many as 48 cases, almost 500 bottles.

Richard has found the ideal product on which to bring his marketing skills to bear, and he is enthusiastic about the opportunities that working for himself provides. 'Having worked for institutions all my life, it is a great change to be self-employed. When things go well you can take all the credit yourself and you are in charge of your own destiny.'

Chapter and Verse

VALERIE McALISTER: *Bookseller*

Valerie McAlister ceased full-time employment several years ago to raise a family. She subsequently obtained a part-time sales job but had to leave that job for family reasons. She remained unemployed for six years until October 1992 when she applied for an Action for Community Employment (ACE) post with Larne Community Enterprises. ACE is a temporary employment scheme in Northern Ireland to help long-term unemployed people back into work.

She was successful in obtaining the post of Home Visitation Officer which involved visiting elderly people living on their own to identify social and welfare needs.

The project manager of Larne Community Enterprises states that when Valerie McAlister first joined ACE she was very much lacking in confidence, having been away from the workplace for so long. However, the work experience and training provided by ACE caused something of a transformation and Valerie became so successful at her job that she was offered a supervisory post (Home Visitation Co-ordinator).

ACE employees are encouraged to make use of the ACE Enterprise Scheme (AES) which is designed to encourage ACE employees to create new businesses. To facilitate the transition to self-employment, employees are permitted to trade commercially for a period of up to 13 weeks while remaining employed by ACE.

Towards the end of her ACE placement Valerie came up with the idea of setting up her own business (a bookshop selling bargain books) and made an application for assistance under AES.

Valerie McAlister's application was approved and following a period of enterprise training she opened her bookshop ('Chapter and Verse') in January 1994. Valerie left ACE in April 1994 and she is making a success of the business.

In a letter of thanks to the ACE project manager Valerie states: 'I started my job in ACE with a lot of doubts and trepidation as to whether I would cope with it but you were always at hand to encourage me and instil a new confidence in me during those moments of doubt.

'My job entailed being responsible for the team of home visitors and the van crew and this responsibility gave me added confidence in my own abilities. Last year you talked about a business start course during one of our meetings and this made me start thinking seriously about trying to fulfil a lifelong ambition of running my own business.

'I have now completed the Enterprise course and I will be opening a bookshop within a few weeks.

'Before working for your organisation I would not have had the confidence or ability to achieve this goal and words can never fully express my gratitude for helping me to do so.'

Driving Force

GARY McEWAN (26): *HGV instructor*

Gary McEwan initially trained and worked as an HGV instructor, but after being made redundant he spent a year unemployed. He then approached Glasgow Opportunities, his local Enterprise Agency, with the idea of setting up a business to exploit a market gap he had noticed when he was employed: that of after-care, or helping HGV trainees to find work after qualifying.

Advisers at the Enterprise Agency suggested that Gary should apply for financial help from the Prince's Youth Business Trust. After completing the Glasgow Opportunities accountancy and sales courses, he drew up a business plan with their help and duly approached the PYBT, who agreed to give him a grant of £1,500 and a low-interest loan of £5,000, which covered the capital costs of the business.

Gary's business, Associated Freight Training, has been markedly successful: to date, 95 per cent of the trainees on their books, many of whom were previously unemployed, have gained work in the Glasgow area. He now attracts customers from all over Scotland. In 1993 he won a £3,000 award at the UK Livewire Final, when he was judged Entrepreneur of the Year and in April 1994 his company won another £1,000 from Livewire as the business that had made the most progress over the last year. 'That money,' he says, 'will enable me to buy a bus to extend my training activities. Eventually, I want to have a complete training centre which offers examinations.'

He emphasises that the most important step he took was his initial approach to Glasgow Opportunities, and encourages others to do the same in their area. 'Approach your local Enterprise Agency, get talking, and end the isolation that being without a job can bring,' he advises.

Bread and Buffers

HUGH McMAHON (44): *Sandwich bar*

Two years ago Hugh McMahon passed through Billericay train station twice a day commuting to work in London. Today he no longer travels with the commuters but instead provides them with a service. At 41 Hugh McMahon was made redundant from the job he had had since he left school. Now he runs a sandwich bar, Bread and Buffers, on Billericay station.

'I had worked in the production department of a magazine publisher. After I was made redundant I applied for jobs in the same area but got nothing.' Eight months' unemployment followed, during which time Hugh became sure that the solution to his problems would be to establish his own business. 'I was 99 per cent sure it was what I wanted to do.' He approached Essex Enterprise and suggested the possibility of starting a sandwich bar.

His advisers were enthusiastic about his proposal and started him on a business start-up scheme for four months (one day a week). 'Although I had worked for such a long time I knew very little about running a business, and the course was a great help,' he remembered. Having completed this, Hugh was enrolled on the Enterprise Allowance Scheme and received a basic income while establishing himself.

Finding the right premises presented new problems and it was some time before a vacancy appeared on Billericay BR station. Hugh used the last of his redundancy money to refit the shop and started trading in the autumn of 1992. The way of life is very different from the days when he had to commute to London each day. 'The hours are long and the work is hard, but I have no regrets,' he said.

Enterprising Folk

GLEN AND GARY MILLER (27): *Folk group*

Sherburn twins Glen and Gary left school at 18 and sought jobs locally. Gary worked for the County Council as a clerk on a temporary basis until his placement expired, and he was subsequently unemployed for approximately two years. Similarly, Glen worked as a local government trainee accountant for the Treasury Department, but later spent a year out of work.

Together they lived on their unemployment benefit and financed their folk band with money which they had saved while in the sixth form at school. Glen claims that they had both always wanted to do something in the music business. They had played in pubs and in other venues in the past but not on what they would call a serious level.

Members of the band did attend a pre-start-up course at the Chester-le-Street and Durham Enterprise Agency, which was geared towards helping them to develop their own business plan. They worked closely with the agency, receiving much advice and more specialist information relevant to their particular business. On approaching both the PYBT and other Enterprise schemes they were told that their business plan was one of the best ever seen and they were in no real need of support although they did in fact receive the minimum enterprise allowance.

Known as The Whisky Priests, they had little experience of performing in public and were initially, like a lot of bands, relatively unknown. It was hard work for the five of them: they bought music periodicals, went to libraries, and searched through the Yellow Pages looking for venues in which to play. For weeks and weeks they pursued this work and very gradually they were able to increase their fee as they became more well-known.

The band's entourage now consists of five full-time members and they frequently employ others, such as a sound engineer, on a casual basis, particularly when they are on tour. Session musicians also work for them part-time on a sub-contract if they are short of a player.

They now use agents to organise most of their work abroad, which has taken them

Glen and Gary Miller and The Whisky Priests.

to Austria, Holland, Belgium and Germany, among other places. Glen claims that it is more than a hobby now, but their success means that they do have less time to spend on their music because they now have other matters, such as administration, to attend to. However, they do realise that, 'we are lucky to be able to earn a living from something we enjoy'.

Glen manages most of the accounts, claiming to use common sense for a lot of the work. Some time ago he did a two-year accountancy course at New College, Durham, as well as working as a trainee accountant, and this experience has obviously helped.

The band's success is due mainly to a persistent determination to progress and produce popular material. As a band they have produced three albums which have proved very popular, particularly on the Continent.

After one and a half years spent laying the foundations, the rewards are now evident. They are planning several foreign tours next year, and are also exploring the possibility of performing in the USA.

A Clean Sweep

ANNE MORRIS: *Industrial cleaning service*

Anne Morris wanted a career in the film industry, so she left her home town of Liverpool to take a degree course in film and video studies at Hull. On graduation, she moved to London but found it impossible to get any kind of job, let alone one in her chosen field. 'It was incredibly difficult,' she says. 'It was so demoralising to go down to the job centre and not find anything, not even something for which I needed no training.'

There followed seven months of job-searching. Apart from the question of money, Anne stresses the psychological strain that goes with unemployment. 'I suppose I wasn't unemployed for that long, and I kept myself occupied; but even so it made me doubt my ability. I lost confidence frighteningly fast. I don't know how people cope when they are out of work for a very long time.'

It was in the face of such a prospect that Anne considered establishing herself in business. Before committing herself to anything, she enrolled on a four-month full-time course at Downham Business Centre in south London (funded by SOLOTEC in Bromley). 'The course covered all aspects of running a business,' she says. 'I wouldn't have wanted to set up on my own without this training. It made sure I knew what I was doing.' The confidence Anne had lost while she was unemployed soon returned. 'It is so important to get your confidence back, and to remember that there are still things you can do,' she stresses.

During her time on the course, she decided on the idea of setting up a domestic and industrial cleaning service. 'It was a long way from film studies,' she admits, 'but I knew it would work.' She found there was a gap in the market for this kind of service in her home area of Forest Hill in south-east London. With help from advisers on the course she drew up a business plan which was submitted to the Prince's Youth Business Trust (PYBT), who approved it and granted her a low-interest loan of £3,000.

Anne's background in the media enabled her to mount a successful and professional advertising campaign, which involved the distribution of 20,000 leaflets locally, and a series of advertisements in local newspapers.

Her persistence was rewarded. Just over a year after starting, she now employs 17 people on a part-time basis, and the company's turnover is more than £60,000. Her own experience of unemployment has shaped her attitude to those she now employs: her philosophy is to employ 'those who have most difficulty in finding work, particularly single mothers. I try to make schedules flexible to fit in with their lives.' She also works part-time at Catford Centre for the unemployed: 'It is such a help when I can explain to people here that I have also experienced unemployment,' she says. 'It means they know I'm not talking down to them.'

On the Record

ADAM AND JASON PERRY (23): *Mobile recording unit*

Identical twins Adam and Jason Perry both graduated from college in graphic design and spent a year looking for work in this field before deciding to try to get into the music business, an ambition of theirs since they set up a band at the age of 14. Perhaps the main objective was to get off the dole. 'You can only watch *Home and Away* twice a day for so long,' remembers Jason.

They had been filling in some of their spare time by recording friends' music for free. This gave them the idea of setting up a mobile recording system which would allow them to reach customers who would not normally venture into a studio. Both twins stress the importance of the original idea: they were filling a previous gap in the market.

They approached the PYBT with their idea for The Four-Wheeled Groove Machine, and were given a £1,500 grant and a £2,000 loan for buying equipment, as well as the services of a financial adviser who visits them every month. They also joined the Enterprise Training Scheme for three months, which gave them structured advice and support, and then spent a further three months on the Enterprise Rehearsal Scheme. This was followed by 29 weeks' Enterprise Allowance payments. 'There is masses of help around,' comments Adam. 'You just have to dredge up all your enthusiasm.'

The brothers also worked hard at generating interest by word of mouth. They bought a van and announced that they would record anywhere, and would even write songs for their customers. The whole venture has been a resounding success in London and the surrounding area, and this has allowed them to set up their own band, A, which has just signed a major recording contract. Now operating as Alien Studios, they are looking to establish a permanent base in Camden or Soho.

The pair advise others seeking to get out of unemployment to 'be willing to do anything, and don't expect miracles in the first year'.

Auto Start

DONALD RIDDELL (22): *Car repairs*

Upon leaving school, Donald Riddell worked in a local garage for five years serving his apprenticeship as a motor mechanic. Through no fault of his own however he was to find himself out of work.

After a spell of six months of unemployment, he decided go self-employed, using the skills that he had acquired during his apprenticeship.

Having located suitable premises and arranged acceptable terms and conditions with the landlord, Donald set himself up in business as a motor mechanic providing vehicle repairs and servicing.

Finance was of course a major consideration. Donald who was 21 obtained funding from the Prince's Scottish Youth Business Trust (PSYBT) and from Western Isles Enterprise's New Start programme (WINS) in addition to his own personal funds and has traded successfully since February 1993.

Donald has quickly established a good reputation for his work and in 1994 Riddell Auto Repairs was recognised as The Most Promising Newcomer in the Highlands & Islands Business Awards.

Food for Thought

CHRIS SAUL: *Doughnut maker*

Chris Saul worked as a computer operations support analyst until he was made redundant in July 1990. While he was scanning the small ads looking for work, he came across an article about a shop in Eastbourne which sold freshly made American-style doughnuts. He and his wife Ellen immediately felt that this would be an interesting idea for a small business. They decided to make use of Chris's redundancy pay to create a new career for themselves. To raise the necessary capital, they sold their London house and moved to rented accommodation in Dorset.

Knowing nothing about catering, they took research very seriously, and went to Canada to investigate the art of making real American-style doughnuts. 'There are a lot of doughnut shops in the Ontario area, but finding someone to train us took weeks. We came very close to giving up. However, in the end we learned all about the ingredients and baking methods and came back with a list of the 30 flavours we now make,' says Chris. The couple even tested the recipes on local shoppers before setting up. 'Exeter's favourite is the caramel creme doughnut, topped with caramel and injected with vanilla custard.'

Although they had decided not to borrow any money, it was obvious that they would need advice in establishing and managing the financial side of the business. They approached the Devon and Cornwall TEC, where, among other things, they learned how to draw up their business plan and to prepare a cash flow forecast. The help they received was quite general – 'obviously, they couldn't give us advice specifically in the art of making doughnuts' – but has proved invaluable, as has the continued support provided by their quarterly assessments.

Today Chris feels it is their determination to succeed that has had the greatest effect. 'You need to have a unique idea, to be open to all possibilities, and not to allow yourself to be distracted.'

Taking the Plunge

BOB SCULLION AND ALLAN RICE: *Diving centre*

Bob Scullion had already been self-employed once before but had not enjoyed working a 40-hour week without any financial gain, so he and his partner at the time had agreed to close down the business.

From there Bob took a job as a doorman at a local nightclub and became friends with the manager, Allan. They had both arranged holidays and decided to take diving lessons together before they went, qualifying after several weeks.

One afternoon they were preparing to dive and realised they didn't have any air in their tanks. 'It was impossible to get any. We were able to fill up our tanks at the centre where we had taken our lessons but only at restricted times. This was when we identified a need for an air supply.' They decided to put an air supply into Bob's house which was close to the sea and make it available to other divers, advertising locally, but when they applied for planning permission they were turned down. Undefeated, they decided to look for premises to set up in. Bob and Allan realised that this would require more money than they could raise themselves and so, with advice from a friend who was already in business, they put together a business plan.

Looking around for loans and information on premises, they stumbled across Business Link South Tyneside (part of the TEC) where they explained their situation. The staff made an appointment for them both to speak to June Leech, a business counsellor for TEDCO (an Enterprise Agency). After several sessions with June it was agreed that their business plan was now viable and they successfully applied for a Tyneside Enterprise Allowance award. This in itself was still not enough but they were again successful in obtaining a loan from another Enterprise Agency.

At that time Allan was forced to go into hospital for an operation so Bob started to look around for premises and discovered that most rents were much more than they could afford. However, he eventually came across premises which the council were letting at a more reasonable rate and raced into hospital to get Allan to sign the papers.

They finally got the keys and with the help of their partners decorated the shop and fitted it out. 'When we started out our main income came from the air supply but very quickly money began coming in from equipment sales. We found people were coming into the shop to fill their tanks and buying the equipment on display.'

Continued success has meant that Bob and Allan are now planning on starting a diving school which will involve contracting out work to a self-employed instructor. 'Neither of us are qualified to instruct quite yet and with all our time being taken up with the shop this seems to be the best solution at the moment.'

Get the Picture?

HILARY SHEDEL (29): *Photographer*

While studying for an HND in stage management at the Central School of Speech and Drama in London, Hilary Shedel became heavily involved in photography. She started taking on freelance commissions, mainly actors' *Spotlight* photographs and publicity shots for shows. When the course finished, she decided to pursue a career in photography, and started to work for professional photographic companies in London.

in photography, and started to work for professional photographic companies in London.

After three years working in, and running, photographic laboratories, acquiring as much 'on the job' experience as possible, she decided to combine her photographic and dark-room skills and set up on her own. She spent eight months unemployed, during which time she explored various different ways of making her ambition a

Shadwell, received advice from the London Enterprise Agency (LENTA), and successfully applied for a £1,100 grant from the PYBT, which along with a £2,000 bank loan, paid for the equipment she initially needed.

Hilary's early training in the theatre helped her compile her client list, which includes actors and actresses and dance and theatre companies. Her work also includes portraiture and PR material for corporate clients, including the Reader's Digest, National Westminster Bank, Brent Council and Tesco Stores. In 1990, she won a national competition to take the official birthday portrait of Prince Charles. She also works as a voluntary photographer for the AIDS charity, the Terence Higgins Trust.

Hilary has found working alone an isolating experience, as 'there's no one to bounce ideas off'. This led her to join a small business support group in London, which provided regular opportunities for discussion. 'That was invaluable,' she says now. 'There were about eight of us, all from the local area, and we'd meet fortnightly and discuss business ideas. If you had a problem like a difficult client who wouldn't pay, or whatever, you could find out how everyone else would handle the situation, as well as being reassured that you weren't the only one with problems.'

She is anxious to stress the impact that running her own business has had on her social life. 'It's a huge commitment. Life totally changes, it becomes impossible to switch off from work. Your social life has to come second, or you just couldn't make the business work.' Her advice to anyone else considering setting up on their own is: 'Talk to people who are in business alone, find out how it affects their lives, and then think about whether you are willing to make the commitment.'

Going for Growth

RACHAEL SPEERS (26): *Plants for hire*

'In the sixth form I had thought about starting my own business, but didn't know what to do and didn't give it much more thought.' On leaving school Rachael Speers went into employment as a bus driver for two years before she left Barrow-in-Furness for Australia. Returning in 1990 at the age of 22 she 'hoped to find a better job than before, but there was nothing around'.

Rachael was unemployed for 20 months, until 1992, when she established her own business, a service hiring out green plants for her local business community. 'I wanted something with good prospects.' The idea she had had while still at school was brought back to life, but this time followed through to its conclusion.

To help her realise her ambition, Rachael's benefit office put her in contact with Furness Business Initiative. The lack of knowledge that had posed a problem before was now remedied. She undertook courses in book-keeping, business administration and marketing and produced a business plan. 'I realised I would have to do something that would not require a lot of capital,' she explained.

Rachael drew on an idea she had seen in Australia: hiring out plants, both indoor and outdoor, to business offices. Her service would include caring for the rented greenery. Although Rachael admits to having 'enjoyed gardening', her proposal was more a business proposition than the result of a hobby. 'I knew that there was only one company doing it, and they were quite a way away, in Kendal.'

Her research was based on speaking to local companies and suggesting the idea. Once her business plan had been approved she started to receive Enterprise Allowance payments and NatWest Bank arranged a £1,000 overdraft for her to cover any initial costs. Foliage Plant Hire began trading in June 1992 and at first Rachael relied on word of mouth, on people she knew in the area, to get things started. 'I built it up from there,' she recalled.

Rachael now services a considerable number of companies in her area as well as providing displays for special occasions. She works by herself from home, getting casual help as she needs it. She buys her plants from local nurseries and is building up a capital base as the number of plants she owns increases.

Although Rachael benefited from the advice and business support she received she now realises that she learns a lot 'on the job'. Having decided she 'might as well have a go', she is happy to expand her company as her business experience increases.

Mediterranean Flavours

PANAGIOTIS AND MARI STAVROS: *Greek taverna*

Following a period living in his native Corfu, Panagiotis Stavros and his Llanrwst-born wife, Mari, returned to Blaenau Ffestiniog. Like many other people in the area they faced unemployment. After being out of work for over a year, the enterprising couple decided to make use of their business and catering experiences in order to open a Greek taverna in the centre of town.

They were to encounter many problems and setbacks before their idea could become a reality. They bought shop premises in the high street but when they applied for permission to convert their shop premises into a taverna they were immediately refused permission and discouraged from even thinking about the idea. After a disastrous period running the premises as a Greek leather shop they applied again and eventually got their 'change of use'.

By this time, however, they had two young children and their financial situation was not at all healthy. They had to sell everything they owned to raise money for the conversion with Panagiotis having to do all the work himself, reusing the existing nails and wood in order to save money. By the time the premises were ready they had been served with a repossession order from the bank, but managed to persuade them that they needed more time. The restaurant finally opened that summer and has become the talk of the town and has since become an ongoing business employing up to ten people at the height of the season. They have a turnover well in excess of £31,000 and a profit margin of approximately 60 per cent. The restaurant is now so busy that they have to operate on a bookings-only basis and frequently have to turn people away.

During the time that they were setting up their business, the couple made full use the advice, guidance and financial support of TARGED (North West Wales TEC). They successfully applied for the Enterprise Allowance Scheme and as Mari explained, 'The Enterprise Allowance that we received was absolutely essential to our determination to establish the taverna. Without the security of the weekly cash flow of £40 each we would have had great doubt about starting the venture.'

Panagiotis and Mari are optimistic about the future and it is their intention to establish a chain of restaurants across North Wales and employ other people to manage them. The couple recently won the first prize of £1,000 in a competition jointly sponsored by TARGED and the NatWest Bank. They intend to reinvest the money in the business in order to extend their kitchen facilities and are now looking at the possibility of obtaining a grant to further finance the work. Panagiotis added, 'We also hope to convert our garden into an outdoor catering area – all we need to do then is import a little sun from Greece!'

On Your Bike

DAVID SWAN (33): *Bicycle shop*

David Swan had worked in the bicycle trade for 15 years when he was made redundant from his post as bike shop manager at the age of 29. He had started working in the trade part-time while still at school, progressing to workshop manager and spending 11 years with various companies. In 1990 the shop he had worked for was forced out of business: 'It was a shock. It was cold, and that made it worse. Winter was the worst time to be made redundant, maybe if it had been summer, I might have been more optimistic.'

As it was, several months into his eight months' unemployment the bleakness of David's situation prompted him to approach the Gloucester Enterprise Agency with the idea which he had always had at the back of his mind of setting up his own bike shop. 'I went on an 'awareness day' that covered the basics of setting up a business,' he says, 'and decided to go for it.' He already knew the field well, but he required more financial expertise, so he took a course in book-keeping, and was helped with the preparation of his business plan. He invested all his savings and redundancy pay in the business and enrolled on the Enterprise Allowance scheme for business start-ups which entitled him to £40 a week for the first six months and £30 for the next six after that.

Almost exactly a year after losing his job, he began trading in premises he had found in Gloucester. Now, two years on, the business is still growing and David is hoping to open a second shop in late 1994. The change in his life has been dramatic. 'You have to be 100 per cent committed,' he stresses. 'Instead of getting a pay packet once a week and rushing out to spend it, I have to be much more careful. When I tell people that I run my own business, they think I must be very rich, but it's not like that at all. I'm glad I've done it, but it hasn't been easy.'

Eastern Promise

IBRAHIM SYED (25): *Importer and retailer*

Even though he was equipped with a degree in Business Studies, Ibrahim Syed was far from confident of finding a job, and indeed was unemployed for seven months after his graduation.

At one of his regular interviews at the benefit office, Ibrahim suggested setting up a business. His adviser immediately recommended contacting the Prince's Youth Business Trust to enquire about the possibility of a grant or a loan. Ibrahim was delighted. 'Just to know such help was available was enough to get me thinking,' he remembers.

It occurred to Ibrahim that there could be a considerable market for goods imported from India. Discovering that there were no outlets for imported ethnic clothing in the north-east, he set up a stall for a day in his town hall in Middlesbrough. Demonstrating his initiative, he obtained merchandise on a sale-or-return basis from a wholesaler in Birmingham, borrowed clothing racks from Littlewoods and mannequins from another shop, and persuaded the local radio station to advertise the event free of charge.

His efforts paid off. 'The demand was far greater than I had expected,' he says, 'and I was able to assess the customers' needs. They wanted more children's clothes and jewellery than I had foreseen, but the main market was for women's clothing.'

The success of this trial venture convinced the Prince's Youth Business Trust (PYBT) of the soundness of Ibrahim's proposal, and they gave him a grant of £1,500 for any capital expenditure and a £5,000 business loan repayable over three years at a low rate of interest. An adviser from the Trust still visits him monthly. With this support, he set up a shop, Anokhee, in Middlesbrough, and imports 70 per cent of his merchandise direct from India. Many of the garments are made to his own designs – appropriately, the shop's name means 'unique' in Urdu.

Ibrahim was one of Livewire's ten finalists for the Enterprise Awards of 1993, and used his prize-money for a stock-buying trip to India. He has recently expanded his business, opening a second store in Newcastle and starting up a wholesale operation.

Addicted to Success

MARTIN THOMAS (25): *Wind and surf shop*

Former Welsh windsurfing champion, Martin Thomas, first became addicted to this energetic sport ten years ago. He had intended to pursue a career in engineering but soon realised that his real vocation lay in a very different direction.

After college he spent seven years working at Rat Rigs in Cardiff, before becoming the Welsh champion in 1990. The win prompted him to leave his job and move to the Spanish resort of Tarifa, an essential destination for all serious board sailors, in order to concentrate solely on windsurfing. There Martin was able to build his knowledge, improve his technique and pick up a few more trophies along the way. Martin knew that actual windsurfing could not provide him with a career in the long term but it was while he was in Spain that he came up with the idea of opening his own wind and surf shop so he could combine business and pleasure and at the same time make use of the experience he had gained in the sport. When the opportunity came up in the summer of 1994 Martin returned to Britain and started making plans.

In order to prove to himself that he could build a viable business without over-committing himself Martin spent several months trading from his parents' garage. Working through the idea in this way gave him an ideal opportunity to test a market that he was convinced existed. Whilst stock levels at home grew Martin looked at many different locations in the county before he finally settled on a site on Island Road, in Barry. 'It's ideal because so many windsurfers use the area around Cold Knap all through the year,' explained Martin.

Cardiff and Vale Enterprise (CAVE) business adviser, Robin Wynne-Hughes, was impressed with Martin's enthusiasm and potential. 'With ten years' experience in the sport Martin's product knowledge is impeccable. He knows his market, has a good rapport with customers and has excellent contacts through his own involvement in the sport – we wish him well!'

The help Martin has received from CAVE is certainly paying off. Earlier this year Martin was awarded the Vale Award for Business Excellence along with a cheque for £600 at the 1994 Livewire Awards.

Dogged Determination

ANGELA WATSON (44): *Dog beautician*

It was at school that Angela first began dog grooming, 28 years ago. On leaving school she spent 18 months working for a pet shop in Bolden. She became disillusioned when promises that she would be able to enjoy a percentage of the earnings failed to materialise and promotion prospects looked minimal.

Deciding that enough was enough, Angela left the pet shop and worked on a part-time basis, finally giving up to have children. Until her youngest children were of nursery age she worked in a bar one or two evenings a week. After about nine years of unemployment and casual work, Angela was keen to do something more. She had heard that Walker Hall in Sunderland ran a business course for women and, on going for an interview, decided that this was that she wanted to do.

The course lasted ten weeks and involved three seminars a week. These were mostly aimed at trying to boost the confidence of women and helping those who wanted to get back to work after a substantial absence from a working environment. Angela and others were taught how to sell themselves at interviews, and encouraged not to take a back seat in the shadow of men once in a job. On a business note, she also learned the correct forms of book-keeping, assessing VAT and estimating tax returns.

applied to her local Business Enterprise Centre to see if she would qualify for the Enterprise Allowance. Her plan was accepted, entitling her to £60 per week for 13 weeks, £40 for 13 weeks, and a further £20 for the remaining 26 weeks.

In addition to providing financial assistance, the centre's business counsellors were on constant standby to answer any queries and to give advice on any matter to do with business. Angela's progress was carefully monitored, and every 13 weeks her progress was reassessed by the Enterprise Centre.

Angela's business is now highly successful. Working from home is convenient for her as she is able to look after her children simultaneously during the school holidays. The business is advertised through friends with pet shops who have put up notices in their windows, and by the local vet. Angela's main contracts are gained in this way and from loyal clients who return again and again.

Angela would recommend the course that she did to anyone; she claims that 'these courses are definitely a good idea as they give people the opportunity to do things for themselves'. It is the success of people such as Angela that illustrates that it is possible to achieve your aim if you pursue it with confidence and determination.

Plumbing New Heights

GEOFF WITHERSPOON: *Plumber*

The West Wales Training and Enterprise Council and Neath College have proved to be true plumbers' mates – twice over. After helping Geoff Witherspoon launch his own plumbing business, the compliment was returned when Geoff set up on his own and took on a trainee from the same course he had attended.

Geoff Witherpoon benefited from an Employment Training course run by the college some years ago and funded by the TEC. He made sufficient progress to launch his own business and today trades successfully from his base at Neath Abbey, West Glamorgan. Recently he decided to expand – and contacted the college in search of an appropriate trainee.

Neath College is one of seven further education establishments in West Glamorgan and Dyfed delivering Learning for Work courses on behalf of the TEC, including a thriving plumbing course. Twelve people were working towards level 2 of the new National Vocational Qualification in domestic plumbing and central heating installation, and Anthony Jones was the fortunate one recruited by Geoff.

Alison Burns, training manager at Neath College, said the success was doubly pleasing: 'Here we have an ex-trainee taking on a present trainee. A course member has not only gone on to find full time employment but is now creating the same opportunity for someone else,' she said.

Neath College is a significant centre for Learning for Works courses, and currently has about 80 trainees learning plumbing, catering, care, clerical and administration including book-keeping and accounting, retail and warehouse, electrical, mechanical and welding engineering and motor vehicle engineering.

Geoff said the initial course had given him the qualifications he needed.

'I had had plenty of experience but I needed a written qualification. I went on to take a course in how to run a business and it all went from there.

'Looking back, I am so glad that I did it. It is the best thing I have ever done and I only wish that I had done it earlier. I have been on my own for two years now and I find it brilliant,' he said.

Cleaning Up

MARK (32) AND GRAHAM (30) WRAY: *Industrial cleaning supplies*

When Mark Wray lost his job as a sheet metal worker in Liverpool, he found few prospects of re-entering the workplace in a way which would put his previous skill to use.

After Mark had suffered two years of unemployment, relieved by occasional short-term casual jobs, his brother Graham came up with the idea of setting up a small business providing industrial cleaning supplies in their home town, Liverpool.

They approached the Prince's Youth Business Trust (PYBT), and were assisted in drawing up a business plan and gaining the necessary administrative expertise as well as receiving a £3000 loan. They were also given a £2000 short-term grant from the youth employment scheme and another loan of £3000 from the inter business project to supplement their weekly Enterprise Allowance.

Mark and Graham's early enthusiasm was tested as they came to understand the harsh realities of business practice. 'Initially, our mood was optimistic,' remembers Mark. 'We thought our company would become large in a short space of time, but we soon realised it wasn't going to be that easy.'

However, they did not let their enthusiasm wane, and their persistence and hard work has meant that today, seven years after setting out, the company enjoys large contracts and a turnover of £500,000, with a full-time staff of eight. Their ambition is now to become 'a million-pound turnover profitable business'.

The Bus Stops Here

DAVID WYATT (28): *Bus services*

After leaving school, David Wyatt got a job with his local bus company in Glossop, Derbyshire. Within five years, he was part of the junior management; but his promotion was shortly followed by redundancy and six months' unemployment.

Realising that there was a lack of public transport in his area, David began to give serious thought to an idea he had been 'nurturing for a long time', that of establishing a bus company to serve his local community in Glossopdale.

His first stop was the Enterprise Agency, who helped him gain a basic grounding in marketing and book-keeping. David is appreciative of this help, but stresses that his success owes just as much to the 'confidence to proceed by trial and error' which he had had from the outset.

Half of his funding came from his redundancy payment while the rest was in the form of an initial loan of £5,000 and a further £1,000 expansion loan from the Prince's Youth Business Trust which he has recently finished paying off.

Now, three years after it was established, The Glossopdale Bus Company has a turnover of £320,000, employs 14 staff and has just invested in three new vehicles. David's initial enthusiasm remains as strong as ever, and he is delighted to be meeting a genuine local demand. For him junior management seems a long way off and, as he says, 'It just goes to show every cloud has a silver lining'.

In Employment

(in alphabetical order)

Burger Graduate

JOSEPH ATWERE (23): *Burger King award winner*

Behind the statistics that confirm GrandMet Trust's reputation as one of the UK's leading employment guidance and training organisations are hundreds of individual success stories. Trainees who overcome the most daunting obstacles to achieve vocational qualifications or succeed in the job market when the odds are really stacked against them, surface with remarkable frequency at the Trust's 80-plus operations centres throughout the country.

One of the high spots of GrandMet Trust's year is the Awards for Achievement programme. Every year the Trust's training centres nominate the outstanding successes amongst their trainees, who compete for a prized award. The overall winner of 1993 in the personal development category, which is for trainees who have often overcome considerable problems to achieve their potential by hard work and effort, was 23-year-old Joseph Atwere of East London.

Joseph grew up on a Liverpool council estate where unemployment was high and crime commonplace. He moved to London when he was 16, but never found a regular job, and had become one of London's growing community of homeless and jobless young people by the time GrandMet discovered him in January 1993.

Joseph was one of the early recruits on the Bridging the Gap programme, an initiative that resulted from a collaboration between GrandMet Trust and its fellow GrandMet operating company, Burger King. It is a customised 12-week training programme for Burger King restaurant staff that was London's first practical solution to the downward spiral created by the no home = no job: no job = no home poverty trap. As one of the world's major fast food operations, with 11 of its 200-plus UK outlets based in central London, where 800 staff are employed, BK was ideally situated to offer training placements that met the special needs of homeless and jobless young Londoners.

Joseph's latent abilities were revealed by the Bridging the Gap programme, which offered him normal salary rates after an initial four-week period. Together with all the other Bridging the Gap trainees who successfully completed the course, Joseph was guaranteed full-time work by Burger King, which also set up a special fund to provide interest-free loans to help new employees pay deposits on their own accommodation. With his new skills, and first-ever working routine, Joseph rediscovered his self-esteem and a positive, optimistic attitude towards his future.

From being unemployed, homeless and without much hope at the beginning of 1993, Joseph had become a valued member of the Burger King team at its newest restaurant in London's Piccadilly at the end of the year. Six months later he had gained a place at the South Bank University in London, to study for a degree in politics and sociology.

On the Right Track

CRAIG BERESFORD: *Delivery driver*

After leaving school, Craig Beresford joined a six-month college course, but it didn't engage his interest, and he dropped out. At around the same time, he became homeless, and moved into a hostel. It was here, after being unemployed for a year and a half, that he heard about a ten-week course designed to help people back into work, which was run by CITEE, a Christian organisation based in Coventry.

The course concentrated on CV and letter-writing skills and role-playing interview practice. Craig particularly valued the opportunity of learning from the other people on the course, who came from a wide variety of backgrounds and age groups.

Having covered the basics, CITEE arranged 'tasters': one or two-day work placements in different fields. Craig was sent to Springfield Wholefoods where, within a few days, he was offered a permanent post as a driver. He has been fully employed since March 1992.

Craig emphasises that by far the most difficult thing for him was remotivation. His period of unemployment, coupled with homelessness, had left him with low self-esteem. 'Finding a job has to be your main goal. You have to give it all you can,' he says.

Warm Reception

CAROL: *Receptionist/typist*

Carol worked for British Telecom for ten years before leaving to look after her three children, who are now aged 16, 14 and six. After 15 years of domestic duties, she decided it was time for her to return to work. She had had experience in a range of clerical work and accounting, but was without any computing or typing skills. She found her first attempts to get work, through visits to her local Job Centre, very demoralising. She was excluded from applying for a number of jobs as soon as she revealed that she had no experience in using computers. Carol found herself virtually unemployable, and it was only after she expressed her frustration at the Job Centre that she was offered the opportunity to retrain.

Carol was concerned that she would not be able to afford to undertake any training, but in fact she was eligible for free training as a 'woman returner' to the labour market. She undertook a Business Administration course with NACRO New Careers Training between September 1993 and April 1994, gaining certificates, with distinction, in computing and typing. She also gained an NVQ Level I in business administration and is currently waiting to be assessed for part of her Level II.

Carol started looking for work in February, and in April was recruited by a local firm as a part-time receptionist and typist - she started immediately after having two interviews with them. She enjoys her work and says she realises now that she would never have worked again had she not gone back to update and extend her skills.

A large part of her success in finding a job is attributed to the skill and enthusiasm of her trainers, as well as the realisation that her years out of paid employment had still contributed to her abilities. 'When I couldn't find a job, I became depressed and didn't know what I would do with the rest of my life. My training revealed skills I hadn't realised I had,' she says, 'but if you've looked after a family for fifteen years you must be good at organising.' Carol sees that her training was a means of channelling experience she already had so that it enhanced her employment prospects, as well as enabling her to develop new skills crucial to employment in the 1990s.

Never Better

REUBEN CLARKE (49): *Hospital deputy training manager*

'Redundancy was the best thing that ever happened to me but only in retrospect. It was absolutely awful at the time.' The positive attitude Reuben Clarke now takes toward the loss of his job six years ago is typical of the change in his whole outlook on life. Yet this confidence was not easily won, and seven years ago Reuben would never have believed that today he would be deputy training manager at Hartlepool Hospital.

When Reuben was made redundant from his job as a salesman he was only too aware that the prospects of his finding work again were not good: 'At 46 I thought I was too old and I had no qualifications at all'. However, even this realism did not prepare him for the 518 rejections he received from retailers and factories. 'The worst thing was that I didn't even get one interview. All I wanted was a chance to sell myself.' No such chance came, and Reuben was unemployed for 18 months. While his bank was very understanding, it proved the final straw when he had to sell clothes and holiday souvenirs to meet day-to-day bills. 'I simply had nothing left to lose,' he remembers.

It was the extreme difficulty of his position that forced Reuben to take the decision that changed the course of his life. His counsellor at the job club (which used to operate as a one-to-one advice scheme called Option 9 until it was abandoned) urged him to apply for a one-year community programme position as a filing system co-ordinator with the local health authority. At first the prospect of trying something outside the area of his previous job was very daunting. 'I was extremely under-confident, and I only wanted the kind of job I knew.'

His counsellor encouraged him to treat the situation in a positive way, to view it as a chance to change direction. Reluctantly he applied and was delighted to be asked for an interview: 'In the interview I was very laid-back. I didn't care, because I didn't expect to get the job.' To his surprise, by the time he arrived home he had received a telephone message asking him to start work the following week. The confidence to change the direction of his search had paid off, and after 18 months he had a job. It was only to last one year, but it was, at last, an opportunity to sell himself; and, by demonstrating his ability, this is exactly what Reuben did.

On completion of his year-long post, Reuben was interviewed for the job of employment training placement officer with Hartlepool General Hospital. Once again he was successful. However, within three weeks he met another hurdle: as part of the Employment Training Scheme (now Adult Training), he was expected to undertake courses leading to National Vocational Qualifications (NVQs) at college in Middlesbrough. Reuben had never taken qualifications before, and it was now almost

20 years since he had left school. The prospect of returning to education terrified him: 'After the first day of the course I just sat in the car, thinking everybody was so much cleverer than me and so much younger. I thought, I just can't do this. I was demoralised by the whole thing.'

Once more encouragement was at hand, this time from a trainer on the course who made him take a positive view of what he was doing. At the end of the two-week course in communications he returned to work and realised, to his delight, that 'without noticing at first, I was doing what I had been taught'. It was this realisation, that the City and Guilds qualifications he was taking actually made a difference to the job he was doing, that gave Reuben the confidence and conviction to continue. 'Qualifications are such a driving force. They allow you to do more and give you the desire and confidence to succeed; they simply open everything up.' To be recognised at work for his success also gave Reuben great confidence: 'Qualifications give you credibility within your organisation, and focus on your ability.'

Even once his job had become permanent Reuben continued to study and take further exams and courses, progressing up the levels of Vocational Qualifications. He has now taken one a year for the past five years. His determination has been rewarded: in April 1993 he achieved what he calls his 'hat trick', gaining the prestigious Licentiateship, a senior award from City and Guilds that recognises success in both the workplace and in qualifications, and was elected to membership of the Institute of Training and Development. He was also nominated as Adult Learner of the Year for his region.

Sweeping Changes

NOAH COOPER (40): *Road-sweeper*

Noah Cooper left school at an early age unable to either read or write. This prevented him from holding down the job he found with the Wessex Water Authority, because he was unable to complete any kind of administration without help. Three years of unemployment saw him making many job applications, assisted by friends, but all were unsuccessful. Despite the prevailing assumption among his friends that, having left school, he would never be literate, Noah was prompted by his marriage and increasing financial responsibilities to ask his social worker for help. He was put in touch with an adult learning instructor, and took a literacy course, involving both home sessions and evening classes. Along with his education, he found his confidence growing rapidly.

His improving skills led the local council to give him a six-month trial as a road-sweeper; and his increasing ability during this time to fill in timesheets, write notes to his supervisor and read road maps, among other tasks, led to the position being made permanent. He is now Shepton Mallet's only road-sweeper.

Noah now attends evening classes and his reading and writing skills have 'dramatically improved'. He also reads regularly to his three children, and even has plans to write a book about his experiences. Literacy and employment have, he says, 'made a man out of me'.

A Personal Training Programme

DAN (47): *Careers adviser*

Dan had a fairly average comprehensive school education, leaving school with two O-levels. During his school years, his main interest was swimming, which he did to a very high standard, only narrowly missing out on selection for the 1964 Olympic Games in Tokyo. Although disappointed, he decided that he could pursue his interest and find suitable work in the leisure industry. Starting as a pool attendant at a local sports centre, he was quickly promoted and was a supervisor by the time he was 19.

Dan then made the move to management in the leisure industry, becoming an assistant manager with a London borough council, and a manager, by the time he was 23, of a prestige leisure centre with significant staff levels and budgetary responsibilities. During this time, he gained a Diploma in Management Studies and an MBA from Kingston Polytechnic. In 1987, he moved to another borough to manage the entire range of leisure services, including sporting facilities, libraries and open spaces. He was responsible for nearly 400 staff and a budget of £8 million.

With the introduction of compulsory competitive tendering, Dan joined a private company which made several successful bids to deliver leisure facilities for the local authority. However, the company was slightly underfunded and experienced cash flow problems. Dan was let down by his partners and, despite mortgaging his house and realising other assets, he was unable to save the business. Having lost his job and his house, Dan felt he was forced to look at other means of turning round his desperate financial position. This resulted in his being sentenced to eighteen months imprisonment for fraud and he was sent to HMP Ford in February 1992. His sentence was reduced on appeal and he was released after five months to a difficult situation: because he was so well known in his field, his conviction would make it hard for him to return to the same area of work.

Dan had spent six months on bail, and during this time had become interested in carpentry – he had restored some antique furniture and had even made himself a workshop. On his release, it seemed sensible to pick up on this new area of interest. Employment Services was unable to offer him a training place, so he approached

NACRO directly and became a trainee in Carpentry and Joinery in August 1992, only two weeks after being released. During this time he gained his City and Guilds qualification, and a year later he successfully applied for a full time trainer position with NACRO New Careers Training.

Although Dan and his wife are living in much reduced circumstances, he feels that his life is back on track. He enjoys training others and has obtained further qualifications since his employment with NACRO: certification in occupational health and safety and a Certificate in Training and Development from national lead bodies in these areas. Dan now feels he would like to develop his training abilities in other areas, possibly using his management experience to move into the field of management training.

Dan was in his mid-40s on his release, and felt that this, in conjunction with being an ex-offender, could have been a significant impediment to becoming employed again. However, he was determined to make the most of difficult circumstances, and helpful advice from prison staff and training in prison which provided useful groundwork helped channel him into the right path on his release. His determination and hard work have paid off, and he has discovered a new area of interest and expertise with considerable future potential.

In the Frame

ANDREW ERSKINE (21): *Trainee production manager*

After six months working in Argos in Aberdeen, Prestwick-born Andrew Erskine returned to his home town and signed on for unemployment benefit. After thoughts about returning to college came to nothing, pressure from his concerned father led to him enquiring about employment training with a view to retraining in another career.

It was arranged for him to train through Radix (a locally-based company which runs training courses) as a picture and mirror frame-maker following a MAPS (machine assembly and processing skills) training plan. A friend's brother mentioned to Andrew that his frame company was expanding and he was taken on through a placement arrangement.

Radix offered a one-day induction course to trainees, involving basic arithmetic and literacy tests, followed up by regular monitoring of the trainees' progress. Andrew was visited every six weeks and his progress at Frame UK was steady.

Financially, Andrew was better off during his period of training: he lived on his £67.20 per fortnight unemployment benefit as well as a further £20 per fortnight plus travel expenses paid to him by Radix. As he lived 18 miles away, he travelled to work on the train each day during his training, and worked hard to achieve the City and Guilds qualification he subsequently earned.

Frame UK were so impressed by Andrew's work that they decided to retain him. Within a month, due to the expansion of the business, three more staff were taken on and Andrew was promoted to trainee production manager. Very recently the entire firm expanded to bigger premises. Andrew enthuses: 'I am on to a good thing.'

Adding Up

DAVE FRANCE (49): *Computer support*

Despite all of the reports in the media and experiences of friends, it is a jolt to know you are not wanted in the jobs market after more than 20 years' experience in your chosen field. This was what happened to Dave France when he was made redundant in 1991 after two decades working with a local stockbroking company.

Following two years of job searching Dave was fortunate enough to become involved in an Information Technology course run by Cardiff and Vale Enterprise, which eventually earned him a place on CAVE's Executive Secondment Scheme.

The course, designed to provide an important insight into the fields of marketing, health and safety, cash flow forecasting and business reviews, opened up a whole new world of job opportunities. Within weeks Dave was seconded to Pritchard Alarms, a small company in desperate need of an expert to help install a recently acquired computer. David Pritchard, of Pritchard Alarms, had approached South Glamorgan TEC who passed the request on to CAVE.

Following a countrywide search for suitable software a programme was soon identified by Business Adviser Vince Williams, and Dave was given the task of evaluating and then installing the system. Thanks to Dave's hard work a whole computerised accounting system was set up, which recently helped Pritchard Alarms achieve accreditation to the British standard BS 5750, part II.

Dave's efforts have earned him a full-time position with Pritchard Alarms, where his role is to help with the administration of this busy local firm, and in particular, to look after the computerized side of the business.

Healthy Position

VIOLET GLEESON (37): *Local health authority worker*

For five years Violet Gleeson worked for the Islington Health Authority in the Mental Health section. When Islington HA merged with Bloomsbury, Violet was forced out of a job because her immediate boss was no longer in charge of the department.

For 18 months, Violet had no job. She had a Pitman's secretarial qualification but was unable to find work. In order to fill in the time she helped out at Friends In Need (FIN), an organisation which cares for elderly people, driving an ambulance which took people to and from the FIN establishment. Keeping herself going with voluntary work was crucial for her.

After six months without work Violet reapplied to the health authority through the normal procedures. It became apparent that she was somewhat overqualified and too senior for the post in question, but soon another job became available, which she got.

Violet points out that the biggest problem for unemployed people is motivation. She admits: 'There were days when I was better off staying in bed. How do you motivate people who are already qualified?' After periods of depression, Violet is now back in employment and happy with her work.

Reaping the Benefit

MARLENE HENDERSON (23): *Administrator*

Marlene Henderson from Inverness was a senior care officer in a Cheshire Home in England for one and a half years before she decided that she fancied a change in career. On moving back to Scotland in August 1991 she registered as unemployed. After six months out of work, Marlene applied for employment training and secured an interview with Microcom at Albyn House.

By March 1992 Marlene was in a work placement there as a trainee, which she greatly enjoyed. She lived on her Social Security allowance and worked extremely hard. In August 1992 the Employment Service advertised for casual administration staff, and Marlene put herself forward.

She was lucky enough to gain one of the posts, as a temporary but full-time administrator, and officially signed off the unemployment register in September 1992. A year on, she enjoys her work, dealing with the reception, new claims and training for work.

On the Wing

ANNE JAMES (52): *Wildfowl Trust warden*

Having lived and worked in Bristol for five years Anne James was content in her job working for the Glassboat Restaurant, by whom she was employed as a driver to carry out deliveries and collect shopping. As a hobby Anne also cared for some 150 swans at Bristol Dock, financed by sponsorship from the council.

Then Anne moved to Belgium with her partner for three months but was unemployed after she returned to England. For nine months she was unable to find work until the unemployment office in Bristol, hearing of her keen interest in birds, suggested she contact the Norton Radstock College with regard to a course they run on bird and animal care.

Anne was enrolled and began the City and Guilds course in September 1992. She was 50 at the time and referred to herself as an 'oldie'. Of attending Norton Radstock twice a week she enthuses: 'I couldn't speak highly enough about the place.' Anne reached the college from Bristol on a bus specially organised for her and the other students. Her course involved learning skills in bird and animal care as well as some basic biology. The other three days a week she worked on a placement at Slimbridge Wildfowl and Wetlands Trust.

On 20 May Anne passed her exams at Norton Radstock and began work full-time at the Trust. She is delighted to have been able to retrain to work in something that was previously an enjoyable hobby, and her recently acquired knowledge has also benefited the swans at Bristol Dock.

Inspiring Confidence

ROBERT JAMES: *Outreach support worker and job club leader*

Robert James was unemployed for two years eight months. Now, thanks to Training for Work, he has a good job as one of the outreach support workers and job club leader at St Botolph's, a centre for homeless people in central London run by GrandMet Trust. The job club operated here is specifically geared to the needs of the homeless unemployed. Robert has worked at St Botolph's since November 1992 and is uniquely qualified to run the job club and offer the advice he does, having been unemployed and homeless himself.

Robert had previously worked in the music industry for some 30 years. At one stage he had his own business in music publishing and orchestral management. But the recession took its toll and his business eventually collapsed in 1990. Due to rising debts and mortgage arrears, he moved into a council flat with a friend, but he had to leave when the tenant moved out. So in May 1992 he was made homeless. He found a hostel place in London and remained there for nine months. Until this time, he had been actively seeking work, sending off many applications each week, but at the hostel his motivation quickly dissolved into despondency. He had no money and the council refused to help him find other suitable accommodation as he was relatively healthy. In retrospect, he said the hostel was one of the worst he has seen and was full of junkies and alcoholics.

He finally got so depressed about his life that he decided to go to the Wapping Job Club in London, which he attended for a week. It was there that he found out about Employment Action, a scheme whereby people use their own skills to work in the community. His placement took him to GrandMet Trust where, because of his background, he was entrusted with the task of fund-raising and marketing. When a job came up at St Botolph's, the Trust offered the position to Robert, as they felt he had a genuine empathy with the homeless people he would be helping. Robert was still living in the hostel at this time and left it only in February 1993.

For Robert, taking the decision to attend a job club meant that he eventually found work. The Employment Action Scheme, which has since been merged with Employment Training to become Training for Work, offered him the chance to be part of the workforce again and to put his wide-ranging experience to good use in the community.

His placement helped restore the confidence and faith he had lost after being unemployed for almost three years. He felt that his life was meaningful again and the placement offered him the chance to get out of the hostel and further change his life. Now, being in the position to help others do the same thing, he knows he can offer advice that is truly tried and tested, giving his work credence and honesty.

When teaching in the job club sessions, he reinforces the necessity of strengthening the skills you have to offer. He knows from his own experience that improving interview technique, compiling a good CV and accompanying letter and improving your telephone manner could mean the difference between securing an interview or being overlooked. Yet he feels it is just as crucial to maintain determination and spirit, which he attempts to bolster by strengthening motivation, confidence and hope: a thing which is doubly difficult if you are unemployed and homeless.

It's All Working Out Fine

IFAN JONES: *Information technology tutor*

Ifan Jones left school with no qualifications. After being unemployed for six months he went on the RESTART scheme to try and get back to work. His first job was with British Car Rentals as a vehicle preparer as well as doing some administration work. He went on to work in a poultry processing plant before enquiring about starting his own car valeting business.

This he did following a business course with Menter Gwynedd. Anglesey Auto Valeting unfortunately became another victim of the recession. So Ifan found himself unemployed once more. At the Job Centre he enquired about receiving some Information Technology Training. He was referred to CTF Training in Llangefni and was offered a place on their IT route the following Monday.

Ifan was introduced to the application side of IT and found himself enjoying it immensely. He soon completed RSA levels 1 and 2 and continued to study at level

3 (Intermediate). He gained a level 3 equivalent qualification through a number of different aspects of IT.

After completing the training he joined a temping agency who within a week found him a placement with the Countryside Council for Wales, as part of their Information Systems Development Unit. Within a week or two he was confident of his duties and familiar with the technology that the company used. He explained, 'The training served me well and I had no problems adjusting to my first post in my newly found vocation.'

From his temping placement he applied for a permanent post as IT tutor at CTF Training and following an interview he was successful. Since becoming IT tutor in September 1993, he has received training in teaching gaining PGCE stage 1 in December 1993 and is due to be assessed for stage 2. He has also completed his Assessor Award.

He is still very much geared to developing his vocation and future in IT and tutoring. Currently he is aiming for a City and Guilds Training and Development level 3, RSA Business Administration level 3 and is very interested in doing a degree in Computer Science through the Open University.

Ifan says 'The switch from trainee to tutor at CTF was scary but I must admit to enjoying every minute of it now!'

Packing Them In

DAVID KNOTT: *Warehouseman*

At 20 years old, Mancunian David Knott had attended various youth training courses but none of them had resulted in his securing a permanent job. He did complete a two-year YTS course in upholstery and subsequently got a job in a carpet factory, but unfortunately this later went into liquidation and David was forced to search for new employment.

It was the Job Centre who put David in touch with the Rathbone Society, who aim to help train people with learning difficulties. David's numeracy and literacy skills were very poor and he lacked much self-confidence.

On top of this, he had also been fighting against illness which made his quest for training more difficult. He was compelled to spend a large amount of time going in and out of hospital and it was some time before he was fit to work again.

Eventually he was able to attend a 44-week course with Rathbone Training on a warehousing option. On this course David, together with several others, was able to learn the necessary skills involved in warehousing and storing goods.

He achieved a full NVQ level 1 and was taken on by his placement, Kwiksave. He works for the company on a fairly part-time basis, only three days a week, but he greatly enjoys it and is hoping to get his hours extended as soon as possible.

Success in Store

DAVID LINDSAY (30): *Sales assistant*

After six months of buying and selling properties parttime, David found himself out of work. He was to spend a total of eight months unemployed, during which the Job Centre recommended to him that he approach Fullemploy with a view to retraining.

This he did, and as a result he completed a three-month full-time course gaining a City and Guilds stage 1 qualification in Information Technology. David learned a lot about computers and improved his interview style. He also learned more about how to deal with people as well as role-playing, telephone management and letter writing.

David claims his Fullemploy training was 'excellent', and a highly constructive use of three months. Since November he has worked for Musical Vision, where he enjoys the work, but he feels he would be confident enough to move on in the not-too-distant future.

David's advice to others who may find themselves in a similar position is: 'Keep trying; ask all your friends if they know of any jobs. It is important to go on a course and maximise your time. Be persistent and get qualifications.'

In Training

LINDA MACDONALD: *Employment training*

Linda MacDonald had worked for over 20 years as a secretary, a landlady and the manager of a timeshare complex when she married and moved to Inverness at the age of 40.

She had no job to go to there, and after eight months' unemployment she started an employment action course run by Community Industry, a training company recently established in the town. The six-month course mainly covered the areas, already familiar to her, of clerical and administrative office work. Having demonstrated her competence and commitment, Linda was offered a full-time job which included responsibility for training other unemployed people. 'This,' she says, 'was a great opportunity and challenge. Training was a completely new area to me.'

She took in-house training courses at Community Industry, covering computer assessment, literacy, numeracy and psychometric testing and soon after began coaching and assessing full time. 'The age-group is very wide – from 16 to 60,' she explains.

Linda has since been promoted from 'participant' to supervisor, then to co-ordinator and finally to area manager and feels that her own experience of unemployment helps her in her dealings with others who are without jobs. 'It is so good,' she says, 'to be able to say that I have been in the same position. People can't think that I'm just sitting there without knowing what it's like.'

Full Circle

STUART MACKAY (43): *Butcher*

Stuart MacKay had wanted a qualification in warehousing when he went on a Training for Work programme but he never expected to end up with a full-time job back behind the counter of the local butcher's shop where he had spent 12 years.

After moving to the Highlands from Glasgow in 1975, Stuart began working at Browns butcher's shop in Nairn and became established there until he decided to go into business on his own and opened a rival shop in 1987. However, after two years he hit problems when new Government health regulations were introduced and Stuart faced the prospect of expensive improvements if his business was to conform to the new guidelines. He felt it was too much of a gamble and instead closed down the business and faced unemployment.

After a few months he secured a warehousing job with a local oil fabrication yard but the uncertain nature of that work was brought home to him two years later when he was one of hundreds of men made redundant.

Father-of-two Stuart was then unemployed for around six months and decided he had to take the initiative to get back into the jobs market. He tried the job club but quickly decided that it wasn't for him. Then a training agency opportunity came up and Stuart felt encouraged to try something totally different. 'I was going to try warehousing. I had been doing that at the fabrication yard and I thought that if I had a qualification it could only help if more jobs came up there in the future.'

He contacted a national training agency and began working towards a City and Guilds Retail Certificate but a job was always going to be the first priority rather than the qualification. Stuart spent about five or six weeks doing office work with the agency but then he was offered the chance of a Training for Work place back at Browns, where he had worked for 12 years! He was overjoyed: 'I had always remained on good terms with the people there and I jumped at the chance to go back'.

Stuart began in January and was due to be placed there for a year but unfortunately the scheme was cut short and after six months he returned to unemployment. However, only a week later a surprise phone call brought the offer of a full-time job at Browns – one of the workers had left and it was felt that Stuart was the ideal person to replace him.

Stuart says he is really enjoying being back with full-time work. 'I couldn't have thought that I would be back at the butcher's shop after all those years – especially as I had been looking for warehousing work. I had even been thinking of leaving the area because of the lack of jobs. If it wasn't for the training agency I probably wouldn't have got back at the butcher's.'

Ferry Happy

DIANE MAXWELL (28): *Office worker*

Diane Maxwell is a 28-year-old single parent with two children aged nine years and three years of age. She worked for five years as a production operative in a local factory before being unemployed for three years.

She commenced the Training and Employment Agency's Job Training Programme after seeing an advert in the local newspaper, and completed training at North East Training Services and Larne College of Further Education. During her period of training she gained word processing qualifications plus units towards an NVQ level 2 in business administration.

Also during her training she commenced a work placement with P&O Ferries in their office at Larne Harbour, and when this was completed she obtained a part time job in the Stena Sealink passenger office at the harbour terminal.

Diane is very enthusiastic about the training programme and states, 'It is a really worthwhile programme and it worked for me. I believe I would never have gained permanent employment without the skills and qualifications I gained whilst on the Job Training Programme.'

Magic Move

SHONA MCCARTHY: *Projects officer*

Shona, a budding, talented young arts enthusiast, was eager to put both her degree in Media Studies and English from the University of Ulster, Coleraine and her creative drama experience in a voluntary capacity with the 'Nervous Energy Education Theatre Company' to the test by opting for a career in journalism. However, after ten months of unemployment she approached Hugh J. O'Boyle Training Ltd, Downpatrick, a long-established managing agent for the Training and Employment Agency to seek further work experience through their Job Training Programme and was placed with Ulster Journals and Fortnight Publications, Belfast.

After gaining valuable skills not only in journalism but also in arts administration, conference organisation and practical computer techniques Shona decided to diversify and refocus her ambition towards a future in the exciting arts domain. Fortunately, at this time a professional post became available in the newly established Northern Ireland Film Council and the members of the interview panel for this important post were extremely impressed with Shona's performance as a highly motivated trainee of the Job Training Programme, offering her a full-time position as executive assistant of the Northern Ireland Film Council (NIFC) and Assistant Director of Cinemagic, the Northern Ireland International Film Festival for Young People.

'Even with all the necessary qualifications the prospect of trying to get a job when leaving university can be extremely daunting, particularly in the present climate of rising unemployment. Nevertheless, if you have the required individual drive I think the Job Training Programme is a worthwhile channel for building up experience in your field of interest whilst at the same time gaining additional practical skills through relevant courses.

'Furthermore, it is imperative that you use this scheme to your own advantage in order to sell your unique attributes to prospective employers and display a high degree of personal commitment and autonomy, proving your own capabilities. The Cinemagic festival is innovative, unique and absorbing.

'I deal with film companies and producers all over the world to create a dynamic event which involves international films, directors and workshops so I have had the opportunity to travel to London, France and America.'

Shona particularly enjoys organising practical workshops for youth through a series of master classes annually taken by experts in the field including Thaddeus O'Sullivan, director of *December Bride* on directing; Jim Sheridan, writer and director of *My Left Foot* on writing, and Adrian Dunbar, writer and actor of *Hear My Song* on acting for films.

Moreover, this leverage allowed her to move on to 'bigger and better things' as she is currently excelling through a recent promotion to Projects Officer and continues to develop her talents in this busy and progressive environment.

'My promotion has meant additional responsibility in terms of monitoring trainees, raising sponsorship for NIFC projects and having sole organisational control for specific events. I will also become involved with some of the other exciting new developments, such as encouraging indigenous film production in Northern Ireland; working to set up a film archive; training provision for film makers and a year-long programme of activities to celebrate the Centenary of Cinema 1995–96.'

IN EMPLOYMENT

Only Logical

MICHAEL: *Computer operator*

Michael had been sentenced to a period of Community Service having been found guilty of driving while banned after a conviction for drink-driving. He had lost his job with an insurance company, where he had been on a salary of £32,000, and had a wife and two children to support. On top of this he had not been able to tell his wife about his conviction which had obviously increased the pressure he was under.

Michael was referred to the Apex Trust's Derbyshire Employment Guidance project at a time when his confidence was extremely low. His lack of motivation led to him missing appointments with the project worker and it seemed as though he would not be able to pick himself up again. However, during one discussion it came to light that one of Michael's leisure interests was computers.

The Apex Trust worker helped to draw up an action plan based around this interest to encourage Michael to develop his knowledge and skills. Eventually he was placed on a Training for Work scheme, during which his self-confidence improved markedly. After completing the course Michael finally found employment as a computer operator. Being employed was the first step to getting back on his feet and Michael began to take control of his life again and give his family the support they needed.

A Sporting Chance

TONY MORRIS (58): *Leisure administrator*

The industrial service company which Tony Morris, a trained engineer, had run for 16 years went out of business in 1987. Tony worked as a pension salesman until he was made redundant in 1991, and he was then unemployed for two years.

When he was signing on one day, an adult education officer suggested that, since he was a keen sportsman and had already acted as a volunteer badminton coach during school holidays, he should take a City and Guilds course in Leisure Administration at Dudley College. 'I had nothing to lose, so I thought I might as well have a go,' he says. He was 55 years old. 'On the first day of the course, I suddenly realised how much younger than me everyone else was,' he remembers. But, encouraged by his tutors, he was undaunted, and passed his exams two months early.

As well as studying, he did some part-time coaching at sports centres, but admits he 'never dared hope' for permanent employment in his area, the West Midlands, 'because most jobs went to younger men'.

He followed this with a further course in management, and believes that it was this that impressed interviewers. 'To see from the CV of someone my age that they are still prepared to learn suggests that they must have something.' He was offered a job as assistant site manager at the Thorne's School in Dudley, including some football and badminton coaching at weekends.

'I got the job the day after my 57th birthday. It was the best present of my life. The job has knocked ten years off my age,' he says.

Carry on Regardless

JOHN MUNRO (30): *Porter*

Nobody can know more about the social consequences and difficulties of being unemployed than John Munro who spent nine years out of work before he finally secured the job he has now at the Royal Northern Infirmary. He admitted 'I felt and was treated like a second-class citizen. Nobody wanted to know me.'

John had worked as a storekeeper near Inverness until illness forced him to take sick leave in March 1984. By the time he recovered he found that his job had been filled by somebody else. He searched for work everywhere as he had a wife and three school-aged children to support. He signed on at the DHSS and regularly went to the Job Centre. It was in 1990 that he saw an advertisement there for a storeman vacancy. He was given the job, which was arranged through the JHP Employment Training Scheme, and worked there for three months, receiving both his unemployment benefit and an extra £10 per week from the scheme.

Unfortunately this was not John's big break. He felt that he was treated unfairly, the final straw coming when he was sacked over a disagreement involving permission for him to take a week's holiday. Unemployed again, John was fed up and his wife was understandably frustrated as he was around all the time. Worse, his confidence was shattered.

Then the Employment Action Scheme placed an advertisement in the Job Centre for a porter in Inverness. He went to the Employment Action office and found the staff very welcoming; they told him of two porters' jobs that were available, so he agreed to take the one that was nearer his home. For six months the EAS paid him an extra £10 per week on top of his unemployment benefit. Later this was extended for a further six months and John was finally employed full-time by the Royal Northern Infirmary on 4 June 1993.

On his first day at the RNI John was nervous but now he is confident and happy. He travels to work on the bus and has the opportunity to do overtime work once or twice a month. He is no longer depressed and plans to remain in his present job for as long as it is available to him.

John's advice to anybody in a similar position to him is to 'go for it'. The JHP scheme had, in his case, proved disappointing, but his perseverance ultimately proved to be vital. Together with the EAS John was able to find work he enjoys after nine years.

Community Care

CHRIS PEMBERTON (48): *Residential social worker*

After having been made redundant and subsequently being unemployed for 21 months, Chris Pemberton has now found a good job, thanks to the help of Action Workwise. After leaving the factory where he worked making clocks Chris began a small enterprise with a partner making fibreglass mouldings. Unfortunately, this venture proved uneconomic and he was left unemployed. He quickly joined a job club to try to increase his chances of securing employment. He achieved his goal, and not only found employment, but he also managed to change career: he is now working as a residential social worker.

As a result of attending the job club, Chris was informed about Action Workwise, a charity set up to help those currently facing unemployment by offering ongoing support, encouragement and practical help. Action Workwise has helped over 400 people and liaises closely with other help agencies, as well as the Employment Service, providing assistance and advice to the individual until his or her situation is resolved.

Chris believes that he would not have his present job without the help of Action Workwise. As a residential social worker in a family therapy unit in Norfolk, he has had a complete change of career: 'The excellent support from all at Action Workwise did a great deal to improve my self-confidence, which in turn made it possible for me to consider such a different job. The realistic mock interviews, using job descriptions I had received, proved decisive and invaluable. I had not previously been good at interviews but I knew I had the ability. Before I had been letting myself down.'

For Chris, the most important thing for an unemployed person is to keep in regular contact with an agency such as Action Workwise. Exercises in self-confidence help to develop improved communication techniques and to keep one's self-esteem buoyant. It is crucial to produce well-presented letters and an up-to-date, accurate CV, especially if it is something you have not considered before, and Chris is convinced that improving your telephone manner can only be favourable as so many people do not realise how they do themselves a disservice on this initial approach.

'I have learned that we are no good to ourselves or anyone else if we have a low opinion of what we can offer an employer. This way, all our potential is lost,' he explained.

An Open Book

PHILIP: *Book-keeper*

Philip had been unemployed for two years when he contacted the specialist job club at the Apex Employment Centre in Bristol. He had found it impossible to find employment and having a criminal record did not make things any easier. By the time he contacted the job club he was very depressed and worried about his financial situation.

After some initial interviews with workers at the centre, Philip realised that his main problem was that he had no idea how to prepare a suitable CV and was not accustomed to interview techniques. With advice and practice this situation soon changed and over a period of six months Philip had applied for over 70 different positions. This perseverance eventually paid off and he was offered the post of book-keeper with a legal firm, which suited his past experience and training.

Philip was delighted and is still very happy in his job. 'I can honestly say that the job club helped to restore my confidence and, in addition to improving my job-seeking skills, it helped to alleviate my general depression and disillusionment .'

A New Cycle

DAVID ROBERTS (58): *Vehicle accessories*

A former executive vice-president found business success with a Deeside-based firm following a Training and Enterprise-funded recruitment scheme.

Dr David Roberts, of Mynydd Isa, found himself out of work and fighting a losing battle for employment after returning to Britain following the completion of his six-year contract with American firm Vitra-fix Inc. Thanks to the Training and Enterprise-funded Executive Placement Programme however, he soon found business success with vehicle towing bracket and accessories manufacturer Dixon-Bates Ltd.

'I had been looking for a suitable job for 12 months and because of my age I found many companies wouldn't even consider me for an interview,' he said.

'Simply by chance I saw an advert in a local paper for a three-month placement scheme managed by the Newtech Innovation Centre in Wrexham, I thought I'd give it a try and have never looked back since.'

Programme co-ordinator Peter Harrison said the benefits are two-fold for the secondees and the companies who employ them. 'The programme is particularly useful for businesses requiring the skills that managers, executives and graduates can offer – while at the same time, boosting the morale of someone who is having problems finding work,' he explained.

Following his three-month term with Dixon-Bates working as consultant on a new bicycle parking rack project, Dr David Roberts was offered a full-time position.

Said quality manager, Clive Smith: 'We were very pleased with Dr David Roberts' achievements over the time he spent with us and were delighted to offer him a more permanent position.

'In our opinion the Management Placement Programme is a valuable approach to recruitment and adds an extremely useful dimension to the interview process as the employer can see how the individual performs in the job – something that cannot be gained from the standard interview situation.'

David continues to lead the Grippa Project and has achieved significant success in bringing this product to the forefront of the market. Demand is building up rapidly both in the United Kingdom and Europe.

Winning Through

GEORGE ROBOTHAM (23): *Computer adviser*

'I want one of those even if I have to buy it,' was George Robotham's first comment on seeing one of GrandMet Trust's coveted Awards for Achievement. George, from Gloucester, was at a London hotel for the annual awards ceremony for GrandMet Trust trainees in 1992.

He waited as names of competitors from around the country were read out. His name did not come up; not, that is, until the overall winner for achievement in personal development was announced. George had won. He could not believe it: 'It just didn't seem possible. I had been afraid to enter in the first place, and I was proud enough to have been nominated, let alone win.'

In Employment

George's award recognised the distance he had come: from the loss of his job, unemployment and a period in prison to becoming an accomplished computer technician and adviser with the leading software company Microsoft. Today he advises clients who call the company with difficulties in their computer systems. George has transformed his life in just two years with his enthusiasm and the help of others: 'You can't just be like a slug or snail – you've got to try to help yourself.'

When George left school in 1988 he started an apprenticeship in engineering with a local company. After a spell in prison he continued training with another company but lost his job and was unemployed for over six months. His probation officer suggested he should approach Fullemploy (a specialist branch of GrandMet Trust for ethnic minorities) in Gloucester. 'I thought I might as well go along. They interviewed me and wanted me to show I was committed by registering to go on a course, which I did.' The course he took was in word-processing and business administration. It was a 15-month course held in weekly sessions. At the same time he undertook courses at Gloucester College (GLOSCAT), achieving a GCSE in accountancy and additional maths. When he finished his courses he was unable to find employment immediately, but was registered with Fullemploy's agency. It was they who placed him with

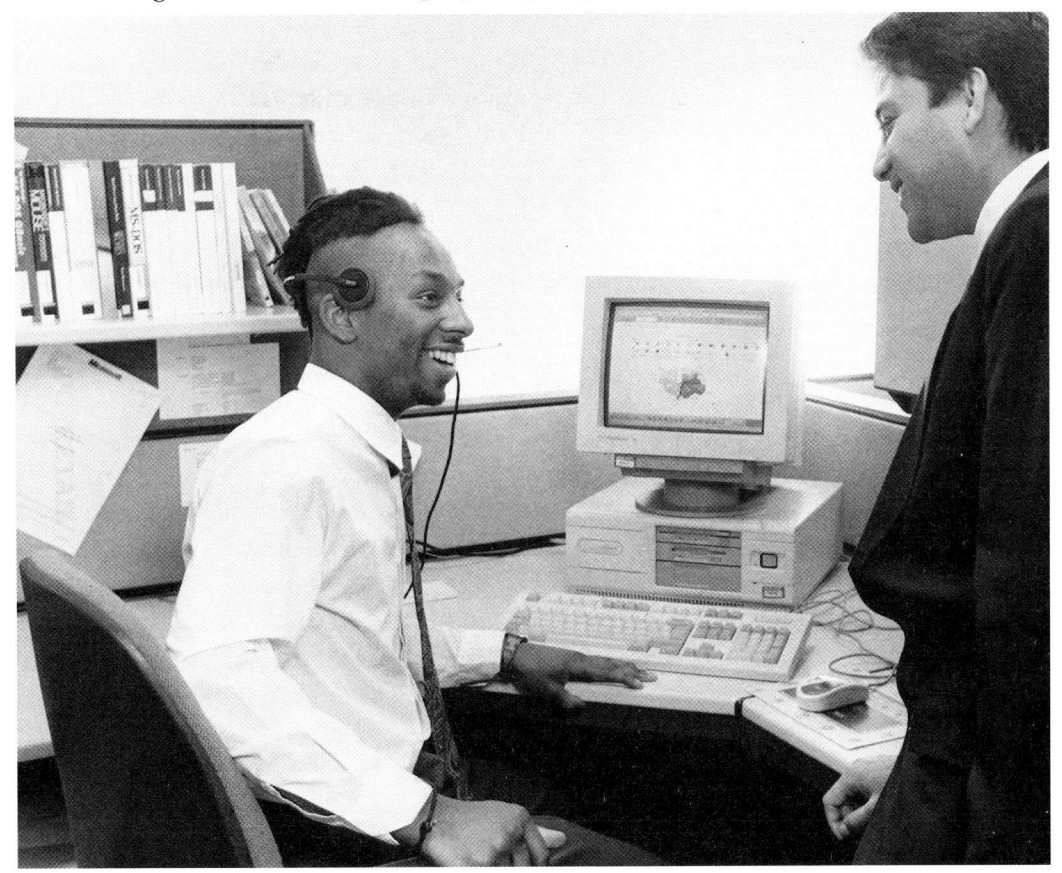

Microsoft: 'Their contacts with the senior bosses in the firm helped me get the placement,' explained George.

George's advisers helped him to prepare for his interview. It was this, he believes, that gave him his break. 'When I went into the interview I knew what to do; I knew how to structure my time, what I wanted to say and how to express it.'

At first he was taken on for a month's trial placement. At the end of this Microsoft recognised George's talents and he was offered a six-month contract which was in turn renewed for a further six months. Ultimately he was given a permanent job. 'At first I had to learn on the job, but I have progressed and have been promoted each year. I look forward to staying on and possibly becoming a manager here.' After years of uncertainty, having a job has given George security: 'I only really felt happy for the first time when my job became permanent.'

Building on Experience

NEIL RORISON (43): *Warehouseman*

Neil Rorison had worked in the building trade for 25 years but he had never heard of the company which gave him full-time employment thanks to a national training agency. Neil was a qualified joiner and had worked on a series of short-term jobs all over Scotland, from Edinburgh to the Shetland Islands, before he found himself out of work for two years. Neil found it difficult to come to terms with a possible future without work. 'I was applying for anything and everything that was coming up on the job market because of boredom and frustration. I was fed up being stuck at home and feeling that I was in a rut.'

In a bid to try something new, Neil contacted the national training agency through his local Job Centre. Having been unsuccessful in the applications he had made for the few jobs that had been advertised, Neil thought a qualification was the best way to improve his chances.

He was placed on a Training for Work programme in warehousing with builders' merchant RMC Catherwood in Inverness where he hoped to qualify for a City and Guilds certificate in wholesale warehousing (level 1). Although the job was different from what he had known before, he was delighted to be back in the building trade.

Neil began the six-month course in July and in November he was told there was a full-time job available with the company if he wanted it. He quickly said yes and is still with the firm, carrying out general store work. Father-of-two Neil explained: 'I believe I got the job on my own merits and experience but it was the training agency which gave me the opportunity. The success of the Training for Work programme really depends on the person who goes for it. I was determined to get back working again and through the course I was given an opportunity. But you have to work at it and show you are keen to get back into working life.'

A Taxing Task

MANJIT SIDHU (25): *Personal tax assistant*

When accountancy student Manjit Sidhu discovered that the firm she had worked for during her summer holidays couldn't offer her a full-time position she began the arduous task of looking for another job.

Starting in December 1991, while still studying part-time for her professional accountancy qualifications, she scoured the Yellow Pages writing to 'every public practice I could think of'.

'I wasn't getting any response at all, not even a reply to my letters. By the time I finished my exams in June I had lost all confidence in ever getting a job at all.'

After contacting her local Job Centre she attended a three-day professional executive course in Wandsworth which covered interview technique and CV writing. 'I'd paid money for one of those CVs done through the post and it was horrendous, my tutor said that if it had come before him he would have thrown it in the bin!'

With the help of the staff there, all experienced recruitment consultants, Manjit left with a 'beautiful laser-printed CV' which was commented upon in subsequent interviews and 'helped me get the job I've got at the moment'.

Next stop was Tooting Job Centre to gain computer experience, because 'any job I applied for I was told: 'No. You've never worked with Lotus 123.'' Starting on the learning skills seminar run by Fullemploy at the beginning of August, Manjit found her tutor to be 'very good, very patient', and adds, 'I learned a lot in the few weeks I was there, including spreadsheets, word processing and a basic grounding in the Lotus system. It would be the equivalent of paying £300 to £400 for a commercial course which, as a student, was the last thing I could afford.'

It was while attending the course that Manjit applied for a job at the *Evening Standard*. Despite extensive preparation at the centre she 'didn't hold out much chance of getting the job' because her first interview was 'short and very basic, they just didn't seem interested'. She was very surprised to be called up for a second interview, but out of seven candidates she was offered the job then and there.

On 21 September 1992, Manjit started as a personal tax assistant at the City accountancy firm Kernon & Co and she has since completed her course at college, becoming a fully qualified ACCA accountant.

Shopping Around

MELADO STEVENS (28): *Sales assistant*

After having been unemployed for two years Melado Stevens found a new and interesting job as a sales assistant at the Body Shop with the help of LEAP (Linked Employment and Accommodation Project). Melado had previously worked in a porcelain factory for more than four years before being made redundant due to cutbacks.

Not the kind of person to sit around doing nothing, Melado enrolled on a one-year computer training course which she found through her local TEC. Yet having successfully completed the course, she still could not find employment and, to make matters worse, she found herself homeless and had to move into a hostel. She lived at the hostel for six months and it was during this time, in August 1992, that she was told about LEAP. The course involves a two-week session of training, covering interview techniques, CV and letter-compilation and confidence-boosting. LEAP then arrange a work placement with a supporting company, in Melado's case the Body Shop, and she was offered a permanent job at their King's Road branch in London in September 1992.

Melado's advice is simple: 'Go on a course. It adds structure to your day, increases your confidence and could even result in a permanent position. If you want it badly enough, it will happen.'

Easy PC

PHILIP STROUD: *Computer administrator*

Philip Stroud, from Birmingham, lost his job at 40, having worked as a carpet salesman for 18 years. He was then unemployed for 12 months before he decided to find out about the types of training available for DTP. 'I wanted to become computer literate and competent and to be able to understand new technology and its use in industry,' he explains.

With the help of Aston Job Centre, he eventually found a place with MicroTech Computer Services, a training organisation affiliated to Birmingham TEC. He completed a course in information technology and, despite feeling out of place due to his age, he finished ahead of class with an NVQ level 3. He was even asked to stay behind as an assistant tutor to help out the rest of his class-mates.

Having started with no knowledge of computers at all, Philip then gained a work placement with a software house for whom he now works as administration executive.

He maintains it is important to thoroughly research the types of training available in order to find the one most suitable for you.

MircoTech was ideal for him because 'the atmosphere was conducive to learning. We were treated like adults, not kids.' In his view there is no replacement for hard work and a willingness to learn. 'Don't sit back and say "teach me", be prepared to meet your tutors halfway.'

A Career at the Bar

LISA TAYLOR (20): *Pub trainee*

When Lisa Taylor left school she had no qualifications and a year ago was unemployed with little prospect of a career. Today, thanks to a Thames Valley Enterprise SkillTrain course, she is in a well-paid job and aims eventually to own her own pub.

Her boss, Michael Doyle, the deputy manager of the George Hotel in Reading, said: 'These courses backed by Thames Valley Enterprise are marvellous because they give many young people who leave school without any qualifications something to aim for. Lisa was the first person I have personally engaged and I would have no hesitation in considering taking on others who are on such courses.'

Lisa's career in the licensed trade took off when she saw a newspaper advertisement by Kudos Leisure seeking trainees to work in pubs and clubs.

'I had attended a number of schools and left with no qualifications. Having been on the dole for six months, I realised that unless I gained some qualifications and experience it would be difficult to get a good job,' explained Lisa, who moved to Reading from London with her parents four years ago.

She was interviewed by Mrs Rita Koatley, an associate of Kudos Leisure which operates the courses under contract with Thames Valley Enterprise, the region's Training and Enterprise Council.

The SkillTrain course lasted six months and it involves one day a week in a classroom, learning book-keeping, stock control, licensing laws and product knowledge. Later Lisa gained the British Institute of Innkeepers level 3 certificate.

Mrs Koatley said: 'Those on the course need to have a placement within the industry to gain practical experience. Lisa went out on her own and approached the George Hotel.'

Here Mr Doyle, who is responsible for all personnel matters at the hotel, takes up the story.

'You tend to shy away from people who are seeking work and yet have no qualifications. They very often have no aim in life and are just wanting to rest their head for a while. But Lisa did have commitment and was extremely keen. She needed to gain experience and last June we agreed to take her on, on a temporary basis for 30 hours a week.

'She has a nice personality, is very good for business and has a good rapport with the customers. They knew she was on a course and urged us to keep her. Last September we decided to take her on the permanent staff and she continued to have one day a week off for course work. Now with a recent pay rise her salary is way in excess of double of what she was receiving when she was on the course.'

Lisa, who is 20, and lives in Coley Avenue, Reading, added: 'The course has helped me tremendously and I am grateful to Thames Valley Enterprise for backing such programmes. Being able to achieve some qualifications gives you greater confidence.

'I love my job working in the bars and it's enjoyable having a job where you meet people and socialise at the same time as earning money. I'd like to become a manageress and eventually own my own pub. Being unemployed is soul-destroying and having a job makes you have a greater degree of self-worth. Anyone wishing to go into the licensed trade should consider going on such a course. I doubt they will regret it.'

Green Shoots of Recovery

JOHN TURNER (57): *Horticultural instructor*

John Turner had worked for the parks department of Runcorn Council (DEVCO) for 17 years, since he qualified for a General Certificate in Horticulture after completing a Royal Horticulture Society course at Byrom Street College in Liverpool. He became a landscape supervisor but lost his job when the Warrington and Runcorn councils were reorganised in 1989. He was lucky enough to get another job as an assistant manager at a garden centre, but unfortunately this only lasted for six months as staff cut-backs again left him out of a job and he began a period of unemployment that would last for over two years.

At 52, John's prospects of finding employment were not good. He was fully aware of this but was nevertheless annoyed by the attitude he encountered at the Job Centres.

'There is nothing worse than being told by someone half your age and experience what you should do and knowing they're wrong. It's humiliating as well as infuriating. There weren't any jobs out there, whatever they said.'

John found the Employment Training Scheme, on which he was placed as a matter of course after six months on the dole, to be of little help and decided instead to put his extensive knowledge and experience to good use in instructing horticulture, something he had done on a basic level in his previous job. The Employment Office were enthusiastic about his suggestion and John started City and Guilds Training and Assessment courses locally at Frodsham College.

After 18 months he had completed the necessary courses to qualify for the City and Guilds 'Adult Trainer Award' and this enabled him to fulfil his wish to teach. 'You learn all methods of instructing on the course. If I had the manual I could probably teach the basics of most things now.'

On completing his course he asked Reasheath Horticultural College, the site of one of his previous placements, whether they might have an opening for him. Impressed by the knowledge he displayed during his placements the college offered him occasional classes to teach, and at the beginning of the New Year they took him on full-time as a horticulture instructor. John is delighted with his new post: 'I now have the chance to show others what I know.'

The Chance to Choose

DEREK TYSON (50): *Hygiene manager*

Five years ago Derek Tyson was forced to move around the country looking for work. Recently he was given the opportunity to change his job and take on one with greater responsibility. 'I started on the shop floor. Now I'm qualified to managerial level, my prospects are so much better.'

When Derek was made redundant from the South Wales colliery where he worked in the maintenance department he returned to his home town of Sunderland. Previously he had had labouring jobs in the town but now he was unable to find any work. After four months of fruitless attempts he and his wife decided to move to the south-east in order to improve Derek's chances. However, even in Surrey it was still 'incredibly difficult to find permanent work'. He took on the odd casual building job, but those apart his unemployment continued for several months.

Ultimately it was an opportunity he saw while doing casual work that led to Derek securing permanent employment. He was doing maintenance work for a bakery when the job of hygiene manager became vacant. 'The money was better than I was getting, so I applied.' He got the job, subject to him undertaking evening class courses in hygiene inspection at the local college, Brookland College, in Weybridge. On completing the classes he was also given the task of instructing other employees. 'It was when I started teaching others that I realised I needed to learn much more, particularly about bakery.'

Derek took up the City and Guilds bakery course, attending in his own time but financed by his company, which led to an NVQ in the subject. For three years Derek took Wednesday as his day off to study at college. This meant that he had to work over the weekend during this whole period. 'It was particularly hard because I had homework to do as well as a family to look after. But these qualifications are the key to a true job; they give you wider scope.'

The determination Derek showed over three years in attaining his NVQ has paid off. He has been offered a more senior job as a quality control manager with another company. Today, rather than being made redundant, Derek is in the position of being able to hand in his notice. 'I have moved from unskilled labour to skilled work, my job prospects are better and I have a much greater understanding of what I am doing.'

Out of the Porsche and into the Pub

ALAN VENNING (37): *Assistant steward*

Attending a Thames Valley Enterprise-backed SkillTrain course beats being on the dole, for the rewards can come quite quickly. This is the advice of father-of-four Alan Venning who a year on is now earning around twice the figure he received in unemployment benefit and income support.

Alan knows what it is like to fall into the poverty trap. Two years ago he was made redundant by Porsche (UK) as a paint and body technician.

'I looked for another job repairing and spraying cars but the pay was so bad. With four children I needed to find a job which paid a reasonable wage. After a year on the dole without any success in finding a suitable job I saw an advertisement in the *Evening Post* saying that Kudos Leisure were looking for management trainees to work in pubs and clubs. Having done some spare time work as a barman, the idea appealed to me.

'When I started on the course I was told there was no immediate financial improvement. I would still receive unemployment benefit and income support plus £10 a week from the Government for being on the course. While there wasn't any increase in my income, I felt being on the course was an investment for the future.'

It lasted for six months and each week there was a six-hour study day which covered book-keeping, stock control, licensing laws, product knowledge and the complexities of Value Added Tax.

'These study days were also useful,' stressed 37-year-old Alan, 'because in the lunch-hour people on the course, who ranged from 18 to 50 years of age, were able to compare notes on their work experience. There was a feeling on the course that everyone was on a learning curve and as we were all in the same boat there was no embarrassment about any mistakes made.'

Much of this SkillTrain course, where participants study for the British Institute of Innkeeping certificate, is spent in practical experience and Kudos Leisure found Alan a placement with the Reading Trade Union and Working Men's Club in Reading.

After obtaining a Grade III certificate from the British Institute of Innkeeping and a basic food hygiene certificate, Alan obtained employment as the assistant steward at the British Legion Club in Tilehurst, where there are 2,000 members.

Club secretary Mrs Julia Cox said of Alan: 'He is hard working and popular with the members. Alan was given the job because he had trained for what is an extremely responsible position.'

Mrs Rita Keatley, an associate of Kudos Leisure, which operates the courses under contract to Thames Valley Enterprise, added: 'When Alan came to us he was stuck in the poverty trap but he realised that what we had to offer was worthwhile.'

His wife Julie said she was happy he had found a rewarding job and he learned a great deal on the course. The hours may be sometimes long but he does have periods during the day to be with his children, Lisa (17), Paul (15), Stewart (9) and Jemma (3) at their home in Eldart Close, Tilehurst.

Alan concluded: 'Eventually I would like to be a manager of a club or own my own club or freehold pub. After going on a Thames Valley Enterprise supported course you soon realise that there is a lot more on the horizon. I would recommend them to anyone who is unemployed.'

Carving A Niche

ROBERT WATSON (23): *Butcher*

While still at school, Robert Watson discovered on a work experience placement that he was very interested in becoming a butcher. He enjoyed the placement so much that on leaving school, equipped with English and history O-level, he soon found work locally, and was employed at Sarah Brownridge in Tadcaster, where he was a butcher improver, for two and a half years.

Unfortunately Robert, ran into trouble with the law and spent nine weeks in prison, thereby losing his position at Sarah Brownridge. On re-entering the employment market he signed on with the DSS and regularly visited the Job Centre. He found the staff there and at the job club pleasant and helpful, but they were unable to find him work.

Robert looked for a job everywhere, visiting industrial estates, factories, and all the butchers in the area. He simply wanted to work and was prepared to do anything. For six months he continued this seemingly fruitless search for employment, kept going by his firm determination and the need to support his wife and their family. He believed that there was no point just sitting at home.

He was convinced that there was work out there if he could only find it. With no car, or even a bike, for transport he walked everywhere, on one occasion covering 28 miles in the same day.

His efforts were finally rewarded when he approached Barry Davies, a butcher in Tadcaster. Barry needed another member of staff but had insufficient funds to pay Robert a proper salary. Undeterred, Robert went back to the Job Centre to ask if there was a scheme that could help him around this problem.

It was the DSS who sent Robert to the Yorkshire Rural Community Council (YRCC). Within ten minutes he was seen by a representative to whom he explained his situation. Two weeks later Robert was working for Barry Davies, receiving both his money from the DSS and an extra £10 per week from the YRCC, which he continued to receive for three months.

By June 1993, Barry Davies was able to employ him on a full-time basis. Robert, now aged 23, is contented there and says: 'I can see myself staying for a good long time.'

On the Books

JEAN WILKINSON (50): *Bookseller*

Jean Wilkinson's confidence was shattered and her morale low when she was unable to find work after the bookshop where she had worked for several years closed down. Jean, in her fifties, had been employed in a variety of jobs at different times: she had worked in a factory for some years and in a bookshop for another three before taking a part-time job in another bookshop for two years.

Jean had been promoted to temporary manager for a while and had much enjoyed this position of responsibility. When the bookshop closed, she was at a loss to know what to do and set about looking for more work. She wrote to a huge number of bookshops in the local area after searching through the Yellow Pages, but even after a couple of interviews she still hadn't found a job.

It then occurred to Jean to do a beginners' computing course at Shipley New Start Centre, which she had recently been told about. She was shown around the centre and given advice about her course. There was a range of other courses on offer but Jean decided to stick with what she had already chosen.

The introductory course lasted for six three-hour sessions. During this time Jean was still registered unemployed and she and her husband were living on his earnings as a supply teacher.

On finishing the course, armed with her updated computer literacy, Jean applied for more posts. She first got a temporary job, a job lasting one month in a bookshop in Bradford and subsequently found work in Leeds on a more permanent basis. She explains that on managing to find work instantly her morale lifted and she regained much of her lost confidence.

Jean's employers have recently merged with another company and they are benefiting from a new computerised system which Jean is, of course, able to operate.

'The hardest thing about being unemployed is knowing what to do with your time,' admits Jean. Now, her confidence restored, she is happy in her job and plans to stay for the foreseeable future.

Showing the Way

WINIFRED WILKINSON (39): *Computer lecturer*

Winifred proudly claims that in life she has 'used everything as a stepping-stone', and this is certainly illustrated by her remarkable progress towards the success she now enjoys.

In 1976 Winifred was a factory worker with no qualifications. She left her job to have children and later discovered that she was unable to return to her job after maternity leave. Until her children were five Winifred remained unemployed. She then decided to take a secretarial course. After completing this she spent almost a year in temporary jobs which further increased her confidence to help her to continue building up her qualifications.

Winifred began a BTEC in computing at Barnsley, a course on which she was the only woman to finish. At first she felt inhibited by the fact that nearly all the other students were not only male but also substantially younger that her. While studying, Winifred had to work part-time to support her family. She boasts cheerily: 'You name it, I've done it!' For a while Winifred worked in a bar, and for six months she did night shifts in a garage, which enabled her to study at the same time.

When BTEC finished in the summer of 1988, she saw an advertisement in the local Job Centre for a part-time tutor in computers, word processing and business studies. She had first realised her ability to communicate with people while at college, when she had helped out fellow students as well as receiving help from them herself.

She got the job, and continued to teach six hours a week at the Centre for Unemployed in Wakefield while she completed an HND in computer studies at Wakefield District College. During her placement year she also worked as a tutor at Whitwood Centre for City and Guilds business computing.

When she achieved her HND, Winifred realised that she had been at college for five years and decided that it might be time for her to branch out and set up a business of her own. This she did in partnership with a friend of hers. The business they formed, Easytech, provided on-site computer training for small businesses. Easytech's success led to Winifred being offered the post of lecturer in Information Technology at Wakefield College and she is now back in full-time employment.

As a young mother of two teenage children Winifred looks back on her progress with satisfaction. She explained: 'You achieve things you thought you'd never have done and then you look a bit higher.' She went on to say that 'throwing people in at the deep end is no good; you have to offer them support and then gradually build up their confidence'.

Winifred has absolutely no regrets about the hard work she did throughout college. She is now reaping the benefits.

Computing Camaraderie

JOHN WRIGHT: *Computer programmer*

Ninteen years was a long time to work for Blue Circle Industries, where John was employed as part of a project team training users of computers. Yet when the company centralised in Basingstoke, John was unable to move there from Leeds and was consequently left unemployed.

He looked around for a similar job but was unsuccessful in finding anything. All the vacancies he enquired about were unsuitable and involved a different field of computing. It was not until after six months of continual searching that John attended a restart interview at Seacroft Unemployment Office. After a further six months he was offered a second restart interview, at which it was suggested that he contact Leeds TEC. There they sponsored him to attend JHP Training in order to study for a City and Guilds diploma in computing.

John's course involved two different parts. He learned to use the Cobol package, which he had never used before. This entailed learning a completely new computer language and programme design. He also underwent training in interview techniques, and was provided with advice for job searching and gaining placements. There were three others who began the course at the same time as John, but by the end only he and one other managed to achieve the City and Guilds qualifications.

The JHP course usually lasts for approximately 12 months, but after only eight John was offered a placement at Blackburn Associates. The placement was full-time and lasted three months. While he was there he wrote specialist programmes for airport systems, and some of his work may be seen in operation in Sweden.

John currently works for Blackburn Associates on a long-term basis. He acknowledges the help he received on his course and even now returns for a Friday lunchtime drink with his tutor. He enjoyed the 'good spirit and camaraderie' which he found on his course and his advice for others who may find themselves in difficult situations is: 'If you know what you want to do, then stick with it and you'll get there in the end'.

A Licence to Stack

HARRY YATES (52): *Forklift driver*

A career in ruins was to be the fate of a 52-year-old Wrexham man until Training and Enterprise-funded training that was to get him 'back on the road'.

Harry Yates of Ruthin spent his working life travelling thousands of miles across the country behind the wheel of specialised vehicles. But after being made redundant from his Mold-based job in September 1993, new safety regulations prevented him finding another career.

'By law anyone driving a specialist vehicle such as forklift trucks, and vehicles over 7.5 tonnes must now have a licence,' Harry explained. 'When I started driving trucks more than 20 years ago there were no such requirements – only when I was forced into looking for another job did I find I wasn't qualified.'

After facing refusals from companies in the area who all demanded the necessary paperwork, Harry faced a bleak future.

'Not only did I lack the paperwork but my age was also against me,' he said. 'It wasn't until Training and Enterprise offered to fund the Road Transport Industry Training Board course that I felt I still had a future.'

Harry attended a course at Wrexham Training and has since achieved a forklift truck licence and the position of stacker truck driver for Wrexham rubber manufacturers Fibrax. 'I am absolutely delighted with the results and the interest shown by Wrexham Training and Wrexham Training and Enterprise – without this licence I faced the rest of my years unemployed.'

Special Needs

(in alphabetical order)

Trained to Train

CLIVE BULMER (49): *Employment trainer*

Clive Bulmer from Chopwell, Tyne and Wear, spent 16 years in the police force. When he suffered a severe injury to his right arm he had no choice but to take medical retirement from the profession he loved.

It took him 18 months to recover properly, during which time he was lucky in receiving a great deal of help. The DRO (disablement resettlement officers) at Consett were very helpful and after an assessment with them, he was sent on a seven-week rehabilitation course with BB Training and Enterprise.

BB Ltd is a large private organisation which runs employment training through training for work. After two weeks with them, Clive decided that he definitely wanted to pursue a computer skills course. In the final week of the course, Clive was given a placement with Lloyd's Training.

He attended an interview on a Monday morning and by the following week he had started work. His employers were keen to take on somebody of a mature age and Clive fitted their requirement. Clive's job involves training people to operate computers, particularly word processing and database software, as well as teaching radio and television servicing, a subject he had studied for a City and Guilds qualification before he joined the police.

He is lucky in that he receives a modest pension from the police force, but in fact this proved disadvantageous when he was looking for work as many employers were keen to take on somebody with absolutely no income. In principle this is understandable, but Clive is anxious to stress that a job is important for self-esteem and morale, as well as to provide an income.

Clive describes his years unemployed as difficult: 'You start looking for excuses'. He stresses the value of 'gainful employment' and the importance of being in work. He is obviously a happier man now and content in his role at Lloyd's Training.

Read All About It

HEATHER CLARK (32): *Journalist*

Heather Clark is a thalidomide victim from Leeds who determinedly overcame her physical disabilities to gain employment. For five and a half years Heather worked full-time in a disabled living centre in Leeds. She had begun there on a voluntary basis and her role snowballed from there. In addition to her job as a receptionist she showed visitors around on arrival, and accumulated many other responsibilities during her time at the centre.

Heather then had another full-time job before leaving to go travelling abroad. She had had at some stage an idea that she would some day like to write, but at this stage she did not purse this. On her return from abroad, she worked in a nursing home part-time, but soon realised that she did not want to spent the rest of her life working as an office administrator.

Heather was keen to enter the world of media, and it was after watching a disability programme on television that she became aware of a journalism course available at Sheffield College, which greatly interested her. She applied to the college and simultaneously contacted RADAR (Royal Association for Disability And Rehabilitation), of whom she had heard through the publication *Disability Now*.

RADAR were extremely helpful, and when she was offered a place at Sheffield

College, Stradborke, they also agreed to pay her course fees as well as living and travelling expenses. They themselves apparently received a donation from an anonymous benefactor to be used specifically to fund disabled students.

The course Heather undertook lasted a year and earned her a certificate in journalism. She finished this at Easter in 1993, and because straight away it is often difficult for trainee journalists to break into full-time work, she decided to go freelance straight away.

Heather says she 'bombarded' various organisations, including Yorkshire Television, with her CV and requests for work, until she was invited by the newsroom at Yorkshire Television to do some research for them over a two-week period. They liked her work so much that she was later asked back and they are now her major client, employing her week by week. Heather enthuses that RADAR were very helpful and supportive and she herself has often returned to help them by showing others an excellent example of what it is possible to achieve.

She feels that disabled people often tend to be more determined and loyal than others because they have to fight more, and give at least 110 per cent in an attempt to prove that they are as capable as able-bodied people. She feels that colleges on the whole need to change their attitudes and their way of thinking as far as disabled people are concerned and become more aware of their capabilities and potential.

In her free time, Heather enjoys carriage-driving and sky-diving and is an advanced motorist. She is indeed a remarkable example of determination and ambition to succeed.

A Helping Hand

PHILIP DOWNS (38): *Disability consultant*

Philip Downs, from Didsbury, Manchester joined the police force in 1972 as a cadet but, tragically, after two years he suffered a severe accident while rehearsing a gymnastics display. This put a rapid end to his police training and he spent over ten years going in and out of hospital. He has been confined to a wheelchair for 20 years now.

Philip was fortunate in that the Police Dependants' Trust provided much support for him, buying him a speech activated computer and other vital equipment. But Philip felt that he needed to do something to keep himself occupied, and as a result established Disabled Living and Design.

His business was not set up without a struggle, however. It took Philip much courage and many years to be able to write even short letters and to regain his self-confidence and morale. Going on holiday for the first time in 17 years, he became aware of how difficult it was for disabled people to manage physically in an unfamiliar environment. He struggled without the assistance of a hoist as he was unable to take most of his kit on holiday with him.

Quoting the phrase, 'Necessity is the mother of invention', Philip felt the need to design portable hoists, sun-beds, loungers and other equipment to be used by disabled people. This he began to do with the help of the University of Manchester's Institute of Science and Technology. Philip developed an easily portable hoist using light fibres, which is important since most carers are women. He designed the hoist using a pencil clenched in his mouth, and later took his plans to various companies, where the design is still awaiting formal approval.

The business is concerned with all those suffering from very minor to very severe disabilities. He estimates the costs of equipment such as speech-activated computers, similar to the one he uses himself, and is also involved in a variety of other projects, such as the sales and marketing of products for smaller companies. He helps to market and sell products such as wheelchair covers and patient-lifters.

Philip admits to occasionally feeling frustrated with his situation. He is unable to be employed formally since he takes longer than most to get ready in the morning. However, he is thankful for the chance to be occupied and claims: 'I really wouldn't want it to be any different.' He has also established the Manchester United Disabled Supporters Association and has arranged for disabled supporters to attend football matches and secure special places.

Philip is contented and sounds cheerful and optimistic, although the income from his business appears to be penalised by his Therapeutic Earnings Allowance, rendering him unable to earn too much. Nevertheless, he has come a very long way from the days when he was initially wheelchair-bound, and he can take satisfaction from the knowledge that his work is helping others similarly disadvantaged.

From Coal to Computers

COLIN JULIAN: *Local council administrative assistant*

A serious motorbike accident brought to an end Colin Julian's 15 years as a miner but started a whole new chapter in his life. After Colin spent a year recuperating and a further 'dire' year unemployed, his local disability rehabilitation officer suggested he went for an interview at the Employment Rehabilitation Centre (ERC) in South Gosforth.

Despite his initial reluctance, the results of a series of aptitude tests and the advice of his instructor prompted him to begin a course that introduced him to the alien world of office work.

'I'd never been in an office before in my life and the only computer I'd seen I played games on,' says Colin. Getting back into a regular nine to five routine was an added benefit as I'd been slouching around doing nothing for such a long time.'

The course, which gave him a basic grounding in time-keeping, typing and computing was 'a tremendous help, and in only six weeks gave me the confidence to start work in a real office – something I could not have faced before.'

Now working for Newcastle City Council Education, Colin is enjoying his forced change of career. 'I was a supervisor at the pits and here I'm just an odd-job man. But there's no way I'd go back. The range of tasks from working with the computers to dealing with enquiries and the constant opportunities to meet people make me a very busy chappie. I love it!'

A Window of Opportunity

EDDIE NOLAN (48): *Domestic assistant*

For the first time in his life 48-year-old Eddie Nolan has a regular job – made possible with a helping hand from the West London Training and Enterprise Council.

Eddie, who lives in Brentford, Middlesex, had never been given the choice of finding employment because of the limited options available to people with special learning needs. All that changed in November 1993 when West TEC launched a new project to help people with learning problems.

Together with the Leaders' Employment Resource, based in Hounslow, an organisation that helps find work for people with learning disabilities, West London TEC offered Eddie and six other people the chance of training leading to employment.

He now works daily at Eldridge House Residential Unit, Feltham, as a domestic assistant. To attain the job, Eddie completed an eight-week course of training and a competitive selection interview. He began work in January 1994, initially helped by a support worker from Leaders. Today, Eddie needs only a guidance role from his support worker and is able to carry out his duties from 10am to 2pm each weekday.

'Eddie's enthusiasm and determination have resulted in him being employed for the first time. This has been a most worthwhile project,' said Judith Parsons, Executive Director of Training and Education at West London TEC, who has been delighted by Eddie's success.

She added: 'We hope to mirror this successful scheme in other parts of West London and it is expected that the partnership between West London TEC and Leaders Employment Resource will continue.'

Clever Computing

DAVID PORTER: *Computer design*

Many people have video cameras and photographers recording their wedding day but few have a television camera crew to contend with. Such was the interest in David Porter and his bride Jill's wedding in July that Ulster Television recorded the event to portray the courage of two people who have both had to overcome the effects of disability to lead what they see as a normal life expectation of education, work and now marriage.

David's visual impairment necessitated him leaving his home in the county town of Omagh, Co Tyrone in Northern Ireland to go to Jordanstown School for the visually impaired near Belfast. He had to leave school to continue his studies at home when his mobility difficulties worsened considerably, requiring him to use a wheelchair. Having spent some years at home he developed an interest in computers and hoped that someday his lifeline to work could be achieved through new technology.

When David heard that the Training and Employment Agency was organising a pilot scheme for home-based computer training he decided to give it a go.

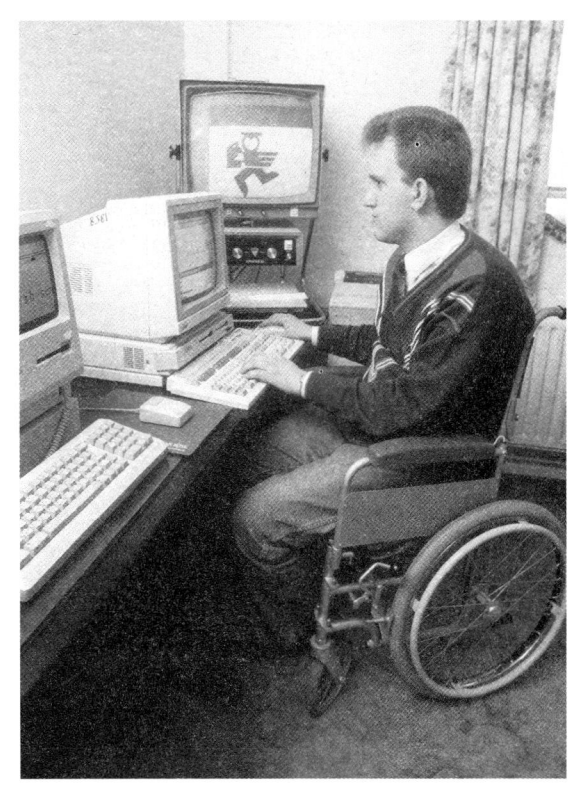

His bedroom was taken over by wires, computer equipment, CCTUs, magnifiers, printers and more wires – all equipment supplied through the Agency's Disablement Advisory Service (DAS).

On successful completion of the course David was placed with the Western Education and Library Board at their Microtech Centre but worked from home where he used an Apple Mac computer to prepare leaflets and forms for printing.

David is still with the Western Education and Library Board where he is now employed full time under the DAS Sheltered Placement Scheme still working from home. He now works with the Archimedes computer system and as well as desktop publishing duties has prepared databases for history, science and language advisers in the training of teaching staff.

David's supervisor visits him at home each week, bringing him work and collecting work which has been completed. David also travels to the Board's Microtech Centre on a regular basis to help him keep in contact with his employer's workplace.

Through his work David has gained the confidence to approach the future positively and his recent marriage to Jill is a further proof of this.

A Talent to Teach

STEVE (34): *Unit manager at a training centre*

Steve was born with a stenosis of the aortic valve – a congenital heart defect – which required open heart surgery in 1968 (one of the first operations of its kind to be performed in South Wales) when he was eight years old. Although Steve did well at school, his ill health meant that he left in 1975 with no formal qualifications. He was lucky, however, and within three weeks was employed locally in the baking and confectionery industry, moving on to a catering job in the local hospital. His growing dissatisfaction with his area of work was exacerbated by health problems and in 1978 he became unemployed on health grounds.

Using his period of unemployment to take stock of career options, Steve put himself on a ten-week disablement and rehabilitation course run by Employment Services. This indicated that he had an ability in engineering skills and machine operation, and, with another lucky break, he gained work with a local engineering company within three weeks of finishing the course.

Steve was made redundant in June 1980, shortly before he was due to be married. That was the start of seven years' unemployment. During that time, Steve experienced the range of feelings common to those who are unemployed in the long term – he lost confidence in his abilities, became dejected and found some of the processes involved in seeking work demoralising. However, he was determined to find paid employment, even taking a job for 13 weeks as part of a floor laying gang, despite the danger the physical activity posed to his health.

In 1986, Steve took part in one of the first Employment Service Restart programmes and attended Merthyr College to undertake computing, computer aided engineering and pneumatic systems. He passed all subjects with credit or distinction and by November 1987 felt sufficiently confident to take on a full time instructor post with NACRO in Merthyr Tydfil as part of their Community Programme. He quickly progressed to becoming assistant training officer, though still in a voluntary capacity, and in September 1988 was able to secure a paid position as a trainer in computing.

Within four years, Steve was the training organiser for Business Administration and Information Technology, responsible for co-ordinating and verifying NVQs. Through the NACRO staff development programme, he has been able to gain further qualifications in training and development. In 1993, he was selected for secondment to Mid-Glamorgan Training and Enterprise Council to form part of the Adult Credits Development Team. Now back with NACRO, he is the Unit Manager, responsible for training and project work and quality issues.

Steve realises now that, although he gained no formal qualifications early in his life, he had developed skills, and was able to develop some of them while unemployed, especially through his hobby of drawing and sketching. Steve says 'with the help of Restart, Merthyr College and NACRO, I made the transition from being long-term unemployed myself to helping the long-term unemployed to achieve their return ticket. Leaving school unqualified meant I didn't really have a measure of my potential and the best thing is that I have surprised myself with my abilities. Although it was difficult, I never lost the commitment and will to find paid employment.'

Engineering an Opening

KEVIN WILKIN (38): *Fitter/machinist*

For ten years Kevin Wilkin enjoyed his life as a glazier but a devastating car accident rendered him unable to continue his job. His injuries included two broken legs, one of which eventually had to be amputated above the knee. He also shattered an elbow joint, fractured his pelvis and suffered numerous internal injuries.

It took Kevin three and a half years to recover and, just as importantly, to regain much of his lost confidence. Despite short-lived despondence when a glass-blowing course he had hoped to do was cancelled, followed by a period of believing that no one would employ him, Kevin continued to look for work. A second accident put Kevin out of action for a further three years, after which he decided that he wanted to retrain.

Kevin's regional medical officer had previously suggested retraining, but on being interviewed at Leicester Employment Rehabilitation Centre, Kevin disliked the thought of the book-keeping and other clerical work towards which he was steered. He was more interested in restoring motorcycles, which he enjoyed as a hobby. So through his disablement officer he secured an interview at Portland College with a view to pursuing a one-year engineering competence course.

Kevin had already begun a model engineering course at a local college so he was able to combine business with pleasure. His course at Portland College lasted 12 months and resulted in him achieving an NVQ level 2 and a City and Guilds qualification. He acquired a knowledge of machinery and became able to read drawings, and by the end of it he was able to work unsupervised and produce high-quality equipment.

Following the completion of his course at Portland College, Kevin worked on a placement for a company in Northampton. Afterwards he spent only a further ten days unemployed before the Job Centre found him a position in engineering. At the interview, Kevin took all his college books and qualifications to show Minns Baluns. They were so impressed with his work that he got the job immediately, and has worked there for several months now, producing radio frequency equipment.

Kevin's advice to others who may be disadvantaged in some way is: 'Don't look upon yourself as unemployable.' After 14 years out of work he claims that it was determination that helped him to retrain, and others should follow his example of using every facility available to them.

Hearts of Oak

FRED WILLIAMS: *Centre co-ordinator*

Fred Williams was employed as a senior social worker with the Eastern Health and Social Services Board. Ten years ago he was knocked down on the Castlereagh Road, Belfast and sustained a major head injury and a variety of bodily injuries such as a broken arm, a broken foot, a fractured pelvis and several broken bones in his neck. He remains unable to walk because of spasticity in his left foot.

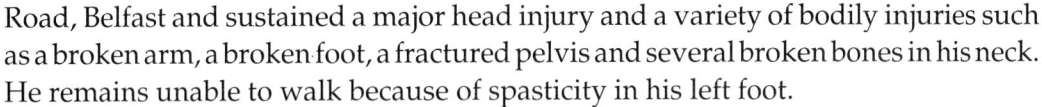

Fred was comatose for six weeks and was in the Royal Victoria Hospital for three and a half months, then a patient in Joss Cardwell for nine months. After that he tried going back to work but still had lots of problems, a major one being limited concentration so he eventually lost his job.

Fred did some work with a voluntary organisation, Victim Support, and learned to use a word processor. 'It was obvious I still wasn't recovered enough to get a job but it was lonely in the house during the day when my wife and kids were out at work and school so I went to the East Belfast Mission four days per week to prevent boredom and turning in on myself.'

Fred then got a part-time job for one year with the Forum for Community Education under the Action for Community Employment Programme (ACE). He then volunteered for three months. Fred's concentration remained impaired: 'When I was tired my emotions would lead to very colourful reactions to situations I found stressful.'

Through his Disablement Employment Adviser in the Training and Employment Agency he got his present job and slowly developed ACORN, a self-help group for disabled people. Fred is now centre co-ordinator for ACORN, a company which provides home visits, lunch out, riding lessons, canoeing, a work scheme and above all company for its members.

A Leap Ahead

FAY YOUNG (29): *Administrative assistant*

Fay Young was unemployed for 12 years, but with the help of LEAP (Linked Accommodation and Employment Project), she found the confidence and skills to get a job at last. She started work in December 1992 and now works regularly with the Housing Corporation in London as an administrative assistant, where she provides administrative and computer support for a number of departments within the corporation.

Having been a heroin addict for nine years, job search motivation was not at the top of her list of priorities. Living in a hostel for homeless people, as well as being registered disabled, meant that her chances of finding work were very slim indeed. Finally, she came off drugs and was told about the LEAP course, which lasts for one month, two weeks of which are spent on an employment placement with a guaranteed job interview at the end. The initial part of the course teaches interview technique, assertiveness and confidence-building. LEAP arranged two placements and Fay was successful on the second, with the Housing Corporation, where she has been covering for maternity and sickness leave since she began.

For Fay, the most important thing is to keep active, even if that means going from one placement to another. 'You have to keep your mind ticking over to ensure that you will be easily able to slot back into a work routine and environment. Be sure of yourself; don't continually knock yourself as others will readily do that for you. Remember that you are worthwhile and have a valid contribution to make.'

If rejection comes, she maintains that you must learn from it, but must also bounce back. Fay thoroughly recommends attending a course like LEAP's, which adds structure to your day, puts you back in touch with routine, introduces you to different people and boosts your confidence. 'Make the most of what you can offer; what have you got to lose?' is Fay's advice.

THE DIRECTORY

Where and how to find help from:

THE BANKS	124
TRAINING & ENTERPRISE COUNCILS	125
LOCAL ENTERPRISE COMPANIES	134
LOCAL ENTERPRISE AGENCIES	136
North East	137
North West	139
Yorkshire & Humberside	142
West Midlands	144
East Midlands & Eastern Region	146
South East	148
South West	153
London	155
Wales	157
Northern Ireland	159
Scotland	161
YOUNG ENTERPRISE	165
BUSINESS LINK	166
TASK FORCES	169
PRINCE'S YOUTH BUSINESS TRUST	171
TUC CENTRES FOR THE UNEMPLOYED	178
SPECIAL NEEDS	187
APEX TRUST	189
NATIONAL ASSOCIATION FOR THE CARE AND RESETTLEMENT OF OFFENDERS (NACRO)	192
VOCATIONAL QUALIFICATIONS	198
GOVERNMENT OFFICES	200
OTHER USEFUL ADDRESSES	202

The Banks

Starting Up a Small Business: How Banks Can Help

by Tony Bird – Regional Executive Director for Lloyds Bank

If you're thinking about setting up a small business, you're not alone. A staggering 45 new firms are launched every hour of every day of the year!

The reasons for setting up are varied. Some people want to be entrepreneurs, seeking independence and control. Others take up self-employment after redundancy, early retirement – or simply due to the need to make a living.

Whether you are a one man band or are planning to run a larger company, it's likely you will bear the brunt of the day-to-day running of the business. It won't be easy – you could be working a 12-hour day, six days a week – but the rewards could be worth all the hard work.

Many new business people will be experts in their own trade, but they may not be good financial planners. That is where your bank can help.

Getting good financial advice is essential – it could be the make or break. If you are putting all you have into a business, then you want a bank that will support you. It doesn't matter whether you are a large or small business or whether you wish to borrow or maintain your accounts in credit, a good relationship between you and your bank is equally important and we understand that if this is to work it must be based on both action and words.

That is why we like you to speak to specially trained business advisers. They will also be able to introduce you to other local support agencies such as the Training and Enterprise Council and the Local Enterprise Agency. We work with these organisations on an ongoing basis to provide you with the right advice as your business grows. We are always 'open for business' and are keen to develop relationships with new customers.

Please remember, coming in to discuss your ideas is free of charge. We're here to help – not just with finance, but with guidance and support when and if it's needed. Please call in at your local branch of Lloyds, Midland, NatWest, Barclays or TSB.

Training and Enterprise Councils (TECs)

This introduction to TECs has been provided by the North London TEC

How can they help small businesses?
What is a TEC or Training and Enterprise Council? What does it do? What is it's relevance to business? There is a popular misconception that the TECs are government organisations whose sole function is to help the unemployed to improve their skills and find work. While TECs rely on government funding, they are in fact, in many cases, companies limited by guarantee, with a board of directors. Their functions are many and varied. Among the most important however are the 'Enterprise' functions, which give them responsibility for helping businesses to grow and develop.

The TECs operate a number of schemes which are of particular assistance to the smaller business. These may be grouped under the headings of:

Advice and Information
Business Development
Finance

Advice and Information
Practical, impartial advice is essential to the success of any business. All TEC's operate an information and advice service. At North London TEC we have the North London Business Information Service which encompasses the library, a telephone enquiry service, a number of on-line databases, European information and most importantly a team of highly experienced business counsellors.

The counsellors come from a variety of backgrounds, ranging from banking to engineering and retail. They have all had senior management experience and each member of the team has a particular area of expertise such as marketing, strategy, exporting or finance. The service is available to businesses trading for more than 18 months and gives them access to experienced advisers who can help them solve their particular business problem.

The EC affects all UK businesses whether through legislation or as a new market to conquer. For the smaller businesses looking to grow and develop, the minefield of European legislation can seem particularly daunting. Most TECs employ a European information officer or manager, who is able to provide advice and guidance on export or import matters. Advice is also available on the numerous grants and loans obtainable from the EC.

Business Development
The majority of TEC Enterprise activity falls into this category. Some of these offerings such as Investors in People (IiP) are national programmes. IiP is a national standard for the effective training and development of people at work. It offers a planned approach to raising business performance by ensuring staff are motivated and can match their organisations' needs in order

to fulfil their business objectives. While it is usually associated with larger organisations IiP can be of great benefit to the smaller business.

At NLTEC, in addition to IiP we offer a wide range of consultancy services, to help with the development needs of smaller businesses.

Business Checks provide the opportunity for a management consultant using proven evaluation methods, to undertake a three day health check within a small company. The process typically includes the following:
- a one and a half day review with key management
- analysis of facts and attitudes
- report with recommendations for further actions.

Making Marketing Work helps smaller businesses maximise the marketing potential of their products or services by providing a strategic review, leading to the development of a marketing plan.

Implementation Consultancy is an initiative to help towards funding for companies committed to implementing action plans developed under one or more of the above mentioned schemes.

Customised Training is a scheme designed to help employers in the NLTEC area with the costs of recruitment and training of people who have been out of work for sometime.

While the above are examples of the help available through NLTEC, other TECs throughout the country operate similar initiatives.

Finance

Raising finance is one of the greatest dilemmas faced by small firms wanting to expand. TECs operate schemes which either directly provide funding or which make sources of funds more accessible. NLTEC operates three schemes, namely LINC, TEAM and London Ventures.

Local Investment Network Company (LINC) puts businesses in touch with groups of investors, in exchange for a share in equity. Introductions are made primarily by means of a monthly bulletin, which is circulated to all registered LINC investors, as well as numerous financial institutions. NLTEC hosts a meeting, giving investors the opportunity to listen to five or six business propositions. LINC operates its own database matching service, to bring together the most suitable opportunities with the appropriate investors.

TEC Enterprise at Midland Bank (TEAM) is a partnership providing local businesses with financial backing, independent business advice and support from NLTEC and Midland Bank. Loans up to £50,000 are available.

London Ventures are fund managers for the London region of Midland Bank Enterprise Fund. This is a direct, fast response venture capital fund, one of a number created in response to the Prince of Wales' request to the City for a low-ceiling, low-cost, quick-reacting fund. NLTEC has created a 'special interest' within the fund for businesses in the area by dedicating loan funds.

Conclusion

It is fair to conclude that TECs have an important role to play in supporting smaller businesses in their efforts to grow and develop. They are actively involved not only in providing training and advice, but also that very important commodity - funding.

Head Office

TEC National Council, 10th Floor, Westminster Tower, 3 Albert Embankment, London SE1 7SP   Tel: 071 735 0010

Chairman: Michael Bett CBE   Director of Policy and Strategy: Chris Humphries

Avon TEC
PO Box 164
St Lawrence House
29-31 Broad Street
Bristol BS99 7HR

Tel: 0272 277116

Chairman: Mr Colin Green
Chief Executive: Mr Pat Hall

AZTEC
Manorgate House
2 Manorgate Road
Kingston-upon-Thames
KT2 7AL

Tel: 081 547 3934

Chairman: Mr David Hill
Chief Executive: Ms Judith Rutherford

Barnsley/Doncaster TEC
Conference Centre
Eldon Street
Barnsley S70 2JL

Tel: 0226 248088

Chairman: Mr Peter Wetzel
Chief Executive: Mr Tony Goulbourn

Bedfordshire TEC
Woburn Court
2 Railton Road
Woburn Road Industrial Estate
Kempston
Beds MK42 7PN

Tel: 0234 843100

Acting Chairman: Mr John Barber
Chief Executive: Ms Diana McMahon MBE

Birmingham TEC
Chaplin Court
80 Hurst Street
Birmingham B5 4TG

Tel: 021 622 4419

Chairman: Mr Charles Darby CBE
Chief Executive: Mr David Cragg

Bolton & Bury TEC
Clive House
Clive Street
Bolton BL1 1ET

Tel: 0204 397350

Chairman: Mr Michael Smyth
Chief Executive: Mr Geoff Critchley

Bradford & District TEC
Fountain Hall
Fountain Street
Bradford BD1 3RA

Tel: 0274 723711

Chair: Mrs Judith Donovan
Chief Executive: Mr Mike Lowe

Calderdale/Kirklees TEC
Park View House
Woodvale Office Park
Woodvale Road
Brighouse HD6 4AB

Tel: 0484 400770

Chair: Mrs Jill Wilson
Chief Executive: Mr Alistair Graham

CAMBSTEC (Central & South Cambridgeshire)
Units 2-3
Trust Court
Chivers Way
The Vision Park
Histon
Cambridge CB4 4PW

Tel: 0223 235633

Chairman: Mr Robert Mallindine
Managing Director: Mr Alan Maltpress

CENTEC (Central London)
12 Grosvenor Crescent
London SW1X 7EE

Tel: 071 411 3500

Chairman: Lord Stockton
Chief Executive: Mrs Gwynneth Flower

Central England TEC
The Oaks
Clewes Road
Redditch B98 7ST

Tel: 0527 545415

Chairman: Mr Terry Morgan
Chief Executive: Mr Rodney Skidmore

CEWTEC (Chester, Ellesmere Port, Wirral)
Block 4
Woodside Business Park
Birkenhead
Wirral L41 1EH

Tel: 051 650 0555

Chairman: Mr John Conlan
Chief Executive: Mr Alan Moody

CILNTEC (City & Inner London North)
80 Great Eastern Street
London EC2A 3DP

Tel: 071 324 2424

Chairman: Mr Hugh Aldous
Chief Executive: Mr Peter Box

County Durham TEC
Valley Street North
Darlington DL1 1TJ

Tel: 0325 351166

Chairman: Mr Bernard Robinson OBE
Chief Executive: Mr David Hall

Coventry & Warwickshire TEC
Brandon Court
Progress Way
Coventry CV3 2TE

Tel: 0203 635666

Chairman: Mr Aaron Jones
Chief Executive: Mr Scott Glover

Cumbria TEC
Venture House
Regents Court
Guard Street
Workington
Cumbria CA14 4EW

Tel: 0900 66991

Chairman: Mr Arthur Sanderson OBE
Chief Executive: Mr Steve Palmer

Devon & Cornwall TEC
Foliot House
Brooklands
Budshead Road
Crownhill
Plymouth PL6 5XR

Tel: 0752 767929

Chairman: Mr Tim Legood
Chief Executive: Mr John Mannell

Dorset TEC
25 Oxford Road
Bournemouth BH8 8EY

Tel: 0202 299284

Chairman: Mr Rex Symons CBE
Chief Executive: Mr John Morrison

Dudley TEC
Dudley Court South
Waterfront East
Level Street
Brierley Hill
West Midlands DY5 1XN

Tel: 0384 485000

Chairman: Mr Philip White
Chief Executive: Mr John Woodall

ELTEC (East Lancashire)
Red Rose Court
Petre Road
Clayton Business Park
Clayton-Le-Moor
Lancashire BB5 5JR

Tel: 0254 301333

Chairman: Mr Tony Cann
Chief Executive: Mr Mark Price

Essex TEC
Redwing House
Hedgerows Business Park
Colchester Road
Chelmsford
Essex CM2 5PB

Tel: 0245 450123

Chairman: Mr Roy Lawrence
Managing Director: Mr Michael Clegg

Gloucestershire TEC
Conway House
33-35 Worcester Street
Gloucester GL1 3AJ

Tel: 0452 524488

Chairman: Mr John Hazelwood CBE
Chief Executive: Mr Graham Hoyle

Greater Nottingham TEC
Marina Road
Castle Marina Park
Nottingham NG7 1TN

Tel: 0602 413313

Chairman: Mr John Williams
Chief Executive: Mr Jim Potts

Greater Peterborough TEC
Unit 4, Blenheim Court
Peppercorn Close
off Lincoln Road
Peterborough PE1 2DU

Tel: 0733 890808

Chairman: Mr Philip Salisbury
Chief Executive: Mr Michael Styles

Gwent TEC
Glyndwr House
Unit B2
Cleppa Park
Newport
Gwent NP9 1YE

Tel: 0633 817777

Chairman: Mr Roger Jones
Chief Executive: Mr David Evans

Hampshire TEC
25 Thackeray Mall
Fareham
Hants PO16 0PQ

Tel: 0329 230099

Chairman: Mr Alan Philpott
Managing Director: Dr Max Wilson

HAWTEC (Hereford & Worcester)
Haswell House
St Nicholas Street
Worcester WR1 1UW

Tel: 0905 723200

Chairman: Mr Barrie Carter
Chief Executive: Mr Alan Curless

Heart of England TEC (Oxfordshire)
26-27 The Quadrant
Abingdon Science Park
Off Barton Lane
Abingdon OX14 3YS

Tel: 0235 553249

Chairman: Mr Julian Blackwell
Chief Executive: Mr Brian McCarthy

Hertfordshire TEC
45 Grosvenor Road
St Albans
Herts AL1 3AW

Tel: 0727 813600

Chairman: Mr Philip Groves
Acting Chief Executive: Judy Green

Humberside TEC
The Maltings
Silvester Square
Silvester Street
Hull HU1 3HL

Tel: 0482 226491

Chairman: Mr Tony Hailey
Managing Director: Mr Peter Fryer

Kent TEC
5th Floor
Mountbatten House
28 Military Road
Chatham
Kent ME4 4JE

Tel: 0634 844411

Chairman: Sir Alastair Morton
Chief Executive: Mr Malcolm Allan

LAWTEC (Lancashire Area West)
4th Floor, Duchy House
96 Lancaster Road
Preston PR1 1HE

Tel: 0772 200035

Chairman: Mr Jonathan Taylor
Managing Director: Mr Tony Bickerstaffe

Leeds TEC
Belgrave Hall
Belgrave Street
Leeds LS2 8DD

Tel: 0532 347666

Chairman: Mr Clive Leach
Chief Executive: Dr Derek Pearce

Leicestershire TEC
Meridian East
Meridian Business Park
Leicester LE3 2WZ

Tel: 0533 651515

Chairman: Mr Martin Henry
Chief Executive: Mr David Nelson

Lincolnshire TEC
Beech House
Witham Park
Waterside South
Lincoln LN5 7JH

Tel: 0522 567765

Chairman: Mr Paul Hodgkinson
Chief Executive: Mr David Rossington

London East TEC
Cityside House
40 Adler Street
London E1 1EE

Tel: 071 377 1866

Chairman: Mr Richard Goddard
Chief Executive: Ms Susan Fey

Manchester TEC
Boulton House
17-21 Chorlton Street
Manchester M1 3HY

Tel: 061 236 7222

Chairman: Mr David Compston
Chief Executive: Mr Paul Read

Merseyside TEC
3rd Floor, Tithebarn House
Tithebarn Street
Liverpool L2 2NZ

Tel: 051 236 0026

Chairman: Mr Barry Moult
Chief Executive: Mrs Linda Bloomfield

METROTEC (Wigan) Ltd
Buckingham Row
Northway
Wigan WN1 1XX

Tel: 0942 36312

Chairman: Mr Richard Vincent
Chief Executive: Mr Bill Badrock

Mid Glamorgan TEC
Unit 17-20 Centre Court
Main Avenue
Treforest Industrial Estate
Pontypridd
Mid Glamorgan CF37 5YL

Tel: 0443 841594

Chairman: Mr John Phillips CBE
Chief Executive: Mr Allen Williams

Milton Keynes & North Buckinghamshire TEC
Old Market Halls
Creed Street
Wolverton
Milton Keynes MK12 5LY

Tel: 0908 222555

Chairman: Mr Peter Muir
Chief Executive: Mr Michael Hind

NORMIDTEC (North & Mid Cheshire)
Spencer House
Dewhurst Road
Birchwood
Warrington WA3 7PP

Tel: 0925 826515

Chairman: Mr Peter Clarke
Chief Executive: Mr Chris Blythe

Norfolk & Waveney TEC
Partnership House
Unit 10, Norwich Business Park
Whiting Road
Norwich NR4 6DJ

Tel: 0603 763812

Chairman: Mr Martin Rickard
Managing Director: Mr John Wooddissee

North Derbyshire TEC
Block C, St Mary's Court
St Mary's Gate
Chesterfield S41 7TD

Tel: 0246 551158

Chairman: Mr Derrick Penrose
Chief Executive: Mr Stuart Almond

North East Wales TEC
Wynnstay Block
Hightown Barracks
Kingsmill Road
Wrexham
Clwyd LL13 8BH

Tel: 0978 290049

Chairman: Mr John Troth OBE
Managing Director: Mr Tim Harris

North London TEC
Dumayne House
1 Fox Lane
Palmers Green
London N13 4AB

Tel: 081 447 9422

Chairman: Mr John Wilkinson
Chief Executive: Mr Mike Nixon

North Nottinghamshire TEC
1st Floor, Block C
Edwinstowe House
High Street
Mansfield NG21 9PR

Tel: 0623 824624

Chairman: Mr Tony Wilkinson
Chief Executive: Mrs Pat Richards

North West London TEC
Kirkfield House
118-120 Station Road
Harrow HA1 2RL

Tel: 081 424 8866

Chairman: Mr Declan O'Farrell
Chief Executive: Mr Roy Bain

North Yorkshire TEC
TEC House
7 Pioneer Business Park
Amy Johnson Way
Clifton Moorgate
York YO3 8TN

Tel: 0904 691939

*Chairman: Mr Colin Shepherd
 OBE
Chief Executive: Mr Roger
 Grasby*

Northamptonshire TEC
Royal Pavilion
Summerhouse Road
Moulton Park Ind Estate
Northampton NN3 1WD

Tel: 0604 671200

*Chairman: Mr Tony
 Stoughton-Harris CBE
Chief Executive: Mr Martyn
 Wylie*

Northumberland TEC
Suite 2, Craster Court
Manor Walk Shopping
 Centre
Cramlington NE23 6XX

Tel: 0670 713303

*Chairman: Mr Bill Clark
Chief Executive: Mr Stephen
 Cowell*

Oldham TEC
Meridian Centre
King Street
Oldham OL8 1EZ

Tel: 061 620 0006

*Chairman: Mr Norman Stoller
 MBE
Acting Chief Executive: Ms
 Lynne Clough*

Powys TEC
1st Floor, St David's House
Newtown
Powys SY16 1RB

Tel: 0686 622494

*Chairman: Mr David Margetts
Chief Executive: Mr James
 Wagstaffe*

QUALITEC (St Helens) Ltd
7 Waterside Court
Technology Campus
St Helens
Merseyside WA9 1UE

Tel: 0744 24433

*Chairman: Mr Gordon Spencer
Chief Executive: Mr John
 Gracie*

Rochdale TEC
St James Place
160-162 Yorkshire Street
Rochdale
Lancs OL16 2DL

Tel: 0706 44909

*Chairman: Mr Harry Moore
Chief Executive: Ms Anne
 Martin*

Rotherham TEC
Moorgate House
Moorgate Road
Rotherham S60 2EN

Tel: 0709 830511

*Chairman: Dr Giles Bloomer
Chief Executive: Mr
 Christopher Duff*

Sandwell TEC
1st Floor
Kingston House
438-450 High Street
West Bromwich
West Midlands B70 9LD

Tel: 021 525 4242

*Chairman: Mr Michael Worley
Chief Executive: Mr John
 Bedingfield*

Sheffield TEC
St Mary's Court
55 St Mary's Road
Sheffield S2 4AQ

Tel: 0742 701911

*Chairman: Mr Doug Liversidge
Chief Executive: Mr Keith
 Davie*

Shropshire TEC
2nd Floor
Hazledine House
Central Square
Telford TF3 4JJ

Tel: 0952 291471

*Chairman: Mr Michael Lowe
Chief Executive: Mr Stephen
 Jury*

SOLOTEC
Lancaster House
7 Elmfield Road
Bromley
Kent BR1 1LT

Tel: 081 313 9232

*Chairman: Mr Ralph Ellis
Chief Executive: Mr John
 Howell*

Somerset TEC
Crescent House
3-7 The Mount
Taunton
Somerset TA1 3TT

Tel: 0823 321188

Chairman: Mr David Gwyther
Chief Executive: Mr Roger Phillips

South & East Cheshire TEC
PO Box 37
Middlewich Industrial & Business Park
Dalton Way
Middlewich
Cheshire CW10 0HU

Tel: 0606 737009

Chairman: Mr Tom Booth CBE
Chief Executive: Mr Richard Guy

South Glamorgan TEC
3-7 Drakes Walk
Waterfront 2000
Atlantic Wharf
Cardiff CF1 5AN

Tel: 0222 451000

Chairman: Mr Eric Crawford
Chief Executive: Mr Paul Sheldon

South Thames TEC
200 Great Dover Street
London SE1 4YB

Tel: 071 403 1990

Chairman: Mr Tim Hoult
Chief Executive: Mr Michael Hanson

Southern Derbyshire TEC
St Helens Court
St Helens Street
Derby DE1 3GY

Tel: 0332 290550

Chairman: Mr Eric Betsworth
Chief Executive: Ms Joy Street

Staffordshire TEC
Festival Way
Festival Park
Stoke on Trent ST1 5TQ

Tel: 0782 202733

Chairman: Mr Charles Mitchell CBE
Chief Executive: Mr Richard Ward

Stockport/High Peak TEC
1 St Peters Square
Stockport SK1 1NN

Tel: 061 477 8830

Chairman: Mr Iain Parker
Chief Executive: Mr Trevor Jones

Suffolk TEC
2nd Floor
Crown House
Crown Street
Ipswich IP1 3HS

Tel: 0473 218951

Chairman: Mr Robin Chesterman OBE
Managing Director: Mr Mike Bax

Sunderland City TEC
Business and Innovation Centre
Sunderland Enterprise Park
Riverside
Sunderland SR5 2TA

Chairman: Mr John Anderson
Managing Director: Mr Jules Preston

Surrey TEC
Technology House
48-54 Goldsworth Road
Woking
Surrey GU21 1LE

Tel: 0483 728190

Chairman: Mr Colin Harris
Managing Director: Mr Richard Wormell

Sussex TEC
2nd Floor
Electrowatt House
North Street
Horsham
West Sussex RH12 1RS

Tel: 0403 271471

Chairman: Dr James Stewart
Acting Chief Executive: Mr Roger Reed

TARGED
North West Wales TEC
1st Floor, Llys Brittania
Parc Menai
Bangor
Gwynedd LL57 4BN

Tel: 0248 671444

Chairman: Mr Geoff Drake
Chief Executive: Miss Enid Rowlands

Teesside TEC
Training & Enterprise House
2 Queens Square
Middlesbrough
Cleveland TS2 1AA

Tel: 0642 231023

Chairman: Mr Les Bell
Chief Executive: to be filled

Thames Valley Enterprise
6th Floor
Kings Point
120 Kings Road
Reading RG1 3BZ

Tel: 0734 568156

Chairman: Mr Russell Nathan
Chief Executive: Mr Roy Knott

Tyneside TEC
Moongate House
5th Avenue Business Park
Team Valley Trading Estate
Gateshead NE11 0HF

Tel: 091 487 5599

Chairman: Mr Chris Sharp
Chief Executive: Mrs Olivia Grant

Wakefield TEC
Grove Hall
60 College Grove Road
Wakefield WF1 3RN

Tel: 0924 299907

Chairman: Mr Jon Wesson
Chief Executive: Mr Geoffrey Badcock

Walsall TEC
5th Floor, Townend House
Townend Square
Walsall WS1 1NS

Tel: 0922 32332

Chairman: Mr Peter Burton
Chief Executive: Mr John Hyde

West London TEC
Sovereign Court
15-21 Staines Road
Hounslow
Middx TW3 3HA

Tel: 081 577 1010

Acting Chairman: Mrs Ann Hacker
Chief Executive: Dr Phil Blackburn

West Wales TEC
3rd Floor
Orchard House
Orchard Street
Swansea
West Glamorgan SA1 5DJ

Tel: 0792 460355

Chairman: Mr Robert Hastie CBE
Chief Executive: Mr Chris Jones

Wight Training & Enterprise
Mill Court
Furrlongs
Newport
Isle of Wight PO30 2AA

Tel: 0983 822818

Chairman: Mr Francis Dabell
Chief Executive: Mr Derek Kozel

Wiltshire TEC
The Bora Building
Westlea Campus
Westlea Down
Swindon
Wilts SN5 7EZ

Tel: 0793 513644

Chairman: Mr John Briffitt
Chief Executive: Mr Tim Boucher

Wolverhampton TEC
Pendeford Business Park
Wobaston Road
Wolverhampton WV9 5HA

Tel: 0902 397787

Chairman: Mr David Thompson
Chief Executive: Mr Peter Latchford

Local Enterprise Companies

In Scotland, Scottish Enterprise and Highlands and Islands Enterprise are responsible for delivering Government training programmes for young people and unemployed adults and also the Business Start-Up scheme, through their respective networks of local enterprise companies (LECs).

Addresses and contact points are given in the following pages:

SCOTTISH ENTERPRISE

Scottish Enterprise
(Head Office)
120 Bothwell Street
Glasgow G2 7JP

Tel: 041 248 2700

Contact: Crawford Beveridge

Scottish Borders Enterprise
Bridge Street
Galashiels TD1 1SW

Tel: 0896 58991

Contact: David Douglas

Dumfries & Galloway
  Enterprise
Cairnsmore House
Bankend Road
Dumfries DG1 4TA

Tel: 0387 54444

Contact: Leah Rafferty

Dunbartonshire Enterprise
Spectrum House
Clydebank Business Park
Clydebank G81 2DR

Tel: 041 951 2121

*Contact: Colin Sword or
  Collette Felippe*

Forth Valley Enterprise
Laurel House
Laurelhill Business Park
Stirling FK7 9JQ

Tel: 07864 51919

Contact: Brian Smail

Fife Enterprise
Huntsmans House
33 Cadham Centre
Glenrothes KY7 6RU

Tel: 0592 621000

*Contact: Mark Snell or Liz
  Sutherland*

Glasgow Development
  Agency
Atrium Court
50 Waterloo Street
Glasgow G2 6HQ

Tel: 041 204 1111

Contact: Mr Billy Bunnis

Grampian Enterprise Ltd
27 Albyn Place
Aberdeen AB1 1YL

Tel: 0224 211500

Contact: Mr Mike Fleming

Lanarkshire Development
  Agency
New Lanarkshire House
Willow Drive
Strathclyde Business Park
Bellshill ML4 3AD

Tel: 0698 745454

Contact: Mr David Quinn

Lothian & Edinburgh
  Enterprise Ltd
Apex House
99 Haymarket Terrace
Edinburgh EH12 5HD

Tel: 031 313 4000

Contact: Mr Bob Moffat

Moray Badenoch &
  Strathspey Enterprise
Elgin Business Centre
Maisondieu Road
Elgin IV30 1RH

Tel: 0343 550567

Contact: Mr Jim McKay

Renfrewshire Enterprise
  Company
25-29 Causeyside Street
Paisley PA1 1UL

Tel: 041 848 0101

Contact: Cath McCready

LOCAL ENTERPRISE COMAPNIES

Scottish Enterprise Tayside
Enterprise House
45 North Lindsay Street
Dundee DD1 1HT

Tel: 0382 23100

Contact: Tayside Bias

Enterprise Ayrshire
17-19 Hill Street
Kilmarnock
Ayrshire KA3 1HA

Tel: 0563 26623

Contact: Anne Currie

HIGHLANDS AND ISLANDS ENTERPRISE

Highlands and Islands
  Enterprise
(Head Office)
Bridge House
20 Bridge Street
Inverness IV1 1QR

Tel: 0463 234171

Contact: Iain Robertson

Argyll & the Islands
  Enterprise
Stag Chambers
Lorne Street
Lochgilphead
Argyll PA31 8LU

Tel: 0546 602281

Contact: Mrs Margaret Dolan

Caithness & Sutherland
  Enterprise
2 Princes Street
Thurso
Caithness KW14 7BQ

Tel: 0847 66115

*Contact: Mrs Anne-Marie
  Monteforte*

Inverness & Nairn
  Enterprise
Castle Wynd
Inverness IV2 3DW

Tel: 0463 713504

*Contact: Mrs Ryvonne Crook
and Mr Mark Mackintosh*

Lochaber Ltd
St Mary's House
Gordon Square
Fort William

Tel: 0397 704326

*Contact: Miss Jacqueline
  McKenna*

Orkney Enterprise
14 Queen Street
Kirkwall
Orkney KW15 1JE

Tel: 0856 874638

Contact: Mr Harvey Stevenson

Ross & Cromarty Enterprise
62 High Street
Invergordon
Ross and Cromarty
IV18 0DH

Tel: 0349 853666

Contact: Mrs Marion Mackay

Shetland Enterprise
The Toll Clock Shopping
  Centre
26 North Road
Lerwick
Shetland ZE1 0PE

Tel: 0595 3177

*Contact: Mrs Valerie
  Terneman*

Skye & Lochalsh Enterprise
King's House
The Green
Portree
Isle of Skye IV51 9ER

Tel: 0478 612841

Contact: Miss Linda Johnston

Western Isles Enterprise
3 Harbour View
Cromwell Street Quay
Stornoway PA87 2DF

Tel: 0851 703905

Contact: Mr Murdo Morrison

Local Enterprise Agencies

Local Enterprise Agencies and Trusts are independent not-for-profit organisations, offering a range of help and assistance to new and existing businesses on a confidential basis.

Over the last 20 years, the importance of small businesses to the economy in terms of jobs and wealth creation has been increasingly recognised and never more so than today. Firms with fewer than 20 employees are the lifeblood of the economy, comprising 96 per cent of the near 3 million businesses in the UK, providing more than a third of all private sector jobs; and generating a fifth of national turnover. It is generally accepted that businesses who make use of the advice, training and other support provided by Agencies and Trusts and similar organisations are more likely to survive, develop and grow.

Business in the Community (BITC) and Scottish Business in the Community have enjoyed a long and close relationship with Agencies and Trusts in the UK. They were first conceived in the 1970s to help businesses to start up and grow, thereby creating jobs and wealth. They were a pioneering example of the way that businesses, local authorities, central government and the voluntary sector could work together to develop the local economy.

The core service that Agencies and Trusts provide is information and advice. Over the years they have also developed a range of other services to help local businesses, including consultancy, training courses, work or office space, and raising finance.

Agencies and Trusts are funded in a variety of ways, including cash or in-kind sponsorship from local businesses and local authorities; through delivering services or managing projects under contract to, for example, Training and Enterprise Councils and Local Enterprise Companies; providing office or workspace; and funding from the European Commission.

Business in the Community and Scottish Business in the Community remain committed to the work done by Agencies and Trusts, the values they represent and the opportunities they provide for the private and public sectors to work together.

Business in the Community (BITC) is the leading authority on the promotion of corporate community involvement. Their mission is to make community involvement a natural part of successful business practice and to increase the quality and extent of business involvement in the community.

BITC is an independent organisation, financed by contributions from over 400 member companies with special project funding from both the public and private sectors. Supported by a network of 11 regional offices, BITC's personnel work closely with member companies to:

- promote business partnerships with local and central government, the voluntary sector and trade unions;
- collect and share examples of good practice;
- provide expert advice on developing and communicating community involvement programmes;
- achieve practical action by matching business resources with community needs;
- conduct a year-round programme of events to stimulate debate and develop new approaches in addressing community involvement issues.

Such partnerships are now widespread in tackling a range of economic, educational and social issues. They include Training and Enterprise Councils (in England and Wales), Local Enterprise Companies (in Scotland) and Education Business Partnerships (EBPs), to mention just a few.

Most Agencies and Trusts are companies limited by guarantee. They were originally defined by statute under section 48, Finance Act 1982 (later incorporated under S.79 Income and Corporation Taxes Act 1988). Cash or in-kind support from businesses to Agencies and Trusts approved under the Act is tax deductible. Registration as an approved Agency or Trust is the responsibility of the Department of Trade and Industry in England and that of the Scottish, Welsh and Nothern Ireland Offices.

Since 1970 their number has grown to more than 400. This has been achieved through the support of more than 6,000 businesses and other organisations who between them provide several million pounds' worth of sponsorship each year. Agencies and Trusts help thousands of businesses each year, both new and established, and make a major contribution to the health and success of the economy of their area.

For several years BITC acted as the unofficial umbrella organisation for local enterprise agencies in England and Wales. Now, however, the agencies have taken on this responsibility themselves through establishing their own associations which seek to influence local, regional and national strategies to assist businesses to develop and prosper. Agencies in Northern Ireland have also established their own association. Details of the associations appear at the beginning of each section of the directory. The associations in England have also established a national federation. Further information about the federation can be obtained from John Guest, Chief Executive, Federation of Enterprise Agencies, c/o Cadbury Schweppes, Bourneville, Birmingham B30 2LU, Tel: 021 458 2000.

These changes do not apply to Scotland where Scottish Business in the Community continues to act as the umbrella organisation for local enterprise trusts.

Head Office

DTI, Small Firms and
   Business Links Division
c/o Employment
   Department
St Mary House
Moorfoot
Sheffield S1 4PQ

Tel: 0742 597500

North East

Chester-le-Street & City of
   Durham
Newcastle Road
Chester-le-Street
Co Durham DH3 3TS

Tel: 091 389 2648

   Durham City
   Tel: 091 384 5407

Chairman: Terence Carney,
   Terence Carney Solicitors
Chief Executive: Ronald Batty

Cleveland Business
   Development Agency
New Exchange Buildings
Queens Square
Middlesbrough
Cleveland TS2 1AA

Tel: 0642 231389

   Stockton on Tees
   Tel: 0642 617964

Chairman: David Bowles,
   Northern Development
   Company
Chief Executive: Eric Sugden

Darlington Business Venture
4 Woodland Road
Darlington
Co Durham DL3 7PJ

Tel: 0325 480891

Chairman: Richard Coad,
   Armstrong Watson
Chief Executive: Alan Coultas

Derwentside Industrial
   Development Agency
Berry Edge Road
Consett
Co Durham DH8 5EU
Tel: 0207 509124

Chairman: John Tait, Barclays
   Bank plc
Chief Executive: Eddie
   Hutchinson

RETURN TICKET

Design Works
William Street
Felling
Gateshead
Tyne & Wear NE10 0JP

Tel: 091 495 0066

*Chairman: David Irwin,
 Project North East*
Chief Executive: Richard Clark

East Durham Development
 Agency
Fourth Floor
Lee House
Peterlee
Co Durham SR8 1BB

Tel: 091 586 3366

Chairman: Robert Taylor
*Chief Executive: Ken
 Greenfield*

Hartlepool Enterprise
 Agency Ltd
Suite 2
Municipal Buildings
Church Square
Hartlepool
Cleveland TS24 7ER

Tel: 0429 221216

*Chairman: Keith Thomas, Keith
 Thomas Associates*
Chief Executive: Ian Robertson

Hartlepool New
 Development Support Ltd
Suite 6-7
Municipal Buildings
Church Square
Hartlepool TS24 7ER

Tel: 0429 867100

 Redcar
 Tel: 0642 487005

*Chairman: Colin Doram,
 Hartlepool College of Further
 Education*
Chief Executive: Ronald Preece

North East Innovation
 Centre
Saltmeadows Road
Gateshead
Tyne & Wear NE8 3AH

Tel: 091 490 1222

Chairman: Eric Davey
*Chief Executive: Dr James
 Hedley*

Northumberland Business
 Centre
Southgate
Morpeth
Northumberland NE61 2EH

Tel: 0670 533933

Chairman: Alec McNichol
*Chief Executive: Graham
 Adams*

Project North East
Hawthorn House
Forth Banks
Newcastle Upon Tyne
NE1 3SG

Tel: 091 261 7856

 1 Pink Lane, Newcastle
 Tel: 091 261 6009

 25 Low Friar Street
 Tel: 091 222 1113

*Chairman: Rev Canon Peter
 Dodd, Northumberland
 Industrial Mission*
Chief Executive: David Irwin

The Development Agency of
 Sedgefield District
 (SASDA)
Bede House
St Cuthberts Way
Aycliffe Industrial Estate
Newton Aycliffe
Co Durham DL5 6DX

Tel: 0325 307270

*Chairman: John Pitts, Legal
 Aid Board*
*Chief Executive: John William
 Robson*

South East Northumberland
 Enterprise Trust (SENET)
20 School Road
Bedlington Station
Northumberland NE22 7JB

Tel: 0670 828686

 Ashington
 Tel: 0670 811690

 Blyth
 Tel: 0670 365558

*Chairman: William Patterson,
 British Alcan (Lynemouth)*
Chief Executive: Thomas Dean

Teesdale Enterprise Agency
39 Galgate
Barnard Castle
Co Durham DL12 8EJ

Tel: 0833 31851

Chairman: Jack Johnson
*Chief Executive: Kenneth Lee,
 Glaxo Operations UK Ltd*

The Tyneside Economic
Development Company
Ltd
Business Enterprise Centre
Eldon Street
South Shields
Tyne & Wear NE33 5JR

Tel: 091 455 4300

*Chairman: Albert Elliott, South
Tyneside MBC*
*Chief Executive: Anthony
Tompkins, Rolls Royce
Industrial Power Group*

Tyne & Wear Enterprise
Trust Ltd
Portman House
Portland Road
Newcastle Upon Tyne
NE2 1AQ

Tel: 091 261 4838

   Market Street, Newcastle
   Tel: 091 230 5989

   St Thomas Street,
   Newcastle
   Tel: 091 232 4895

   Oystershell Lane,
   Newcastle
   Tel: 091 233 0770

   Birtley
   Tel: 091 492 0022

   West Street, Gateshead
   Tel: 091 477 5544

   Saltmeadows Road,
   Gateshead
   Tel: 091 490 1155

   Newburn
   Tel: 091 229 0231

   North Shields
   Tel: 091 296 4477

Sunderland Business &
Enterprise Centre
Tel: 091 510 9191

Washington
Tel: 091 417 0511

*Chairman: Councillor T Daniel
Marshall*
Chief Executive: Alan Arthur

Wear Valley Enterprise
Agency Ltd
Auckland New Business
Centre
Bishop Auckland
Co Durham DL14 9TX

Tel: 0388 450505

*Chairman: John Elliott, EBAC
Ltd*
*Chief Executive: Peter
Gawthrop*

North West

Agency for Economic
Development
44 Moss Lane West
Moss Side
Manchester M15 5PD

Tel: 061 226 9434

*Chairman: Peter Walker, The
Co-operative Bank plc*
Chief Executive: Volney Harris

Blackburn & District
Enterprise Trust Ltd
14 Richmond Terrace
Blackburn
Lancs BB1 7BH

Tel: 0254 664747

   Darwen
   Tel: 0254 702476

*Chairman: Geoffrey Livesey
OBE, Cobble Ltd*
Chief Executive: Ken Whittaker

Blackpool & Fylde Business
Agency Ltd
20 Queen Street
Blackpool
FY1 1PD

Tel: 0253 294929

*Chairman: David Tomkins,
Barclays Bank plc*
*Chief Executive: Dennis
Scheib, National Savings*

Bolton Business Ventures
Ltd
46 Lower Bridgeman Street
Bolton BL2 1DG

Tel: 0204 391400

*Chairman: Mrs Jean Wilson,
Vernacare Ltd*
*Chief Executive: Paul
Davidson*

Burnley Enterprise Trust Ltd
Burnley Business Centre
Bank Parade
Burnley BB11 1UQ

Tel: 0282 411320

*Chairman: Dr Stuart
Kellington, Burnley College*
Chief Executive: Michael Green

Bury Partnership
Business Centre
Kay Street
Bury BL9 6BU

Tel: 061 763 1781

*Chairman: Toni Hankins, Row
Hankins Components*
Chief Executive: John Weir

Business for Lancaster Ltd
St Leonard's House
St Leonardgate
Lancaster
Lancs LA1 1NN

Tel: 0524 66222

*Chairman: Raymond Emery,
Forbo Kingfisher Ltd*
*Executive Director: Mrs J
Elizabeth Horsley*

Business in Liverpool Ltd
Merseyside Innovation
 Centre
31 Mount Pleasant
Liverpool L3 5TF

Tel: 051 709 1231/1366

Chairman: Roger James
Chief Executive: Allan Cooper

Business Initiatives Carlisle
The Enterprise Centre
James Street
Carlisle CA2 5BB

Tel: 0228 34120

*Chairman: Graham Kelly,
Barclays Bank plc*
Chief Executive: Bruce Clarke

Business Link Ltd
62 Church Street
Runcorn
Cheshire WA7 1LD

Tel: 0928 563037

 Widnes
 Tel: 051 423 6688

*Chairman: Alan Hill, Halton
Borough Council*
Chief Executive: Alan Griffiths

Chester & Ellesmere Port
 Enterprise Agency Ltd
Chester Enterprise Centre
Hoole Bridge
Chester CH2 3NE

Tel: 0244 311474

 Great Sutton
 Tel: 051 348 0744

*Chairman: Robert Hodson,
Manweb plc*
Chief Executive: Richard Holt

Chorley Local Enterprise
 Agency Ltd
2 Southport Road
Chorley PR7 1LD

Tel: 0257 266166

*Chairman: Dennis Benson,
Leyland DAF*
*Executive Director: Mrs Susan
Mann*

Cumbria Rural Enterprise
 Agency
Unit 1
Lake District Business Park
Mintbridge Road
Kendal LA9 6LZ

Tel: 0529 726624

Chairman: John Dunning
Chief Executive: Nick Jepps

Furness Enterprise Ltd
Local Business Division
Trinity Enterprise Centre
Furness Business Park
Ironworks Road
Barrow-in-Furness
Cumbria LA14 2PN

Tel: 0229 822132

Chairman: Alan Forsyth
General Manager: John Barker

Hyndburn Enterprise Trust
 Ltd
Suites 4-6 Arcade Offices
Church Street
Accrington BB5 2EH

Tel: 0254 390000

Chairman: Donald G Brogden
*Chief Executive: Mrs Aileen
Evans*

Into Business Ltd
Brunswick Small Business
 Centre
Brunswick Business Park
Liverpool L3 4BD

Tel: 051 709 2375

*Chairman: John Brown,
Midland Bank plc*
*Managing Director: James
Duffy*

Knowsley Business Advice
 Agency
Knowsley Business Resource
 Centre
Admin Building
Admin Road
Knowsley Industrial Park
Kirkby
Knowsley L33 7TX

Tel: 051 548 3245

*Chairman: David Dorrity,
Delco Electronics*
*Chief Executive: Lyndon R
Symonds*

LOCAL ENTERPRISE AGENCIES

Manchester Business Venture
c/o Manchester Chamber of Commerce and Industry
Churchgate House
56 Oxford Street
Manchester M60 7HJ

Tel: 061 236 0153

   Cheetham Hill
   Tel: 061 740 2233

Chairman: Michael Prior, Kidsons Impey
Manager: Martin Singer

Oldham Enterprise Agency
The Meridan Centre
King Street
Oldham OL8 1EZ

Tel: 061 665 1225

Chairman: Dr Richard Fenby
Chief Executive: Ed Stacey

Pendle Enterprise Trust Ltd
16 Carr Road
Nelson
Lancs BB9 7JS

Tel: 0282 698001

   Barnoldswick
   Tel: 0282 698001

Chairman: Ronald Foster
Chief Executive: Ronald Morrish

Preston Business Venture Ltd
Premier House
Church Street
Preston PR1 3BQ

Tel: 0772 825723

Chairman: Keith McGavin
Chief Executive: Mrs Susan Watkinson

Ribble Valley Enterprise Agency Ltd
Bank House
York Street
Clitheroe BB7 2DL

Tel: 0200 22110

Chairman: G Martin Hill, ICI Chemicals & Polymers Ltd
Chief Executive: Mrs Aileen Evans

Rochdale Enterprise Group
Generation Centre
Dane Street
Rochdale OL12 6XB

Tel: 0706 356250

Chairman: Chris Dykins, Slingco Ltd
Chief Executive: Bruce Harris

Rossendale Enterprise Trust
29 Kay Street
Rawtenstall
Rossendale
Lancs BB4 7LS

Tel: 0706 229838

Chairman: Neville Cormack OBE, Greenwood & Coope Ltd
Chief Executive: Mrs Joyce Livesey

The Community of St Helens Trust
Business Development Centre
St Helens Technology Campus
Waterside
St Helens WA9 1UB

Tel: 0744 453989

Chairman: Sir Antony Pilkington, Pilkington plc
Director: Brian Andrews, Pilkington plc

Salford 100 Venture
Stamford House
361 Chapel Street
Salford
Manchester M3 5JY

Tel: 061 835 1166

Chairman: Geoffrey Wilson, Phoenix Initiative
Chief Executive: Michael Finnie

South Cheshire Opportunity for Private Enterprise (SCOPE)
Scope House
Weston Road
Crewe
Cheshire CW1 1DD

Tel: 0270 589569

   Mimon Street, Crewe
   Tel: 0270 589569

   Congleton
   Tel: 0260 270027

Chairman: Vic Harris, Rolls Royce Motor Cars Ltd
General Manager: Cheryl Johnson

South Ribble Business Venture Ltd
Leyland DAF Spurrier Gatehouse
Centurion Way
Farington, Leyland
Preston PR5 2GR

Tel: 0772 422242

Chairman: Jim Breakell, Willis Corroon
Chief Executive: Ron Gates

South Sefton Enterprise
  Agency
South Sefton Business
  Centre
Canal Street
Bootle
Merseyside L20 8AH

Tel: 051 933 0024

Chairman: David Price
Manager: Colleen Bold

Southport Marketing &
  Enterprise Bureau
Gordon House
Leicester Street
Southport PR9 0ER

Tel: 0704 544173

Chairman: Robert Thomson
Chief Executive: Neil
  Annandale

Stockport Business Venture
Errwood Park House
Crossley Road
Heaton Chapel
Stockport SK4 5BH

Tel: 061 432 3770

Chairman: Norman Walker
  OBE, Dyer Environmental
  Controls Ltd
Chief Executive: Bill Hurren

Tameside Business Advice
  Service
Charlestown Industrial
  Estate
Turner Street
Ashton-under-Lyne
Tameside
Lancs OL6 8NS

Tel: 061 339 8960

Chief Executive: Kenneth
  Ackroyd, Tameside MBC

Trafford Business Venture
Third Floor
Acre House
Town Square
Sale M33 1XZ

Tel: 061 905 2950

  Trafford Park
  Tel: 061 848 4302

Chairman: Martin Lester
Chief Executive: Stephen
  Conroy

Vale Royal Enterprise
  Agency
Verdin Exchange
High Street
Winsford
Cheshire CW7 2AN

Tel: 0606 861300

Chairman: Robert Collicutt,
  Brunner Mond
General Manager: Mrs Lisa
  Pritchard

Warrington Business Venture
Warrington Business Park
Long Lane
Warrington WA2 8TX

Tel: 0925 33309

Chairman: Anthony Mills,
  BNFL
Director: Peter Robinson

West Cumbria Partnership
Thirlmere Building
50 Lakes Road
Derwent Howe
Workington CA14 3YP

Tel: 0900 65656

Chairman: Kenneth Dixon
Director of Operations: Ms
  Barbara Stephens

West Lancashire Enterprise
  Trust Ltd
The Malt House
48 Southport Road
Ormskirk L39 1OR

Tel: 0695 575488

  1 Westgate, Skelmersdale
  Tel: 0695 29977

Chairman: Ieuan Davies
Chief Executive: Graham
  Looker

Wigan & District Chamber
  of Commerce
Buckingham Row
Northway
Wigan WN1 1XX

Tel: 0942 324547

Chairman: David Page
Chief Executive: Geoff Birkett

Wyre Business Agency Ltd
Wheeler House
Burn Hall Estate
Fleetwood Road North
Fleetwood FY7 8RS

Tel: 0253 828265

Chairman: Ian Henderson, ICI
  plc
Chief Executive: Derek Wheeler

Yorkshire & Humberside

Barnsley Business &
  Innovation Centre
Innovation Way
Barnsley S75 1JL

Tel: 0226 249590

Chairman: The Rt Hon Lord
  Mason of Barnsley PC
Chief Executive: Dr Brian King

Local Enterprise Agencies

Barnsley Enterprise Centre
The Enterprise Centre
1 Pontefract Road
Barnsley S71 1AJ

Tel: 0226 774000

   Thurnscoe
   Tel: 0709 881951

Director: Richard Davies
Chief Executive: John Price

Bradford Enterprise Agency
Commerce House
24 Kirkgate
Bradford
West Yorks BD1 1QB

Tel: 0274 734359

Chairman: Jack Smith
Director: John Smith

Calderdale Business Advice
   Centre
OP56
Dean Clough Industrial Park
Halifax
West Yorks HX3 5AX

Tel: 0422 345631

Chairman: David Horsman,
   Wilkinson Woodward &
   Ludlam
Chief Executive: Arthur
   Stonebridge

Chapeltown & Harehills
   Enterprises Ltd (CHEL)
CHEL
26 Roundhay Road
Chapeltown
Leeds LS7 1AB

Tel: 0532 425996

Chairman: David Springer
Chief Executive: Ravinder Ghir
   Singh

Dales Enterprise Agency Ltd
21-23 High Street
Gargrave
Skipton
North Yorks BD23 3RP

Tel: 0756 748194

   Ingleton
   Tel: 05242 41701

Chairman: Alan Webb,
   Shepherd Baker
Chief Executive: Peter Goulden

DonBAC The Doncaster
   Enterprise Agency
19-21 Hallgate
Doncaster DN1 3NA

Tel: 0302 340320

Chairman: James Bennett
Chief Executive: Brian Crangle

Grimsby & Cleethorpes
   Area Enterprise Agency
   Ltd
10-14 Hainton Avenue
Grimsby DN32 9BB

Tel: 0472 241869

Chairman: Tony Hudson,
   Chem Dry (Northern) Ltd
Chief Executive: Mike Tink,
   United Biscuits (UK) Ltd

Hambleton &
   Richmondshire Business
   Enterprise Centre
Enterprise House
Bridge Street
Bedale DL8 2AD

Tel: 0677 423737

Chairman: Brian Bainbridge
Chief Executive: James Brown

Hull Business Advice Centre
34-38 Beverley Road
Hull HU1 1YE

Tel: 0482 27266

   Riverview Road
   Tel: 0482 883367

   Annie Reed Road
   Tel: 0482 870876

Chairman: Tony Hunt, BP
   Chemicals
Chief Executive: Derek Bell

Institute of Asian Business
Equity Chambers
40 Piccadilly
Bradford BD1 7NN

Tel: 0274 734444

Chairman: Mohinder Singh,
   Majesty Enterprises
Chief Executive: Dayal Sharma

Kirklees & Wakefield
   Venture Trust
Kirklees Enterprise Agency
Unit 6, Batley Ent Centre
513 Batley Road
Batley WF17 8JY

Tel: 0924 420302

   Wakefield Enterprise Agency
   147 Westgate
   Wakefield WF2 9RY
   Tel: 0484 201343

   Huddersfield
   Tel: 0484 427212

   Castleford
   Tel: 0977 519625

   South Elmsall
   Tel: 0977 645141

Chairman: Stephen Oakee,
   Chadwick Lawrence
Chief Executive: Mrs Christine
   Tolson

Leeds Business Venture
1st Floor
County House
82 Vicar Lane
Leeds LS1 7JH

Tel: 0532 446474

*Chairman: A K Dickinson,
 Barclays Bank plc*
Director: E Vevers

Orchard Park & North Hull
 Enterprises Ltd
Dane Park Road
Orchard Park
Hull HU6 9AR

Tel: 0482 806952

*Chairman: James Mulgrove,
 Hull City Council*
*Chief Executive: Robert
 Edmondson*

Rotherham Enterprise
 Agency Ltd
10 Church Street
Rotherham S60 1PD

Tel: 0709 823590

   Rawmarsh
   Tel: 0709 526498

*Chairman: Peter Moran,
 Beatson Clark plc*
Chief Executive: John Clayton

Scarborough Enterprise
 Agency
The Sitwell Centre
Sitwell Street
Scarborough YO12 5EX

Tel: 0723 354454

*Chairman: Councillor Michael
 Pitts*
*Executive Director: Brian
 Wood*

Sheffield Enterprise Agency
 Ltd
23 Shepherd Street
Sheffield
South Yorks S3 7BA

Tel: 0742 755721

*Chairman: Jonathan Hunt,
 Wake Smith & Company*
Chief Executive: Ian Cruddas

South Humber Business
 Advice Centre Ltd
7 Market Place
Brigg
South Humberside
DN20 8HA

Tel: 0652 657637

*Chairman: John Clugston,
 Clugston Ltd*
*Chief Executive: Derek
 Marshall*

Vale of York Small Business
 Association Ltd
1 Davygate
York YO1 2QE

Tel: 0904 641401

   Harrogate Enterprise
    Centre
   Claro Road
   Harrogate NG1 4AT
   Tel: 0423 500032
   Director: John Kennett

   Selby Enterprise Centre
   23 Finkle Street
   Selby YO3 0DT
   Tel: 0757 705567
   Director: Keith Knowles

*Chairman: Ian Traynor,
 Traynor Kitching &
 Associates*
Chief Executive: Mike Rigby

Whitby & District Business
 Development Agency Ltd
St Hilda's Business Centre
The Ropery
Whitby
North Yorks YO22 4ET

Tel: 0947 600827

*Chairman: Moira Thomson,
 Francis E Thomson Ltd*
Chief Executive: Peter Noble

York Enterprise Ltd
York Enterprise Centre
1 Davygate
York YO1 2QE

Tel: 0904 646803

*Chairman: Graham Millar,
 Nestle Rowntree*
*Chief Executive: Norman
 Whyte, National
 Westminster Bank plc*

The Young Business Project
The Fishergate Centre
4 Fishergate
York YO1 4AB

Tel: 0904 610045

Manager: Simon Daubeney

West Midlands

Birmingham Venture
Chamber of Commerce
 House
75 Harborne Road
Edgbaston
Birmingham B15 3DH

Tel: 021 454 6171

Chairman: Bernard Stevens
*Chief Executive: Derek
 Bullivant*

LOCAL ENTERPRISE AGENCIES

Black Business in Birmingham
15 The Square
111 Broad Street
Birmingham B15 1AS

Tel: 021 631 2860

Chairman: Athelston Sealey, Tastees Bakery Ltd
Chief Executive: Olufemi Kolade

Burton Enterprise Agency Ltd
Suites 15-17
Imex Business Park
Shobnall Road
Burton-upon-Trent
Staffs DE14 2AU

Tel: 0283 37151

   Lichfield
   Tel: 0543 258863

Chairman: Derek Radnor
Chief Executive: Peter St John-Harris

Cannock & Burntwood Enterprise Agency Ltd
80 High Green
Cannock
Staffs WS11 1BE

Tel: 0543 571978

Chairman: David Linford, F & E V Linford
Executive Director: A Hulbert

Coventry Business Centre Ltd
Christchurch House
Greyfriars Lane
Coventry CV1 2GY

Tel: 0203 552781

Chairman: Councillor J D Berry, Coventry City Council
Executive Director: John Gibney

Dudley Business Venture
Stanton House
10 Castle Street
Dudley
West Midlands DY1 1LQ

Tel: 0384 231283

Chairman: Graham Knowles, Hulbert Group
Chief Executive: Derek Brind

North Staffordshire & District Business Initiative
Commerce House
Festival Park
Etruria
Stoke-on-Trent ST1 5BE

Tel: 0782 279013

Chairman: Terry Forster, Michelin Tyre plc
Chief Executive: Wanda Ford, KPMG Peat Marwick

Redditch Enterprise Agency Ltd
Sandwell Enterprise Ltd
Rubicon Centre
17 Broad Ground Road
Lakeside
Redditch
Worcs B98 8YP

Tel: 0527 501122

   Bromsgrove
   Tel: 0527 73232

Chairman: Bernard Slater, Slater Yendall Engineering Ltd
Chief Executive: Peter Blacklock, United Biscuits (UK) Ltd

Sandwell Enterprise Ltd
Sandwell Business Advice Centre
Victoria Street
West Bromwich
Sandwell B70 8ET

Tel: 021 500 5412

Chairman: Graham MacKenzie, United Engineering Steels Ltd
Chief Executive: Alfred William Woodhouse

Shropshire Enterprise Trust Ltd
Business Development Centre
Stafford Park 4
Telford
Shopshire TF3 3BA

Tel: 0952 290782/3/4

Chairman: Bob Taylor, Insuwall Ltd
Managing Director: Ernie Houghton MBE

Solihull Business Enterprise Ltd
142 Lode Lane
Solihull B91 2HP

Tel: 021 704 1456

Chairman: John Taylor MP
Executive Director: Fred Smallman

Stafford Enterprise Ltd
23a Goalgate Street
Stafford ST16 2NT

Tel: 0785 57057

Chairman: Lord Nelson of Stafford
Chief Executive: Douglas Marston, Tesco plc

Staffordshire Development
  Association
The Business Advice Centre
Shire Hall
Market Street
Stafford ST16 2LQ

Tel: 0785 277370

*Chairman: Stuart Lyons, CBE,
  Royal Doulton Ltd*
Chief Executive: Ian Cass

Walsall Enterprise Agency Ltd
139-144 Lichfield Street
Walsall WS1 1SE

Tel: 0922 646614

   Caldmore Green
   Tel: 0992 646300

   Willenhall
   Tel: 021 609 7105

*Chairman: Councillor Mike
  Bird, Walsall Metropolitan
  Borough Council*
Chief Executive: Peter O'Brien

Warwickshire Enterprise
  Agency Ltd
The Business Centre
Third Floor
William House
Clarendon Court
The Parade
Leamington Spa CV32 4DG

Tel: 0926 433344

   Atherstone
   Tel: 0827 611741

   Nuneaton
   Tel: 0203 375469

   Rugby
   Tel: 0788 551388

   Stratford Upon Avon
   Tel: 0789 297335

Stoneleigh Park
Tel: 0203 696986

Chairman: Robert Solt
Chief Executive: Denis Malone

Wolverhampton Enterprise
  Ltd
Lich Chambers
Exchange Street
Wolverhampton WV1 1TS

Tel: 0902 312095

*Chairman: Councillor Jim
  Inglis*
Chief Executive: Fred Pickerill

East Midlands & Eastern Region

Bassetlaw Enterprise
  Agency
96 Bridge Street
Worksop
Nottinghamshire S80 1AJ

Tel: 0909 487344

   Retford
   Tel: 0777 706770

   Sutton-in-Ashfield
   Tel: 0623 443597

*Chairman: Anthony Wilkinson,
  Wilkinson Hardware*
Managing Director: Bob Cutts

Cambridge Enterprise
  Agency Ltd
71a Lensfield Road
Cambridge CB2 1EN

Tel: 0223 323553

*Chairman: Tony Barraclough,
  Bain Clarkson Ltd*
*Chief Executive: Malcolm
  Watson, Lloyds Bank plc*

Derby & Derbyshire
  Business Venture
Derven House
32 Friar Gate
Derby DE1 1BX

Tel: 0332 360345

Chairman: John Woodward
Chief Executive: Emanuel Gatt

Fens Business Enterprise
  Trust Ltd (FENBET)
Fenland Business Centre
Longhill Road
March
Cambs PE15 0BJ

Tel: 0354 660900

*Chairman: Colin Lazenby, C A
  Lazenby Associates*
*Chief Executive: Stuart
  Hamilton*

First Enterprise Business
  Agency
88-90 Radford Road
Nottingham NG7 5FU

Tel: 0602 423772

*Chairman: Sullay Jalloh,
  University of Nottingham*
*Chief Executive: Jonathon
  Olaofe*

Great Yarmouth Business
  Advisory Service Ltd
Queens Road Business
  Centre
Queens Road
Great Yarmouth NR30 3HT

Tel: 0493 850204

*Chairman: John Norton,
  Ventureforth Group*
*Managing Director: John
  Jennings*

Huntingdonshire Enterprise
  Agency Ltd
49 High Street
Huntingdon PE18 6AQ

Tel: 0480 450028

Chairman: Andrew Semple
Chief Executive: David
  McDonnell, British Gas

Ipswich Enterprise Agency
  (IPSENTA)
The Suffolk Enterprise Centre
Russell Road
Ipswich IP1 2DE

Tel: 0473 259832

    Sudbury Enterprise Agency
    Tel: 0787 73927

Chairman: James H Crowe,
  British Rail
Chief Executive: Mervyn A W
  James

Kettering Business Venture
  Trust
Venture House
4 Robinson Way
Telford Way Ind. Estate
Kettering NN6 8PP

Tel: 0536 513840

Chairman: Terry Freer SATRA
Chief Executive: Edward George

Lincoln Enterprise Agency
Innovation Centre
West Yard
Ropewalk
Lincoln LN6 7DQ

Tel: 0522 540775

    Horncastle
    Tel: 0507 522227

    Louth
    Tel: 0507 608888

    Mablethorpe
    Tel: 0507 473591

    Skegness
    Tel: 0754 610630

Chairman: Maurice Gates
  MBE, Micrometric
  Techniques Ltd
Chief Executive: Denis Wilson

Lowestoft Enterprise Trust Ltd
Waveney Business
  Development Centre
40 Gordon Road
Lowestoft
Suffolk NR32 1NL

Tel: 0502 563286

Chairman: Peter Comins
Executive Director: Iris
  Shuttleworth

Mansfield Sutton & Kirkby
  Enterprise Partnership
The Old Town Hall
Market Place
Mansfield NG18 1HX

Tel: 0623 21773

    Sutton-in-Ashfield
    Tel: 0623 21773

Chairman: Howard Baggaley,
  Baggaley Group
Chief Executive: Bernard Wale

Mid Anglian Enterprise
  Agency Ltd
9 Whiting Street
Bury St Edmunds
Suffolk IP33 1NX

Tel: 0284 760206

Chairman: Andrew Dickson,
  BDO Binder Hamlyn
  Insurance Brokers
Chief Executive: Albert Cook

Newark Enterprise Trust
The Firs
67 London Road
Newark
Notts NG24 1RZ

Tel: 0636 640666

Chairman: Charles Bright,
  Consultancy Europe
Chief Executive: Brian Tindale

North Derbyshire Enterprise
  Agency
Enterprise House
123 Saltergate
Chesterfield
Derbys S40 1NH

Tel: 0246 207379

    Buxton
    Tel: 0298 74000

    Glossop
    Tel: 0457 868003

Chairman: David Robinson
Chief Executive: Michael
  Horner

Northamptonshire
  Enterprise Agency Ltd
Royal Pavilion
2 Summerhouse Road
Moulton Park
Northampton NN5 6BJ

Tel: 0604 671400

    Wellingborough
    Tel: 0933 440448

Chairman: Jim Harker,
  Northamptonshire County
  Council
Chief Executive: David Mann

Norwich Enterprise Agency
Trust
112 Barrack Street
Norwich NR1 3TX

Tel: 0603 613023

*Chairman: Barry Tarling,
Rhone Poulenc Ltd*
Chief Executive: Peter Smith

Nottinghamshire Business
Venture
Business Information &
Advice Centre
309 Haydn Road
Sherwood
Nottingham NG5 1DG

Tel: 0602 691151

*Chairman: Roger Hursthouse,
Pannell Kerr Forster*
*Chief Executive: Gordon
Mackenzie*

Peterborough Enterprise
Programme
Winchester Place
80 Thorpe Road
Peterborough PE3 6HZ

Tel: 0733 310159

Maxwell Road
Tel: 0733 390707

*Chairman: David Weekes,
Greenwoods Solicitors*
Director: Paul Child

South Lincolnshire
Enterprise Agency
Station Road (East)
Grantham
Lincs NG31 6HX

Tel: 0476 68970

Spalding
Tel: 0775 711393

Sleaford
Tel: 0526 833833

*Chairman: John Hindmarch,
Duncan & Toplis*
*Chief Executive: Mrs
Jacqueline Smith*

West Norfolk Enterprise
Agency Trust Ltd
Enterprise Works
Bergen Way
King's Lynn PE30 2JR

Tel: 0553 764127

*Chairman: Sir Jeremy Bagge,
Stradsett Estates*
Executive Director: Peter Bargh

South East

Basildon & District Local
Enterprise Agency Ltd
c/o Samson House Ltd
Unit 16
Arterial Road
Laindon
Basildon SS15 6DR

Tel: 0268 410400

*Chairman: Max Kochmann,
Pafra Ltd*
*Chief Executive: Dennis
Pigden*

Basingstoke & Andover
Enterprise Centre
75 Church Street
Basingstoke
Hants RG21 1QT

Tel: 0256 54041

Andover
Tel: 0264 332092

Stockbridge
Tel: 0264 332092

*Chairman: Councillor Eileen
Haseldon, Test Valley
Borough Council*
Chief Executive: Colin Close

BECENTA Bedfordshire
Enterprise Agency
The Business Centre
Kimpton Road
Luton LU2 0LB

Tel: 0582 452288/23456

Bedford
Tel: 0234 327422

President: Sam Whitbread
*Chairman: David Wallis,
Vauxhall Motors*
*Chief Executive and Director:
The Reverend Derek Upcott*

Berkshire & Southern
Buckinghamshire
Enterprise Agency
7-11 Station Road
Reading RG1 1LG

Tel: 0734 585715

Acre Road
Tel: 0734 312433

High Wycombe
Tel: 0494 473093

Newbury
Tel: 0635 523472

Slough
Tel: 0753 550276

Chesham
Tel: 0494 778818

Wokingham
Tel: 0734 770960

*Chairman: Gareth Gimblett,
Berkshire County Council*
*Chief Executive: John Hiscocks,
Berkshire County Council*

Local Enterprise Agencies

Blackwater Valley
  Enterprise Trust
Princes Gardens
High Street
Aldershot GU11 1BJ

Tel: 0252 319272

  Camberley
  Tel: 0276 22226

  Farnham
  Tel: 0252 722598

  Fleet
  Tel: 0252 811603

*Chairman: Anthony Bracking,
  S C Johnson Wax*
Chief Executive: Walter Oakey

Braintree District Enterprise
  Agency Ltd
Town Hall Centre
Braintree
Essex CM7 6YG

Tel: 0376 328221

  Saffron Walden
  Tel: 0799 516516

  Great Dunmow
  Tel: 0799 510480

Chairman: Alan Murton
Director: Brian Palmer

Brentwood Enterprise
  Agency Ltd
Brentwood Training Centre
Essex Way
Warley
Brentwood
Essex CM13 3AX

Tel: 0277 213405

*Chairman: Roger Norris, W H
  Norris & Sons*
*Chief Executive: James
  Campbell*

Brighton & Hove Business
  Enterprise Agency
23 Old Steine
Brighton BN1 1EL

Tel: 0273 688882

*Chairman: Bruce Nichol,
  Ewbank Preece Group*
*Chief Executive: Michael Hogg
  (Sponsored by British
  Railways Board)*

Chelmsford Enterprise
  Agency
Unit 3, Robjohns House
Navigation Road
Chelmsford CM2 6ND

Tel: 0245 496712

*Chairman: Keith Andrew, Co-
  operative Bank*
*Chief Executive: Mrs Patricia
  Gard*

Colchester Business
  Enterprise Agency Ltd
154 Magdalen Street
Colchester CO1 2JX

Tel: 0206 48833

  Maldon
  Tel: 0621 851884

*Chairman: William Pavry,
  Paxman's Diesels*
Chief Executive: Graeme Garden

Crawley & Central Sussex
  Enterprise Agency Ltd
6 Spencers Road
Crawley RH11 7DA

Tel: 0293 538670

*Chairman: Anthony Hare,
  Hurston Insurance
  Consultants*
Chief Executive: Sean Haimes

Dacorum Enterprise Agency
83 Marlowes
Hemel Hempstead HP1 1LF

Tel: 0442 232333

*Chairman: David Furnell,
  Furnell Transport*
Chief Executive: Dion Wilson

Downs Enterprise Agency Ltd
St James Training Centre
St Pancras
Chichester PO19 4NN

Tel: 0243 778077

  Horsham
  Tel: 0403 218077

*Chairman: David Skelton,
  Metcraft Ltd*
*Chief Executive: Tom Tyrwhitt
  Drake, Zeneca*

Eastbourne & District
  Enterprise Agency Ltd
Minster House
Business Development Centre
York Road
Eastbourne BN21 4ST

Tel: 0323 644470

*Chairman: W A (Bill) Honey,
  Honey Barrett & Co*
Chief Executive: George Collier

Enterprise Ashford Ltd
The Enterprise Centre
Old Railway Works
Newtown Road
Ashford
Kent TN24 0PD

Tel: 0233 630307

*Chairman: Francis Hewson,
  Geerings of Ahsford Ltd*
*Managing Director: Alan
  Duncan*

Enterprise Tendring Ltd
27a Pier Avenue
Clacton-on-Sea
Essex CO15 1QE

Tel: 0255 421225

*Chairman: John Curry,
 Astralux Dynamics Ltd*
*Chief Executive: Mrs Christine
 Curry*

Essex Business Centre
Church Street
Chelmsford
Essex CM1 1NH

Tel: 0245 283030

    Basildon
    Tel: 0268 728078

    Clacton-on-Sea
    Tel: 0255 221116/552012

    Braintree
    Tel: 0376 550218

    Maldon
    Tel: 0621 851884

    Ongar
    Tel: 0277 362944

*Chairman: Michael Rose, Essex
 County Council*
*Chief Executive: Alan Menzies,
 Essex County Council*

Forest Enterprise Agency
 Trust Ltd
Feat House
Rear of Swimming Pool
Traps Hill
Loughton
Essex IG10 1SZ

Tel: 081 508 7435

Chairman: Mrs Ann Miller
*Chief Executive: Robert Vice,
 Benefits Agency*

Gravesham Enterprise
 Agency
The Maltings Enterprise
 Centre Ltd
Lower Higham Road
Gravesend
Kent DA12 2LY

Tel: 0474 327118

Chairman: Ron Dewar
Director: Michael Fitzpatrick

Great Weald Enterprise
 Agency
Peach Hall
Trench Road
Tonbridge
Kent TN10 3HA

Tel: 0732 360133

*Chairman: Drummond Brams,
 Spain Brothers & Co*
*Chief Executive: Miss Janet
 Sergison*

Guernsey Enterprise Agency
States Arcade
Market Square
St Peter Port
Guernsey
Channel Islands GY1 1HD

Tel: 0481 710043

*Chairman: Jim Le Pelley, Le
 Pelley & Tosteuin Advocates*
Director: Meg Heyworth

Harlow Enterprise Agency Ltd
19 The Rows
The High
Harlow
Essex CM20 1DD

Tel: 0279 438077

    Hertford
    Tel: 0992 503456

*Chairman: Jack Wratten,
 British Petroleum*
*Co-directors: David Matthew,
 Bank of England*
*Dr Philip Chapman, Glaxo
 Manufacturing Services*
*Stephey Dooley, Bank of
 England*

Hastings Business Venture Ltd
18 Cornwallis Gardens
Hastings
East Sussex TN34 1LP

Tel: 0424 433333

    Rye
    Tel: 0797 222293

*Chairman: Martin Oliver,
 Prudential Assurance Co Ltd*
*Chief Executive: Ian
 McCullagh*

Hertsmere Enterprise
 Agency
The Enterprise Centre
Cranborne Road
Potters Bar
Herts EN6 3DQ

Tel: 0707 660270

*Chief Executive: John
 Farnsworth*

Isle of Wight Enterprise
 Agency Ltd
6 Town Lane
Newport
Isle of Wight PO30 1JU

Tel: 0983 529120

Chairman: Mike Oatley
*Chief Executive: John
 Wolfenden*

LOCAL ENTERPRISE AGENCIES

Letchworth Business Centre
Avenue One
Business Park
Letchworth Garden City
Herts SG6 2HB

Tel: 0462 678272

Chief Executive: Mrs Sue Cheshire

Maidstone Enterprise
  Agency
Enterprise Centre
Wren House
64 Lower Stone Street
Maidstone
Kent ME15 6NA

Tel: 0622 675547/757802

Chairman: Tony Extance
Chief Executive: Geoff McCue

Medway Enterprise Agency
  Ltd
Unit 1, Sabre Court
Valentine Close
Gillingham Business Park
Gillingham
Kent ME8 0RW

Tel: 0634 366565

    Chatham
    Tel: 0634 844340

Chief Executive: Mrs Linda Wolk

Milton Keynes Business
  Venture
Medina House
314 Silbury Boulevard
Central Milton Keynes
Bucks MK9 2AE

Tel: 0908 660044

    Bletchley
    Tel: 0908 368071

Kiln Farm
Tel: 0908 564464

Chairman: David Winks, KPMG Peat Marwick
Chief Executive: Colin Offor

North Oxfordshire Business
  Venture Ltd
2nd Floor, Globe House
Calthorpe Street
Banbury
Oxon OX16 8EX

Tel: 0295 267900

Chairman: John Harper, Chestertons
Executive Director: Tim Nattrass

North West Kent Enterprise
  Agency Ltd
Kestner Engineering Works
Station Road
Greenhithe
Kent DA9 9DD

Tel: 0322 381885

Chairman: Frederick Shaw, Kestner Engineering Co Ltd
Managing Director: Michael Fitzpatrick

Shepway Business Advisory
  Panel Ltd
34 Bouverie Squares
Folkestone CT20 1BA

Tel: 0303 259162

    New Romney
    Tel: 0679 64611

    Lydd
    Tel: 0679 20999

Chairman: Lt Comdr Richard Colville
Chief Executive: Peter Patten

South East Essex Business
  Enterprise Agency
362 Chartwell Square
Southend-on-Sea SS2 5SP

Tel: 0702 464443

Chairman: Brian Isaacs
Chief Executive: Terry Pasmore, Ford Motor Company Ltd

South East Hampshire
  Enterprise Agencies
27 Guildhall Walk
Portsmouth PO1 2RY

Tel: 0705 833321

    Alton
    Tel: 0420 87577

    Gosport
    Tel: 0705 586621

    Petersfield
    Tel: 0730 261767

    Fareham
    Tel: 0329 825882

    Havant
    Tel: 0705 492425

    Liss
    Tel: 0730 894583

    Waterlooville
    Tel: 0705 231006

Chairman: Nigel Atkinson, George Gale & Co
Chief Executive: Tim Austin

Southampton Enterprise
  Agency
Solent Business Centre
Millbrook Road West
Southampton SO1 1HW

Tel: 0703 788088

Chairman: Wilfred Wright MBE
Chief Executive: Barrie Levy

Southend Enterprise Agency
845 London Road
Westcliff on Sea
Essex SS0 9SZ

Tel: 0702 471118

Chairman: Anthony Vincent, Asset House of Brackley
Chief Executive: Mrs Sylvia Vincent

St Albans Enterprise Agency
Unit 6G
St Albans Enterprise Centre
Long Spring
Porters Wood
St Albans AL3 6EN

Tel: 0727 837760

Chairman: Kenneth Jenkins
Chief Executive: Kenneth Hughesman

Stevenage Business Initiative
Business & Technology Centre
Bessemer Drive
Stevenage SG1 2DX

Tel: 0438 315733

Chairman: Steve Hollingsworth, British Aerospace Defence Ltd (Dynamics Division)
Chief Executive: Roy Pride

Surrey Business Enterprise Agency Ltd
19a High Street
Woking GU21 1BW

Tel: 0483 728434

Egham
Tel: 0784 439215

Epsom
Tel: 0372 749211

Guildford
Tel: 0483 303662

Redhill
Tel: 0737 773202

Chairman: Paul Coleman
Managing Director: Michael Instone

Swale Enterprise Agency
Broad Oak Enterprise Village
Broad Oak Road
Sittingbourne
Kent ME9 8AQ

Tel: 0795 427623

Chairman: George Holdstock, McCabe Ford & Williams
Chief Executive: Mrs Jenny Aldridge

Thame Business Advice Centre
Seacourt Tower
West Way
Oxford OX2 0JP

Tel: 0865 249279

Chairman: Julian Blackwell, The Blackwell Group
Chief Executive: Kim Hills Spedding

The Enterprise Agency of East Kent
45 North Lane
Canterbury CT2 7EF

Tel: 0227 470234

Margate
Tel: 0843 290205

Deal
Tel: 0304 367673

Chairman: Alexander de Gelsey, Sericol International Ltd
Chief Executive: Wynford Jones

Thurrock Local Enterprise Agency
1 New Road
Grays
Essex RM17 6NY

Tel: 0375 374362

Chairman: Robin Atkinson, Esso (UK) Ltd
Chief Executive: John Harrington

Watford Enterprise Agency
Unit 010
Wenta Business Centre
Colne Way
Watford WD2 4ND

Tel: 0923 247373

Chief Executive: Ken Hards

Welwyn & Hatfield Enterprise Agency Ltd
The Enterprise Centre
Cranborne Road
Potters Bar
Herts EN6 3DQ

Tel: 0707 664169

Chairman: William Couzens, Couzens Chartered Accountants
Director: Kenneth Sumeray

West Sussex Area Enterprise Centre Ltd
69a Chapel Road
Worthing
West Sussex BN11 1HR

Tel: 0903 231499

Chairman: Michael Thrower, Northbrook College
Chief Executive: Mrs Brenda McCurdie

South West

Bath Enterprise Ltd
Green Park Station
Green Park Road
Bath BA1 1JB

Tel: 0225 338383

Chairman: David Evans
Chief Executive: Roger Williams

Bristol & Avon Enterprise Agency
The Coach House
2 Upper York Street
Bristol BS2 8QN

Tel: 0272 272222

Chairman: Edward Price
Chief Executive: Keith Oxtoby

Bristol Black Business Association
9 Lower Ashley Road
St Agnes
Bristol BS2 9QA

Tel: 0272 550916/550935

Chairman: Martin Stewart
Chief Executive: Dennis de'Cordova

Business Enterprise Exeter
39 Marsh Green Road
Marsh Barton
Exeter
Devon EX2 8PN

Tel: 0392 56060

Chairman: Dick Downer
Chief Executive: Mike Lillywhite

Community Service Volunteers
Avon Enterprise Centre
56 Baldwin Street
Bristol
Avon BS1 1QN

Tel: 0272 225555

General Manager: John Eynon-Williams

Dorset Enterprise Agency
1 Britannia Road
Parkstone
Poole
Dorset BH14 8AZ

Tel: 0202 748333

Chairman: Rex Symons CBE, Dorset TEC
Chief Executive: Peter Johnson

East Bristol Enterprise Agency
42 Chelsea Road
Easton
Bristol BS5 6AF

Tel: 0272 554812

Chairman: Danny Savage
Director: Viv Rayner

East Devon Small Industries Group
115 Border Road
Heathpark
Honiton
Devon EX14 8BT

Tel: 0404 41806

Chairman: Allen Cooper
Chief Executive: Geoffrey Hulley

Enterprise Plymouth Ltd
City Business Park
Stoke
Plymouth PL3 4BB

Tel: 0752 569211

Chairman: Richard Pengelly, Bromhead & Co
Chief Executive: Andrew Ashley

Enterprise Tamar Ltd
National School
St Thomas Road
Launceston
Cornwall PL15 8BU

Tel: 0566 775632

Liskeard
Tel: 0579 344433

Tavistock
Tel: 0566 775632

Chairman: Michael Stone, David S Smith Packaging Ltd
Chief Executive: David Stanbury

Fame Serving Business
Vallis House
Robins Lane
Frome
Somerset BA11 3EG

Tel: 0373 452000

Chairman: Chris Harrison
Chief Executive: Martin Knights

Gloucestershire Enterprise Agency
Enterprise House
19-21 Brunswick Road
Gloucester GL1 1HG

Tel: 0452 501411

Chairman: David Seed, Gloucestershire County Council
Chief Executive: Mike Blackie

Return Ticket

Great Western Enterprise Ltd
Great Western Business
 Centre
Emlyn Square
Swindon
Wiltshire SN1 5BP

Tel: 0793 488088

> Rodbourne
> Tel: 0793 514055

> Cheney Manor
> Tel: 0793 512612

> Marlborough
> Business Advice Centre
> Tel: 0672 515715

*Chairman: Rama Nand-lal,
 Cranfield Institute of
 Technology (RMCS)
Managing Director: Norman
 Hayes*

North Wiltshire Enterprise
3-4 New Road
Chippenham
Wilts SN15 1EJ

Tel: 0249 659275

*Chairman, Consultative Board:
 William Wyldbore-Smith
Local Director: Mrs Jean
 Archer*

Hartcliffe & Withywood
 Ventures Ltd
HWV Block
Bishport Avenue
Hartcliffe
Bristol BS13 0RL

Tel: 0272 784865

*Chairman: Graham Parker
Chief Executive: Pat Mundy*

Hebron House Enterprise
Hebron House
Sion Road
Bedminster
Bristol BS9 3BD

Tel: 0272 637634

*Chairman: David Brockington,
 University of the West of
 England
Chief Executive: Susan
 Lowman*

Mid Devon Enterprise
 Agency
The Factory
Tiverton EX16 5LL

Tel: 0884 255629

*Chairman: Reg Waddington
Chief Executive: Michael Dunk*

Restormel Local Enterprise
 Trust Ltd
Westhaul Park
Par Moor Road
St Austell PL25 4RF

Tel: 0726 813079

> Newquay
> Tel: 0726 813079

*Chairman: Mr Barry Grime
Chief Executive: David
 Waddington*

Sedgemoor Enterprise
 Agency Ltd
Cellophane House
Wylds Road
Bridgwater TA6 4BH

Tel: 0278 452978

*Chairman: Arthur Moss,
 Decon Engineering
Chief Executive: Ian Billinge*

South Hams Agency for
 Rural Development
Tindle Centre
Kings Arms Passage
Fore Street
Devon TQ7 1AB

Tel: 0548 856850

> Dartington
> Tel: 0803 862271

*Chairman: Alan Strowger,
 Beers, Solicitors
Chief Executive: Mrs Suzanne
 Massingham*

South Somerset & West
 Dorset Enterprise Agency
Unit 4
Yeovil Business Centre
Hounstone Business Park
Yeovil BA22 8WA

Tel: 0935 79813

*Chairman: Sir Anthony Jay,
 Video Arts
Chief Executive: Richard Tracey*

South Wiltshire Enterprise
 Agency
22 Bedwin Street
Salisbury SP6 3UT

Tel: 0722 411052

*Chairman: William Jarratt,
 MidCountry Ltd
Chief Executive: Richard James*

Taunton District Enterprise
 Centre
23 High Street
Taunton TA1 3PJ

Tel: 0823 336600

*Chairman: Ralph Platt, Relyon
 Ltd
Chief Executive: Chris Clarke*

LOCAL ENTERPRISE AGENCIES

Teignbridge Enterprise Agency
The Tindle Centre
St Marychurch Road
Newton Abbot TQ12 4UQ

Tel: 0626 67534

Chairman: James Putz
Chief Executive: Leslie Saye

The North Devon Enterprise Agency Ltd
Yelland Centre
West Yelland
Barnstaple
North Devon EX31 3EZ

Tel: 0271 861215

Chairman: John Urquhart MBE
Chief Executive: Tony Jennings

Torbay Enterprise Agency
Brunel Business Centre
Torquay Road
Paignton TQ3 2AH

Tel: 0803 666662

Chairman: M Dobson, GMS Consultancy Ltd
Chief Executive: M Wortley

West Cornwall Enterprise Trust
Lloyds Bank Chambers
Market Square
Camborne
Cornwall TR14 8JT

Tel: 0209 714914

  Penzance
  Tel: 0736 330336

  Falmouth
  Tel: 0326 375536

Chairman: C E Brown, BT plc
Chief Executive: R N Smith

West Somerset Enterprise Agency
Vennland Centre
Ponsford Road
Minehead TA24 5DX

Tel: 0643 707500

Chairman: Dennis Taylor, West Somerset Railway
Enterprise Centre Manager: Gill Howard

West Wiltshire Enterprise Business Development Centre
College Road
Trowbridge BA14 0ER

Tel: 0225 774222

Chairman: John Hardwick
Chief Executive: Norman Pierce

Weston & Woodspring Enterprise Agency
Elizabeth House
30-32 Boulevard
Weston-Super-Mare
Avon BS23 1NF

Tel: 0934 418118

Chairman: Robert Wayne, BWOC Ltd
Chief Executive: Ms Angela Hicks

London

Brent Business Venture Ltd
77a Cricklewood Broadway
London NW2 3HT

Tel: 081 450 6270

  Harlesden
  Tel: 081 838 2117

Chairman: Brian Beanland, Guinness Brewing (GB)
Chief Executive: Ms Clair Ferguson

Bromley Enterprise Agency Trust Ltd
7 Palace Grove
Bromley
Kent BR1 3HA

Tel: 081 290 6568

Chairman: Gordon Young
Director: Colin Parham

Camden Enterprise Agency
57 Pratt Street
Camden Town
London NW1 0DP

Tel: 071 482 2128

Chairman: Colin Smith, National Freight Consortium plc
Chief Executive: Mrs Jane Howden

Croydon Business Venture
Acorn House
74-94 Cherry Orchard Road
Croydon
Surrey CR0 6BA

Tel: 081 681 8339

Chairman: Geoffrey Dove, The Dove Group plc
Chief Execuive: Sydney Laurence

Deptford Enterprise Agency
146 Deptford High Street
London SE8 3PQ

Tel: 081 692 9204

Chairman: Kidebi Wanume, Kidebi & Co Solicitors
Chief Executive: Joe Greenland

Docklands Enterprise Centre
11 Marshalsea Road
London SE1 1EP

Tel: 071 357 7581

Chairman: Neil Spence, London Docklands Development Corporation
Centre Manager: Raymond Hook, Midland Bank plc

East London Small Business Centre Ltd
76 Wentworth Street
London E1 7SE

Tel: 071 377 8821

Chairman: Stephen Brooks, Morgan Grenfell Co Ltd
Chief Executive: Mike King

Enfield Enterprise Agency
2-3 Knights Chambers
32 South Mall
Edmonton Green
London N9 0TL

Tel: 081 807 5333

  Cheshunt
  Tel: 081 345 5371

  Hertford
  Tel: 0992 503456

  Wood Green
  Tel: 081 365 8388

Chairman: Ian Ferguson
Chief Executive: John Lindsay

Enterprise Ealing Ltd
Windmill Business Centre
2-4 Windmill Lane
Southall UB2 4NJ

Tel: 081 843 1188

Chairman: Denzil Lewis, Allied Lyons

Executive Director: Jenny Evans, National Westminster Bank plc

Hackney Business Venture
277 Mare Street
Hackney
London E8 1HB

Tel: 081 533 4599

Chairman: David Willetts, Reeve Hepburn
Chief Executive: Sally Johnson

Hammersmith & Fulham Business Resources Ltd
The Lilla Huset
191 Talgarth Road
London W6 8B

Tel: 081 748 3352

Chairman: Alan Thompson
Managing Director: Barbara Hamilton

Harrow Enterprise Agency
Enterprise House
297 Pinner Road
Harrow HA1 4HS

Tel: 081 427 6188

Chairman: Dr I Farrell, Harrow School
Chief Executive: David Hill

Hillingdon Enterprise Agency
400a Long Lane
Hillingdon
Middx UB10 9PG

Tel: 0895 273433

Chairman: Anthony Sansom, Kingston Smith
Chief Executive: Alan Lane

London Enterprise Agency
4 Snow Hill
London EC1A 2BS

Tel: 071 236 3000

Chairman: Robin Heal, BP
Chief Executive: Brian Wright

Manor Gardens Enterprise Centre Ltd
10-18 Manor Gardens
Islington
London N7 6JY

071 272 8944

Chairman: Philip Prain, Kleinwort Benson
Chief Executive: Patrick Quarry

Merton Enterprise Agency
12th Floor, Civic Centre
London Road
Morden
Surrey SM4 5DX

Tel: 081 545 3067

Chairman: Howard Hills
Chief Executive: Harry Corben

North East Thames Business Advisory Centre
Marshalls Chambers
80a South Street
Romford
Essex RM1 1RP

Tel: 0708 766438

  Barking
  Tel: 0708 766438

  Ilford
  Tel: 081 553 4029

Chairman: Geoffrey Price
Chief Executive: Ulrik Middelboe

North London Business
   Development Agency
35-37 Blackstock Road
Finsbury Park
London N4 2LF

Tel: 071 359 7405

*Chairman: Anthony Wade
   MBE, Dyke & Dryden Ltd
Chief Executive: Emmanuel
   Cotter MBE*

Portobello Trust
14 Conlan Street
London W10 5AR

Tel: 081 969 4562

*Chairman: Father Michael
   Hollings
Chief Executive: Neil Johnston*

Richmond Upon Thames
   Enterprise Agency
55 Heath Road
Twickenham
Middx TW1 4AW

Tel: 081 891 3742

Chairman: Paul Turrell

South London Business
   Initiative
Brixton Small Business Centre
444 Brixton Road
London SW9 8EJ

Tel: 071 274 4000 (ext 384)

   8 Nursey Road
   Tel: 071 738 7707

   Peckham
   Tel: 071 252 8280

*Chairman: Sir Patrick Sheehy,
   BAT Industries plc
Chief Executive: Dr Walter
   Baker MBE*

Sutton Enterprise Agency
11 Lower Road
Sutton
Surrey SM1 4QJ

Tel: 081 643 9430

*Chairman: Robert Bennett
Chief Executive: John Wren*

The Barnet Enterprise Trust
Victory House
62-64 East Barnet Road
New Barnet
Herts EN4 8RQ

Tel: 081 447 0110

*Chairman: Ian Ferguson
Chief Executive: Peter Lovell*

Wandsworth Enterprise
   Agency
4th Floor, Woburn House
155-159 Falcon Road
London SW11 2PD

Tel: 071 924 2811

*Chairman: Jeff Crawford
Chief Executive: Alex Amponsah*

West London Enterprise
   Agency Ltd
94 High Street
Hounslow TW3 1NH

Tel: 081 570 3269

*Chairman: Norman Davis,
   RMC plc
Chief Executive: Alan Bossom*

Westminster Enterprise Agency
69-71 Praed Street
Paddington W2 1NS

Tel: 071 706 4266

*Chairman: Kenneth Rushton,
   ICI plc
Director: John Skinner*

Wales

Antur Dwyryd
Osmond Terrace
Penrhyndeudraeth
Gwynedd LL48 6PA

Tel: 0766 771345

*Chairman: James Morris
Chief Executive: Dafydd Wyn
   Jones*

Antur Menai
Llys y Bont
Parc Menai
Bangor
Gwynedd LL57 4BN

Tel: 0248 670627

*Chairman: Richard
   Cuthbertson, DMM
   International Ltd
Chief Executive: Peter McOwan*

Antur Teifi
Parc Busnes
Aberarard
Castle Newydd Emlyn
Dyfed SA38 9DB

Tel: 0239 710238

   Sgwar Emlyn
   Tel: 0239 711114

   Aberteifi
   Tel: 0239 621828

   Caerfryddin
   Tel: 267 236576

   Llandeddr-Pont-Steffan
   Tel: 0570 423619

*Chairman: Gareth Evans,
   Carmarthenshire College of
   Technology & Art
Chief Executive: Wynfford
   James*

Bersham Enterprise
Bersham Enterprise Centre
Plas Grono Road
Rhostyllen
Wrexham LL14 4ED

Tel: 0978 352614

*Chairman: David Messham,
    Clwyd County Council*
*Chief Executive: Mrs Morag
    Murphy*

Cardiff & Vale Enterprise
127 Bute Street
Cardiff CF1 5LE

Tel: 0222 494411

   Sully
   Tel: 0446 739799

Chairman: Brian Margrett
Chief Executive: Peter Fortune

Clwydfro Enterprise Agency
Llysfasi
Ruthin
Clwyd LL15 2LB

Tel: 0978 790414

   Chirk
   Tel: 0691 773291

*Chairman: Councillor Glyn
    Hughes, Clwyd County
    Council*
*Managing Executive: Arwyn
    Jones, Clwyd County Council*

Deeside Enterprise Trust Ltd
Deeside Enterprise Centre
Rowleys Drive
Shotton
Deeside CH5 1PP

Tel: 0244 830003

Chairman: Harvey Davies
Chief Executive: Norman Sturt

Delyn Business Partnership
Greenfield Business Centre
Greenfield
Holywell
Clwyd CH8 7QB

Tel: 0352 711747

*Chairman: Richard Evans,
    Midland Bank plc*
Chief Executive: Brian Scoffield

Dinefwr Enterprise
    Company
Betws Park Workshops
Park Street
Ammanford
Dyfed SA18 2ET

Tel: 0269 596655

   Llandeilo
   Tel: 0558 823863

*Chairman: Huw Jones, T
    Richard Jones (Betws) Ltd*
Chief Executive: Bill Bishop

Enterprise Taff Ely Ogwr
    Partnership Ltd
Enterprise Centre
Brynn Road
Tondu
Bridgend CF32 9BS

Tel: 0656 724414

   Pontypridd
   Tel: 0443 485724

   Maesteg
   Tel: 0656 737752

Chairman: Derek Morgan
Chief Executive: Gareth Bray

Innovation Wales (SEWBIC)
    Ltd
Cardiff Business Technology
    Centre
Senghennydd Road
Cardiff CF2 4AY

Tel: 0222 667041

Chairman: Eurof Evans
*Chief Executive: Douglas
    Hampson*

Llanelli Enterprise Company
100 Trostre Road
Llanelli
Dyfed SA15 2EA

Tel: 0554 772122

Chairman: Tom Norreys OBE
Chief Executive: Tony Giles

MADE and EDP Ltd
Gadlys Enterprise Centre
Gadlys
Aberdare
Mid Glamorgan CF44 8DL

Tel: 0685 882515

*Chairman: Brian Langley,
    Lloyds Bank plc*
Chief Executive: J Alan Jones

Neath Development
    Partnership
7 Water Street
Neath
West Glamorgan SA11 3EP

Tel: 0639 634111

*Chairman: John Wildman
    MBE, Hogget Bowers*
*Chief Executive: Eamonn
    Kinsella*

Newport and Gwent
  Enterprise
Enterprise Way
Off Bolt Street
Newport
Gwent NP9 2AQ

Tel: 0633 254041

*Chairman: Don Corbett,
  National Power plc*
Chief Executive: Alan Prosper

Pembrokeshire Business
  Initiative
PBI Haverfordwest Business
  Centre
Lombard Chambers
14 High Street
Haverfordwest SA61 2LD

Tel: 0437 767655

  Fishguard
  Tel: 0348 872888

  Milford Haven
  Tel: 0646 695300

  Pembroke Dock
  Tel: 0646 621394

*Chairman: John Phillips, P &
  O/Tankships*
*Chief Executive: Richard
  Packman*

Rhondda Development
  Agency
RDA Enterprise Centre
Caemawr Industrial Estate
Treorchy
Rhondda CF42 6EJ

Tel: 0443 440720

*Chairman: David Yendoll,
  Allied Steel & Wire*
Chief Executive: John Hitchen

West Glamorgan Enterprise
  Trust
Pontardulais Workshops
Tyn-y-Bonau Road
Pontardulais
Swansea SA4 1RS

Tel: 0792 885197

  Ysguborfach Street
  Tel: 0792 475345

  Abernant
  Tel: 0269 823840

  Glyncorrwg
  Tel: 0639 85122

*Chairman: Jeffrey Payne,
  Payne & Co*
Manager: Tony Morgan

Northern Ireland

Action Recourse Centre
103-107 York Street
Belfast BT15 1AB

Tel: 0232 328000

Chairman: William McKay

Ards Small Business Centre
Jubilee Road
Newtownards
Co Down B23 4YH

Tel: 0247 819787

*Chairman: Ray Donnan,
  Donnan & Co*
Chief Executive: Trevor Topping

Ballymena Business
  Development Centre
Galgorm Industrial Estate
Fenaghy Road
Ballymena
Co Antrim

Tel: 0266 658618

*Chairman: William Wright, R
  Wright & Son (Coachworks)
  Ltd*
Chief Executive: Ian Niblock

Business Incubation Systems
  Ltd
Brookfield Business Centre
333 Crumlin Road
Belfast BT14 7EA

Tel: 0232 745241

*Chairman: Father Myles
  Kavanagh, Flax Trust*
Chief Executive: Shane Wolsey

Craigavon Industrial
  Development Organisation
Craigavon Enterprise Centre
Carn Industrial Area
Portadown
Craigavon
Co Armagh BT63 5RH

Tel: 0762 333393

Chairman: Jim McCammick
Chief Executive: Jim Smith

Dungannon Enterprise Centre
2 Coalisland Road
Dungannon
Co Tyrone BT71 6JT

Tel: 0868 723489

Chairperson: Frank Higgins
*Chief Executive: Brian
  MacAuley*

Eurocentre West Ltd
Pennyburn Industrial Estate
Bruncrana Road
Derry City BT48 0LU

Tel: 0504 364015

Chairman: Brendan Duddy
Chief Executive: Denis Feeney

Fermanagh Enterprise Ltd
Enniskillen Enterprise Centre
Down Street
Enniskillen
Co Fermanagh

Tel: 0365 323117/327348

Chairman: John O'Kane
Centre Manager: John Treacy

Glenshane Community
  Development Ltd
Glenshame Enterprise
  Centre
414a Ballyquin Road
Dungiven BT47 4NQ

Tel: 05047 42494

  Limavady
  Tel: 05047 62323

Chairman: John McNicholl

Glenwood Enterprises Ltd
Springbank Industrial Estate
Pembroke Loop Road
Dunmurry
Belfast BT17 0QL

Tel: 0232 610311

Chairman: Gerry Keenan
Chief Executive: J J Grugan

Jobspace (NI) Ltd
45 Saul Road
Downpatrick
Co Down BT30 6PA

Tel: 0396 616416

  Ballynahinch
  Tel: 0238 563338

  Downpatrick
  Tel: 0396 616392

Chairman: Edward McGrady
*Chief Executive: Joe
  McCoubrey*

Lisburn Enterprise
  Organisation Ltd
Enterprise Crescent
Ballinderry Road
Lisburn
Co Antrim BT28 2SA

Tel: 0846 661160

Chairman: Mr W G Smyth
*Chief Executive: Ms Miamh
  Goggin*

Omagh Enterprise Co Ltd
Omagh Business Complex
Fortrush Industrial Estate
Derry Road
Omagh
Co Tyrone BT78 5LS

Tel: 0662 249494

Chairman: Brian McGrath

Newry & Mourne Enterprise
  Agency
Enterprise House
Win Business Park
Canal Quay
Newry BT35 6PH

Tel: 0693 67011

*Chairman: Eamonn
  Fitzpatrick, FM Systems Ltd*
*Chief Executive: Ms Margaret
  Andrews*

North Antrim Development
2 Riada Avenue
Garryduff Road
Ballymoney
Co Antrim BT53 7LH

Tel: 02656 66133

  Garryduff Road
  Tel: 02656 66133

  Ballycastle
  Tel: 02656 63737

Chairman: William Crymble
Manager: Francis Henderson

North Down Development
  Organisation Ltd
Enterprise House
2-4 Balloo Avenue
Balloo Industrial Estate
Bangor BT19 7QT

Tel: 0247 271525

Chairman: Alan Logan
*Chief Executive: Mrs Lynne
  Vance*

Townsend Enterprise Park Ltd
Townsend Street
Belfast BT13 2ES

Tel: 0232 894500

*Chairman: Frank Murphy
  ADVEC*
*Chief Executive: Ms Colleen
  Miller*

Westlink Enterprise Centre
30-50 Distillery Street
Belfast BT12 5BJ

Tel: 0232 331549

Chairman: Michael Hurrell
*Chief Executive: Kevin
  McGlennon*

Workspace (Draperstown) Ltd
5 7 Tobermore Road
Draperstown
Derry BT45 7AG

Tel: 0648 28113

  Magherafelt
  Tel: 0648 31032

*Chairman: John Donnelly,
  MDF Engineering/Panther*
*Chief Executive: Patsy
  McShane*

Scotland

Aberdeen Enterprise Trust
6 Albyn Grove
Aberdeen AB1 6SQ

Tel: 0224 582599

Chairman: Kenneth Murray
Chief Executive: Ian Grant (Shell UK Exploration & Production)

Alloa Clackmannan Enterprise
Alloa Business Centre
Alloa, FL10 3SA

Tel: 0259 721454

Chairman: James Bowden
Chief Executive: Alan Stewart

Asset Trust Ltd
The APL Centre
Stevenston Industrial Estate
Stevenston
Ayrshire KA20 3LR

Tel: 0294 61555

   Vista Training
   Tel: 0294 68000

Chairman: Richard Colwell
Chief Executive: Cairns Campbell

Ayr Locality Enterprise Resource Trust (ALERT)
Ayr Business Centre
16 Smith Street
Ayr KA7 1TD

Tel: 0292 264181

   Girvan
   Tel: 0465 5038

Chairman: William Barr, Barr Ltd
Chief Executive: Bill Dunn

Campbeltown & Kintyre Enterprise Trust Ltd
Hazelburn Business Park
Millknowe
Campbeltown
Argyll PA29 6XD

Tel: 0586 552246

Chairman: Peter McKinlay, Scottish Homes

Clydebank Economic Development Co Ltd
Phoenix House
7 South Avenue
Clydebank Business Park
Clydebank G81 2LG

Tel: 041 951 1131

Chairman: James Roxburgh, J C Roxborough & Co
Chief Executive: Alastair Muir

Clydesdale Development Company
Clydesdale Business Centre
129 Hyndford Road
Lanark ML11 9AU

Tel: 0555 665064

Chairman: Arthur Bell, Scotland Direct
Chief Executive: Christopher Travis

Cumbernauld and Kilsyth Enterprise Trust
10-14 Market Street
Kilsyth G65 0BD

Tel: 0236 825500

Chairman: David Millan, Cumbernauld Development Corporation
Chief Executive: Alicia Bruce

Cumnock & Doon Enterprise Trust
Enterprise Centre
Caponacre Industrial Estate
Cumnock
Ayrshire KA18 1SH

Tel: 0290 421159

Chairman: Alex MacDonald
Chief Executive: Colin Williamson

Dumbarton District Enterprise Trust
2/2 Vale of Leven Industrial Estate
Dumbarton G82 3PD

Tel: 0389 50005

   Helensburgh
   Tel: 0436 79090

Chairman: Colin Sherwood, British Petroleum
Chief Executive: Charles Shanlin

Dundee Enterprise Trust
Dudhope Castle
Barrack Road
Dundee DD3 6HF

Tel: 0382 26002

Chairman: Alex Murdoch, C J Lang
Managing Director: David Morrison

East End Executive (Glasgow) Ltd
Unit C8, Building 5
Templeton Business Centre
62 Templeton Street
Glasgow G40 1DA

Tel: 041 554 8656

Clydeford Drive
Tel: 041 554 2319

Chairman: James Cope, Frys Metals Ltd
Chief Executive: John Kilpatrick

East Kilbride Business Centre
PO Box 1
4 Platthorn Road
East Kilbride G74 1NW

Tel: 03552 38456

Chairman: Ray Kirk
Chief Executive: Mrs Linda McDowall

Edinburgh Old Town Renewal Trust
8 Advocates Close
357 High Street
Edinburgh EH1 1PS

Tel: 031 225 8818

Chairman: Graham Ross
Chief Executive: Jim Johnson

Enterprise Levenmouth Ltd
Levenmouth Business Centre
Riverside Road
Leven
Fife KY8 4LT

Tel: 0333 421112

Chairman: Robert Gough, Fife Regional Council
Chief Executive: McLaren Young

Falkirk Enterprise Action Trust
Newhouse Business Park
Newhouse Road
Grangemouth FK3 8LL

Tel: 0324 665500

Chairman: R W Gow, Zeneca/ICI
Chief Executive: John Hoggan

Garnock Valley Development Executive Ltd
4 Main Street
Kilbirnie
Ayrshire KA25 7BY

Tel: 0505 685455

Chairman: James Jenning, Strathclyde Regional Council
Chief Executive: Johan Madsen

Glasgow North Ltd
St Rollox House
130 Springburn Road
Glasgow G21 1YA

Tel: 041 552 5413

Chairman: Francis McAveety, City of Glasgow District Council
Chief Executive: Francis Lyons

Glasgow Opportunities
7 West George Street
Glasgow G2 1EQ

Tel: 041 221 0955

Chairman: Peter Paisley, TSB Bank Scotland plc
Chief Executive: Agnes Samuel

Glenrothes Enterprise Trust
Unit 6, Pentland Court
Saltire Centre
Glenrothes
Fife KY6 2DA

Tel: 0592 630595/630599

Chairman: Colin Bowron
Chief Executive: Arthur Stutt

Gordon Enterprise Trust
Business Development Centre
Thainstone Agricultural Centre
Thainstone
Inverurie
Aberdeenshire AB51 9WU

Tel: 0467 621166

Alford
Tel: 0975 562906

Ellon
Tel: 0358 24405

Huntly
Tel: 0466 792101

Westhill
Tel: 0224 740718

Chairman: William Bruce, Bruce & Partners
Chief Executive: Jackie Hall

Hamilton Enterprise Development Company
Barncluith Business Centre
Townhead Street
Hamilton ML3 7DP

Tel: 0698 429425

Chairman: David Evans, Marks & Spencer
Chief Executive: Ronald Smith

Highland Opportunity Ltd
Development Department
Regional Buildings
Glenurquhart Road
Inverness IV3 5NX

Tel: 0463 702000

Chairman: James Munro, Highland Regional Council
Chief Executive: Hugh Black, Highland Regional Council

Highland Perthshire
  Development Company Ltd
21 Bonnethill Road
Pitlochry
Perthshire PH16 5BS

Tel: 0796 472697

Chairman: John Cameron
Executive Director: Gil Orr

Inverclyde Enterprise Trust
64-66 West Blackhall Street
Greenock PA15 1XG

Tel: 0475 892191

Chairman: Dr Dominic McKay,
  Kinloch Electronics Ltd
Chief Executive: James Barr

Kilmarnock Venture
  Enterprise Trust
Royal Bank Buildings
1 The Cross
Kilmarnock KA1 1LS

Tel: 0563 44602

Chairman: David Drummond
Chief Executive: Gordon
  Rutherford

Kincardine and Deeside
  Enterprise Trust Ltd
Unit 1
Aboyne Business Centre
Huntly Road
Aboyne
Aberdeenshire AB34 5HE

Tel: 03398 87222

Chairman: Hugh Smith, Albyn
  of Stonehaven
Chief Executive: Bill Marshall

Midlothian Enterprise Trust
29a Eskbank Road
Dalkeith
Midlothian EH22 1HJ

Tel: 031 654 1234

Chairman: Ms Isabel Anderson,
  Drummond Miller WS
Chief Executive: Gregor Murray

Monklands Enterprise
  Development Company
Units 10 & 32
Coatbridge Business Centre
204 Main Street
Coatbridge
Lanarkshire

Tel: 0236 423281

Chairman: Richard Carter,
  Boots Co plc
Chief Executive: Ian Russell

Moray Enterprise Trust
Units 14-17
Elgin Business Centre
Maisondieu Road
Elgin
Moray IV30 1RH

Tel: 0343 548391

Chairman: Alex Scott, A R
  Scott Chartered Surveyors
Chief Executive: Ron Taylor

Motherwell Enterprise
  Development Company
364 Brandon Street
Motherwell ML1 1XA

Tel: 0698 269333

  Wishaw
  Tel: 0698 359499

Chairman: Harry Porter OBE,
  Motherwell Bridge
Chief Executive: James Hope

North Argyll Development
  Agency
4 George Street
Oban
Argyll PA34 5RX

Tel: 0631 66368

Chairman: Malcolm Mitchie,
  Malcolm Mitchie & Partners

North East Fife Enterprise
  Trust
3 Riverside Court
Cupar
Fife KY15 5JY

Tel: 0334 56360

  Anstruther
  Tel: 0333 312203

Chairman: Robin Rippin
Chief Executive: Richard
  Henning

Paisley & Renfrew
  Enterprise Trust
27a Blackhall Street
Paisley PA1 1TD

Tel: 041 889 0010

  Giffnock
  c/o Eastwood District
    Council
  Tel: 041 638 6511

Chairman: Thomas Graham,
  Ciba Geigy Ltd
Chief Executive: David Logan

Perthshire Enterprise
  Company
1 High Street
Perth PH1 2SY

Tel: 0738 29114

  Auchterarder
  Tel: 0764 62106

Blairgowrie
Tel: 0250 87 4271

Crieff
Tel: 0764 652578

Kinross
Tel: 0577 62189

Chairman: Alan Begg, General Accident plc
Chief Executive: Robert Main

South Fife Enterprise Trust
6 Main Street
Crossgates
Fife KY4 8AJ

Tel: 0383 515053

Chief Executive: David Blues

Stirling Enterprise Trust
John Player Building
Players Road
Stirling FK7 7RP

Tel: 0786 463416

Chairman: Patrick Burt, Central Regional Council
Chief Executive: Derek Gavin

Strathkelvin Enterprise Trust
Southbank House
Southbank Business Park
Kirkintilloch G66 1XQ

Tel: 041 777 7171

Chryston
Tel: 041 779 4047

Chairman: A Craig Fyfe
Chief Executive: Andrew Thomson

The Barras Enterprise Trust
Unit 1, The Barras Centre
54 Carlton Entry
Glasgow G40 2SB

Tel: 041 552 7258

Chairman: Christopher Dunn, Joseph Dunn (Bottlers) Ltd
Chief Executive: James McMorrow, East End Executive

The Capital Enterprise Trust
Allander House
141 Leith Walk
Edinburgh EH6 8NQ

Tel: 031 553 5566

Chairman: Peter O'Malley, Christian Salvesen plc
Chief Executive: Trevor Slater

The Cowal Enterprise Trust
24 Argyll Street
Dunoon PA23 7HJ

Tel: 0369 2023

Chairman: Charles Black
Chief Executive: Ian McRae

West Lothian Enterprise Ltd
19 North Bridge Street
Bathgate
West Lothian EH48 4PJ

Tel: 0506 634024

Chairman: William V R Percy

Wigtown Rural Development Company
Royal Bank Building
44 Victoria Street
Newton Stewart
Wigtownshire DG8 6BT

Tel: 0671 3434

Chairman: Brain Pattinson, Pasolds Sunchild

Young Enterprise

Young Enterprise (YE) is a unique nationwide Business/Education Partnership founded in 1963. It is a registered charity and company limited by guarantee, funded through voluntary contributions from industry and fees charged to YE companies. Some project funding has been received from Government and at local level there is growing support from TECs.

The YE mission is: 'To provide young people aged 15–19 (regardless of ability or background) with an exciting and imaginative practical business experience, enabling them to develop their personal skills, knowledge and understanding of business objectives and the wealth creation process'.

YE is organised through a UK network of over 180 local Boards of volunteers from Industry and Education.

The YE Company Programme and Team Enterprise Programme (for students with learning difficulties and disabilities) links volunteer Business Advisers to a group of students who run a real company for one academic year. A nominated link teacher/lecturer facilitates the programme. An introductory guide and comprehensive business kit contains advice and documentation covering all company functions.

The young people normally meet for approximately two hours per week decide on a company name and product or service; they elect a board, raise capital by selling shares and set out to make and market their product. They encounter real problems, solutions, failures, successes.

At the end of the business year they wind up their company and distribute their profit, often to charity. At a 'shareholders meeting' they make an oral presentation and submit their written report.

Hundreds of special events are organised such as trade fairs, European links (YE is a founder member of YE Europe), management skills seminars, presentation events and an annual competition.

An annual voluntary examination increasingly recognised by employers and administrators is conducted and awarded by the University of Oxford Delegacy of Local Examinations, based on the practical experience gained.

For further information please contact:

Bob Rolls
Young Enterprise
Ewert Place
Summertown
Oxford OX2 7BZ.

Tel: 0865 311180

Business Link

The Business Link concept was announced by the President of the Board of Trade, the Rt Hon Michael Heseltine MP, at the TEC Conference in Birmingham in July 1992. To assist companies to compete in world markets, the President proposed a major new project to establish a national network of 'one stop shops for business', subsequently named Business Links.

Each Business Link exists to provide a full range of business support services to the local business community. The key elements of Business Links are: partnership (bringing together all key business support agencies), services (offering services targeted to meet local business needs), quality (world class service), focus (available to all businesses but particularly those with growth potential), Business Advisers (key staff who will develop long term relationships with companies) and DTI services (a range of DTI, and other Government services which are accessible through each Business Link).

Business Link services will soon include diagnostic checks, consultancy, exports, innovation, design and technology. In future, private sector export consultants will be placed in all the main Business Links and a new network, 'Nearnet' will be created by Innovation and Technology Counsellors within Business Links. This network will consolidate information about local research and technology organisations, patent agents, local higher and further educational institutions, TECs and providers of technical databases. Supporting this local network, 'Supernet' will encourage greater use of national centres of expertise and the existing science and technology base accessed directly, or through Business Links. Also to aid innovation, £1,000 worth of credits will be available from Innovation and Technology Counsellors to help pay for patent searches and the use of specialised equipment or analytical services.

In addition, a new network of Regional Supply Offices will work with Business Links to improve the quality of the local supply base. It will be staffed by people with industrial experience to help companies exploit new sourcing opportunities.

Currently, 22 Business Links have been opened and the aim is for 50 Business Links to be in operation by the end of 1994. Within two years every company in the country will have access to a Business Link.

For further information please contact:

Parminder Summon
Department of Trade & Industry
Small Firms & Business Links Division
Level 2
St Mary's House
c/o Moorfoot
Sheffield S1 4PQ

Tel: 0742 597508

Business Link Barnsley
1 Burleigh Court
Burleigh Street
Barnsley S70 1XY

Tel: 0226 771000

Chief Executive: Rod Machin

Business Link Birmingham
75 Harborne Road
Edgbaston
Birmingham B15 3DH

Tel: 021 6070 8099

Executive Director: Alun Dow

Business Link Congleton
Riverside Mill
Mountbatten Way
Congleton
Cheshire CW12 1DY

Tel: 0260 294500

Chief Executive: Kevin Mellor

Business Link Crewe and Nantwich
Electra House
Electra Way
Crewe Business Park
Crewe
Cheshire CW1 1YX

Tel: 0270 504700

Managing Director: Peter Riley

Business Link Doncaster
White Rose Way
Hyde Park
Doncaster DN4 5ND

Tel: 0302 761000

Chief Executive: Brian Crangle

Business Link Gateshead
Unit 14-15
Interchange Centre
Gateshead
Tyne and Wear NE8 1BH

Tel: 091 477 5544

General Manager: Graham Woosey

Business Link Halton (Runcorn/Widnes)
Halton Business Forum
Victoria Square
Widnes
Cheshire WA8 7QZ

Tel: 051 420 9420

Chief Executive: Chris Evans

Business Link Hereford & Worcester
Crossway House
Holmer Road
Hereford HR4 9SS

Tel: 0432 356699

Chief Executive: John Saunders

Business Link Hertfordshire
45 Grosvenor Road
St Albans
Herts AL1 3AW

Tel: 0727 813400

Chief Executive: Sue Cheshire

Business Link Hinckley
4 Druid Street
Hinckley
Leics

Tel: 0455 891848

Manager: Bernard Jones

Business Link Leicestershire (Leicester)
10 York Road
Leicester LE1 5TS

Tel: 0533 559944

Chief Executive: Tony Grice

Business Link Leominster
Corn Square
Leominster
Hereford HR6 8LR

Tel: 0568 616344

Customer Service Adviser: Mrs Lisa Hodgson

Business Link Macclesfield
Dukes Court
Mill Street
Macclesfield
Cheshire SK11 6NN

Tel: 0625 664400

Chief Executive: Frederick Buckingham-Evans

Business Link Malvern
Brunel House
Portland Road
Malvern
Worcs WR14 2TB

Tel: 0684 567070

Customer Service Adviser: Miss Sarah Secretan

Business Link Manchester
Churchgate House
56 Oxford Street
Manchester M60 7BL

Tel: 061 237 4000

Managing Director: John Browne

Return Ticket

Business Link Newcastle
Anderson House
Market Street East
Newcastle upon Tyne
NE1 6XA

Tel: 091 230 5989

General Manager: Graham Woosey

Business Link North Tyneside
Howard House
Saville Street
North Shields
Tyne and Wear NE30 1NT

Tel: 091 296 4477

General Manager: Graham Woosey

Business Link North West Leicestershire
Unit 5, The Courtyard
Whitwick Business Park
Coalville
Leics LE67 3SA

Tel: 0530 810470

Manager: Elaine Cowan

Business Link Pershore
Council Office
Civic Centre
Pershore
Worcs WR10 1PT

Tel: 0386 555577

Customer Service Adviser: Miss Charlotte Byron

Business Link Poole
4 New Fields Business Park
Stinsford Road
Nuffield Trading Estate
Poole
Dorset BH17 7NF

Tel: 0345 448844

Chief Executive: Beryl Kite

Business Link Salford
Business Link House
Unit 8a
Winders Way
Salford M6 6BU

Tel: 061 237 4000

Branch Manager: Helen Whittaker-Axon

Business Link Shropshire (Telford)
Trevethick House Unit B1
Stafford Park 4
Telford TF3 3BA

Tel: 0345 543210

Manager: Andrew Mason

Business Link South Tyneside
Eldon Street
South Shields
Tyne and Wear NE33 5JE

Tel: 091 455 4300

General Manager: Graham Woosey

Business Link Tameside
Tameside Business Development Centre
Windmill Lane
Denton
Manchester M34 3YA

Tel: 061 237 4000

Branch Manager: Lisa Hoyland

Business Link Trafford Park
Trafford Park Business Centre
Lloyd House
392 3rd Avenue Village
Trafford Park
Manchester M17 1BL

Tel: 061 237 4000

Branch Manager: Julie Williams

Business Link Tyneside
Moongate House
5th Avenue Business Park
Team Valley
Gateshead NE11 0HF

Tel: 091 491 6161

General Manager: Graham Woosey

Business Link West Cornwall
The West Cornwall Enterprise Centre
Cardrew Industrial Estate
Redruth
Cornwall TR15 1SS

Tel: 0209 314555

Chief Executive: Tony Mansell

Business Link Metropolitan Wigan
Buckingham Row
Northway
Wigan WN1 1XX

Tel: 0942 324547

Chief Executive: Adrian Hardy

Business Link Worcester
Commerce House
10 The Moors
Worcester WR1 3EE

Tel: 0905 22877

Customer Service Adviser: Mrs Stephanie Bowyer

Task Forces

The Government is commited to improving the quality of life in towns and cities through economic, social and environmental regeneration. In supporting this aim Task Forces concentrate on the economic regeneration of designated inner city areas, by improving local people's employment prospects, stimulating enterprise development, and strengthening the capacity of communities to meet their needs.

The Task Forces programme has four main objectives:

- to increase employment prospects for Task Force area residents, by identifying and removing barriers to their employment, and by creating and safeguarding jobs;
- to improve the employability of local people by raising skill levels, and supporting training programmes aimed at specific jobs or identified gaps in the labour market;
- to promote local enterprise development through support for enterprise training, financial and managerial assistance;
- to support education initiatives which improve attainment and access to employment.

To achieve these objectives Task Forces aim to:

- develop an economic regeneration strategy for the area, to improve the co-ordination of different Government programmes and the activities of local authorities, the voluntary sector, and the private sector;
- stimulate economic activity in the area by pump-priming private sector involvement and investment;
- strengthen the capacity of local organisations to undertake economic development, including employment, training, education and business support activities;
- target the needs of specific disadvantaged groups, especially ethnic minorities;
- develop community services, improve the environment, and reduce crime by supporting initiatives which provide training or jobs;
- develop innovatory approaches which are capable of wider application.

Task Forces work strategically to identify local problems and opportunities. They determine their intentions and priorities (including an agreed exist strategy) through annual action plans. Since Task Forces are temporary in nature, they work with other key actors and organisations to improve the capacity of the local community to sustain the regeneration of the area after the Task Force leaves. In addition, Task Forces support projects which promote the creation and safeguarding of jobs, the provision of education and training programmes, and the direct support of businesses.

The effectiveness of the work of Task Forces is monitored internally, and evaluated externally, so that lessons learned can be applied not only to other Task Forces, but also to mainstream Government programmes.

BRADFORD

2 Legrems Terrace
Fieldhead Business Centre
Listerhills Road
Bradford BD7 1LN

Tel: 0274 725656

Contact: Gurdev Dahele

LIVERPOOL
 (GRANBY/TOXTETH)

129B Lodge Lane
Toxteth
Liverpool L8 0QF

Tel: 051 734 5289

Contact: Chris Curry

PLYMOUTH

27-29 Marlborough Street
Devonport
Plymouth PL1 4AE

Tel: 0752 606575

Contact: Richard Cohen

DERBY

6th Floor, St Peter's House
Gower Street
Derby DE1 1SB

Tel: 0332 298800

Contact: Ken Lussey

MANCHESTER
 (MOSS SIDE & HULME)

97 Princess Road
Moss Side
Manchester M14 4TH

Tel: 061 226 8899

Contact: Tony Durrant

SOUTH TYNESIDE

81 Ellison Street
Jarrow
Tyne & Wear NE32 3JU

Tel: 091 428 2000

Contact: Rosemary Gray

BIRMINGHAM
 (NEWTOWN/
 LADYWOOD)

Unit 301A
The Argent Centre
60 Frederick Street
Hockley
Birmingham B1 3HS

Tel: 021 693 4933

Contact: Godfrey Allen

BIRMINGHAM
 (EAST)

Unit 42
Waterlinks House
Richard Street
Nechells
Birmingham B7 4AA

Tel: 021 359 3141

Contact: Christine Heard

CLEVELAND
 (STOCKTON &
 THORNABY)

1st Floor
Bayheath House
Prince Regent Street
Stockton-on-Tees
Cleveland TS18 1DF

Tel: 0642 633344

Contact: Jeremy Sherlock

HULL

75 Beverley Road
Hull HU3 1XN

Tel: 0482 23939

Contact: Martin Seymour

NOTTINGHAM

2 Radford Road
Hyson Green
Nottingham
Notts NG7 5FS

Tel: 0602 421565

Contact: John Whitworth

WIRRAL

Unit 20-22
Woodside Business Park
Woodside
Birkenhead
Wirral L41 1EH

Tel: 051 650 1699

Contact: John Leaker

LONDON AREA
 (DEPTFORD)

Unit 1
City Link Court
471-473 New Cross Road
London SE14 6TA

Tel: 081 694 9276

Contact: Milton Lee

LONDON AREA
 (HACKNEY)

Unit 16b Dalston Cross
 Shopping Centre
Kingsland High Street
London E8 2LX

Tel: 071 275 7100

Contact: Graham Duncan

LONDON AREA
 (TOTTENHAM)

Unit 305
Haringey Technopark
Ashley Road
London N17 9LN

Tel: 081 880 4100

Contact: Dr Anne Gray

The Prince's Youth Business Trust

The Prince's Youth Business Trust is a UK based charity with the Prince of Wales as its president which helps young people in all parts of England, Wales and Northern Ireland to set up or develop their own small businesses. Its underlying aim is, however, greater than that. As its Mission Statement puts it 'it helps young people who would not otherwise have the opportunity to develop their self-confidence, achieve economic independence, fulfil their ambitions and contribute to the community through the medium of self-employment'.

What kinds of people do we help?
The Trust gives its support to young people between the ages of 18 and 29 (or up to 30 in the case of the disabled applicants).

The Trust is particularly concerned to help the unemployed, those from ethnic minority communities, disabled applicants, young offenders, those from decaying inner cities and areas of rural deprivation – indeed all those disadvantaged in any number of different ways, be they social, economic, environmental or physical.

Applicants must have a viable business idea, with the enthusiasm and determination to succeed. They must also have tried but failed to raise all the necessary finance – the Trust is a source of last-resort funding.

Some of the people we help have never had a job, others have lost their jobs through lay-off, illness or other causes. Some have left school barely able to read or write. Others have academic qualifications. What they all have in common is that, without the Trust's help, they would not be able to develop their entrepreneurial skills.

What help do we provide?
Financial help comes in three forms:
Loans of up to £5,000 are available on better terms than those normally obtainable from commercial sources. This money can be used for stock, equipment, or working capital. Second loans of up to £5,000 may be given for expansion to those under the age of 30 who have already received the Trust's financial support.
Grants of up to £1,500 are available to individuals, or £3,000 to groups of young people wanting to start their own business. This money may be used for tools, equipment, transport, professional fees and insurance but not for working capital, rent, rates, raw materials or stock.
Test Marketing grants up to £250 are given to applicants to test a market when there is not enough proof of a need for services they are thinking of providing.

As important as money, is the additional non-financial help which we give. This comes in three forms.
Everyone who receives the Trust's financial support is also allocated a *business adviser*, one of 5,000 volunteers, who may run their own business or may perhaps be an accountant, a marketing expert or a lawyer and is prepared to devote a few hours a month to keeping a friendly eye on the new entrepreneur.
Having received start-up support, there are many *marketing opportunities* available to the young people. Not only does the Trust stage an annual trade show of its own but it also arranges space in other exhibitions, enabling the young people to display their wares to large and appropriate audiences.

Finally, all young people receiving the Trust's support are directed to some form of *enterprise training*, both pre-start and post-start and this is provided by a wide variety of training agencies in the community.

Thanks to the generosity of supporters the Trust can also offer young entrepreneurs all manner of other services, some on a nationwide basis and others in particular areas. These include advantageous start-up insurance, free legal services, free membership of a breakdown service for motorists, free publicity and video training packages on a variety of subjects.

What kind of businesses do we help?
The range of businesses supported by the Trust covers almost every kind of activity which can be set up with the relatively small amounts of finance available and include high-tech computer concerns, window cleaners, fashion designers, mobile hairdressers, craftsmen and women of every kind working in wood, leather, glass and ceramics. There are caterers, whose output ranges from banquets to sandwiches and a world-wide selection of ethnic foods. There are artists and designers, plumbers and electricians - the list is endless.

How is it paid for?
More than 5,000 donors, large and small, have made it possible for the Trust to offer its help to large numbers of people over the years. Some of these donors are private individuals, some are local authorities, some are large corporations. Yet others are charities, trust funds and other philanthropic organisations but the largest single backer of the Trust's work is the Employment Department, a department of government which, having scrutinised the work of the Trust, decided that its value to the community was such that it warranted strong government support. It continues to monitor the success of the scheme to ensure that tax payers' money is being spent wisely and productively.

How is it run?
The Trust has only a small head office based in London and the service is delivered mainly through 38 areas throughout the country, each with an area manager supported by a board of volunteer business and other local figures who decide the allocation of funds within a pre-agreed budget.

The Trust's achievements
The key points of the Trust's work may be summarised as follows:
- In any year about 3,400 new young people are helped to set up their own businesses at a cost to the Trust of approximately £10m in loans, grants and support services.
- In the process the Trust gives advice to about 30,000 young people on their future career choices.
- Since its inception more than 22,000 young people have been helped to set up their own small enterprises.
- Independent research has shown that almost two thirds of the businesses supported by the Trust continue to trade beyond three years - better than the average for small businesses generally.
- The average net cost to the Trust of starting up a business is £2,500 - less than the cost of a year on unemployment benefit.
- 40& of new businesses are started up by women.

- Nearly 12% of the awards are made to people from ethnic minority communities.
- 5% of the awards are made to people with disabilities.
- The Trust's small core staff of 220 people is supported by a small army of 5,000 volunteers acting as area board members or business advisers.
- In the past year, participation by supported businesses in marketing events yielded income from those events of approximately £1.5m.
- The Trust's reputation for delivering a quality service in the UK is such that increasingly interest is shown from organisations from outside the UK wishing to consider similar schemes in their own environments.

HEAD OFFICE

The Prince's Youth Business Trust
5th Floor
5 Cleveland Place
London SW1Y 6JJ

Tel: 071 925 2900

Chairman: Sir Christopher Harding
Chief Executive: Jeremy White

REGIONAL ADDRESSES

Bedfordshire, Hertfordshire, Buckinghamshire

PYBT
Popefield
Hatfield Road
Smallford
St Albans
Herts AL4 0HW

Tel: 0707 271474

Contact: Bob Kirkby

Berkshire/Oxfordshire

PYBT
Berkshire Enterprise Agency
Office Suite 2
Old Town Hall
Mansion House Street
Newbury
Berks RG14 5ES

Tel: 0635 523472

Contact: Jack Williams (Area Manager Berkshire)

Tel: 0635 523472

Contact: Michael McGuire (Area Manager Oxfordshire)

Cambridgeshire

PYBT
Montagu House
81 High Street
Huntingdon
Cambs PE18 6EQ

Tel: 0480 456168

Contact: Peter Quest

Cheshire

PYBT
Business Link Ltd
62 Church Street
Runcorn
Cheshire WA7 1LD

Tel: 0928 56150

Contact: David Thornley

Cumbria

PYBT
Ingwell Hall
Westlakes Science & Technology Park
Moor Row
Cumbria CA24 3JZ

Tel: 0946 592677

Contact: Alan Hurst

Derbyshire

PYBT
Derven House
32 Friar Gate
Derby DE1 1DA

Tel: 0332 384483

Contact: Miss Catherine Rylance

Devon & Cornwall

PYBT
The OPUS Suite
6th Floor, Inter-City House
North Road Station
Plymouth PL4 6AA

Tel: 0752 251051

Contact: Andrew Smy

Essex

PYBT
c/o Essex Young Enterprise Centre
33 Nobel Square
Basildon
Essex SS13 1LT

Tel: 0268 728078

Contact: Eddie Cornwell

Gloucestershire

PYBT
Enterprise House
19/21 Brunswick Road
Gloucester G11 1HG

Tel: 0452 307028

Contact: John Harper

Hereford & Worcester

PYBT
c/o Hereford & Worcester County Council
County Buildings
St Mary's Street
Worcester WR1 1TW

Tel: Tel: 0905 765489

Contact: Miss Brenda Howson

Humberside

PYBT
Spacehire (Goole) Ltd
Rawcliffe Road
Goole
North Humberside
DN14 8JW

Tel: 0405 768229

Contacts: Derek Stevenson or Keith Taylor

PYBT
Hull Business Development Centre
34-38 Beverley Road
Hull HU3 1YE

Tel: 0482 215500

Contact: Peter Moores

Kent

PYBT
County Hall
Maidstone
Kent ME14 1XQ

Tel: 0622 694280

Contact: Ron Dunham

Lancashire

PYBT
Norweb plc
Mid-Lancashire Area
Hartingdon Road
Preston PR1 8LE

Tel: 0772 848289

Contact: Jim Lawrenson

Tel: 0772 848338

Contact: John Ollerton

Leicestershire

PYBT
Beaumont Enterprise Centre
Boston Road
Leicester LE4 1HB

Tel: 0533 341222

Contact: Laurie Anderson

Lincolnshire

PYBT
Welton House
Lime Kiln Way
Lincoln LN2 4UW

Tel: 0522 574000

Contact: Terry Gibbon

London East

PYBT
32 Cheshire Street
London E2 6EH

Tel: 071 613 1413

Contact: Ms Gill Daly

London North

PYBT
The Park Business Centre
Kilburn Park Road
London NW6 5LF

Tel: 071 625 8008/9

Contacts: Ms Sally Crombie or Terry Crimmings

London South

PYBT Centre
5 The Pavement
London SW4 0HY

Tel: 071 498 2774

Contact: Tim Lyon

Manchester

PYBT
Howard House
Fitzwarren Street
Salford
Manchester M6 5RS

Tel: 061 737 0999

Contacts: Jim Carr, Graham Hamlin or Graham Sampson

Merseyside

PYBT
Bedford House
Oxford Street
PO Box 147
Liverpool University
Liverpool L69 3BX

Tel: 051 794 3197

Contacts: Don Dunbavin, Allan Cooper or Kevin Smullen

Norfolk

PYBT
c/o Norwich & Norfolk
  Chamber of Commerce
  and Industry
112 Barrack Street
Norwich NR3 1UB

Tel: 0603 625977 x230

Contact: Mrs Anne Lavery

North East

PYBT
c/o Thorn Lighting Ltd
Spennymoor
Co Durham DL16 7HA

Tel: Tues/Thurs
0388 420042 x2504
Tel: Mon/Wed/Fri
0388 605265

Contact: Eddie Doole

PYBT
c/o St Mary's Training &
  Enterprise Centre
Oystershell Lane
Newcastle NE4 5QS

Tel: 091 230 1997

Contact: Mrs Sandra Kennedy

South Tyneside Task Force
81 Ellison Street
Jarrow
Tyne & Wear

Tel: 091 428 2000

Contact: Robert Scott

PYBT
17 High Force Road
Riverside Business Park
Middlesbrough
Cleveland TS2 1RH

Tel: 0642 245400

Contact: Mrs Jan Verrill

PYBT
East Durham Development
  Agency
4th Floor, Lee House
Peterlee
Co Durham SR8 1BB

Tel: 091 586 3366
Tel: 091 518 0205

*Contact: John Mallett
(Area Manager Wearside)*

*Contact: Richard Moffitt
(Area Manager Durham)*

Northamptonshire

PYBT
The Northamptonshire
  Training & Enterprise
  Council
Royal Pavilion
Summerhouse Pavilions
Moulton Park
Northampton NN3 1WD

Tel: 0604 671200

Contact: Brian Lawrence

Northern Ireland

PYBT
103/107 York Street
Belfast BT15 1AB

Tel: 0232 328000

Contact: Jim Toal

Nottinghamshire

PYBT
3 Broadway
Lace Market
Nottingham NG1 1PR

Tel: 0602 484619

Contact: Mrs Yvonne Ellison

PYBT
The Old Town Hall
Market Place
Mansfield
Notts NG18 1HX

Tel: 0623 23740

Contact: Keith Jackson

Shropshire

PYBT
c/o Shropshire TEC
Hazeldine House
Central Square
Telford
Shropshire TF3 4JJ

Tel: 0952 291471 x316

Contact: Clive Hopkins

Southern Counties

PYBT
IBM UK Laboratories Ltd
Hursley Park
Winchester SO21 2JN

Tel: 0962 818798

Contact: John Le Riche

PYBT
TSB Central Banking
  Operation
Trustcard House
1-9 Gloucester Place
Brighton BN1 4BE

Tel: 0273 743052

Contact: John Waskett

PYBT
25 Bourne Valley Road
Branksome
Poole BH12 1HH

Tel: 0202 768027

Contact: Chris Mulford

Staffordshire

PYBT
The Close
Lichfield WS13 7LD

Tel: 0543 253622

*Contacts: Steve Clutterbuck or
  Mrs Rika Meynell*

Suffolk

PYBT
3 Coachman's Court
Old Cattlemarket
Ipswich IP4 1CX

Tel: 0473 289500

Contact: Christopher Baber

Surrey

PYBT
c/o Self Start
1 Balfour Road
Weybridge
Surrey KT13 8HE

Tel: 0932 820241

Contact: Mrs Maureen Tory

Wales North

PYBT
Greenfield Business Centre
Greenfield
Holywell
Clwyd CH8 7QB

Tel: 0352 715471
Tel: 0352 710751

*Contacts: Michael Tierney or
  Bob Haynes*

Wales South/East

PYBT
Fourth Floor
Empire House
Mount Stuart Square
Cardiff CF1 6DN

Tel: 0222 495875

Contact: Nayland Anderson

PYBT
c/o MADE
Gadlys Enterprise Centre
Depot Road
Gadlys
Aberdare
Mid Glamorgan CF44 8DL

Tel: 0685 882515

Contact: Allan Pritchard

Wales West

PYBT
2 Coleshill Terrace
Llanelli
Dyfed SA15 3DB

Tel: 0554 758956

Contact: Rod Rodrigues

West Midlands

PYBT
85/87 Vittoria Street
Hockley
Birmingham
B1 3NU

Tel: 021 236 5095

Contact: Mrs Kathy Williams

Tel: 021 236 3902

Contact: Jack Curtin

Tel: 021 236 5081

Contact:s Gerry Scott, Ted Gray

PYBT
Dudley Metropolitan Borough
EDU, 3 St James's Road
Dudley
West Midlands
DY1 1HZ

Tel: 0384 456000

Contact: Tony Mitton

Western Counties

PYBT
The Coach House
2 Upper York Street
St Pauls
Bristol
BS2 8QN

Tel: 0272 445555

Contact: Neil Saddington

Yorkshire North

PYBT
Unit 2
Claro Court Business Centre
off Skipton Road
Harrogate
HG1 4BA

Tel: 0423 525100

Contact: Ms Angelika Sumpton or Mike Finn

Yorkshire South

PYBT
50 Christ Church Road
Doncaster DN1 2QN

Tel: 0302 367100

Contact: David Houghton

Tel: 0302 367102

Contact: Ms Doreen Jenner

PYBT
Portacabin
Meadowbank House
Meadowbank Road
Rotherham S61 2DY

Tel: 0709 559923

Contact: Ken Dutton

Yorkshire West

PYBT
Suites 8-11
Union business Centre
288 Harrogate Road
Bradford
West Yorkshire BD2 3SP

Tel: 0274 626414

Contacts: Mrs Pauline Seddon, George Ford, Peter Smith or David Fox

TUC Centres for the Unemployed

East Anglia

CAMBRIDGESHIRE

Cambridge Benefit Advice
  Centre
102 Regent Street
Cambridge CB2 1DP

Tel: 0223 353617

Peterborough Step One
  Unemployment Centre
70 The Broadway
Peterborough PE1 1SU

Tel: 0733 310107

NORFOLK

Great Yarmouth Centre for
  the Unemployed &
  Unwaged
Nelson Drill Hall
Great Yarmouth NR30 2LR

Tel: 0493 331432

SUFFOLK

Ipswich TUC Unemployed
  Workers' Centre
16 Old Foundry Road
Ipswich IP4 2DU

Tel: 0473 255652

East Midlands

DERBYSHIRE

Chesterfield Unemployed
  Workers' Centre
54 Saltergate
Chesterfield S40 1JR

Tel: 0246 231441

NORTHAMPTONSHIRE

Kettering Centre for the
  Unemployed
Unit 9A Dryland Street
Kettering NN16 0BE

Tel: 0536 81989

NUTRAC (Northampton)
Junction 7
7 Hazelwood Road
Northampton NN1 1LG

Tel: 0604 39722

NOTTINGHAMSHIRE

Ollerton Unemployed
  Workers' Centre
Old ANX Building
Dukeries Commercial Centre
Whinney Lane
Ollerton NG22 9TD

Tel: 0623 860891

North West

CHESHIRE

Chester Unemployed
  Workers' Centre
George Street
Chester CH1 3EQ

Tel: 0244 381470

Halton TUCURC
Village Hall
Main Street
Halton
Runcorn

Tel: 09285 61141

GREATER MANCHESTER

Bolton Unemployed
  Workers' Advice Centre
Socialist Club
16 Wood Street
Bolton BL1 1LD

Tel: 0204 396560

Bury Unemployed Workers'
  Centre
12 Tithebarn Street
Bury BL9 0JR

Tel: 061 797 4326

Leigh Unemployed
  Workers' Centre
1 Chester Street
Leigh WN7 1LS

Tel: 0942 608464

Manchester Trades Council
Arthur Berry Mechanics Inst
103 Princess Street
Manchester

Tameside TCU
32 Fold Avenue
Droylsden
Manchester M35 7DE

Oldham Centre for the
  Unemployed
Firth House
Firth Street
Oldham OL1 1QA

Tel: 061 652 0726

Salford TUC Centre for the
  Unemployed
84-86 Liverpool Road
Eccles
Salford M30 0WB

Tel: 061 789 2999

Wigan Unemployed
  Workers' Centre
11 New Market Street
Wigan WN1 1SE

Tel: 0942 495924

LANCASHIRE

Blackpool Unemployed
  Workers' Centre
Parish Centre
Talbot Road
Blackpool FY1 1LB

Tel: 0253 295955

Sally Marlow Community
  and Resource Centre
144-148 St James Street
Burnley

Tel: 0282 24362

Chorley Unemployed Centre
29 Granville Road
Chorley PR6 0HZ

Unemployed Open House
  Resource Centre
305 Grimshaw Street
Preston PR1 3DD

Tel: 0772 201690

Skelmersdale Unemployed
  Workers' Centre
160 Birkrig
Digmoor
Skelmersdale

Tel: 0965 21919

MERSEYSIDE

Ellesmere Port Unemployed
  Resource Centre
King Street
Ellesmere Port L65 4SZ

Tel: 051 355 0233

Huyton Unemployed Centre
Lathom Road Community
  Centre
Huyton L36 9UD

Tel: 051 489 7313

Kirkby Unemployed Centre
Westhead Avenue
Kirkby L33 0XN

Tel: 051 548 0001

MTUCURC
24 Hardman Street
Liverpool L1 9AX

Tel: 051 709 3995

Prescot & Whitston TUC &
  URC
c/o Council Officer
High Street
Prescot L34 3LH

Tel: 051 426 8262

Wallasey Unemployed
  Workers' Centre
108 Seaview Road
Wallasey L45 4LD

Tel: 051 639 8472

Bedington Unemployed
  Community Resource Centre
101 New Chester Road
New Ferry
Wirral L62 4RA

Tel: 051 645 4058/4076

Northern

CUMBRIA

Workington Centre for the
  Unemployed
Trades Hall
39 Brow Top
Workington CA14 5DP

Tel: 0900 61874

DURHAM

Darlington Unemployed
  Workers' Centre
Old Town Hall
Horsemarket
Darlington DL1 5PU

Tel: 0325 380733

Scotland

NORTHUMBERLAND

Wansbeck Community
 Initiatives Centre
Kennilworth Road
Ashington NE63 8AH

Tel: 0670 853619

Blyth Unemployed Workers'
 Centre
22-26 Bowes Street
Blyth NE24 1BD

Tel: 0670 353817

TYNE & WEAR

Newcastle & Gateshead
 Centre Against
 Unemployment
4 The Cloth Market
Newcastle

Tel: 091 232 4606

North Shields People Centre
51 Bedford Street
North Shields NE29 0AB

Tel: 091 258 7411

Sunderland TUC
 Unemployed Wkrs Centre
19 Villiers Street
Sunderland SR1 1LE

Tel: 091 514 4888

Wallsend Peoples' Centre
Ground Floor
Memorial Hall
Frank Street
Wallsend NE28 6RN

Tel: 091 263 5029

AYRSHIRE

Ayr Unemployed Workers'
 Resource Centre
61 Main Street
Ayr KA8 8BU

3 Towns Unemployed
 Workers' Centre
18-20 Countless Street
Saltcoats KA21 5RW

GRAMPIAN

Aberdeen Unemployment
 Centre
54 Frederick Street
Aberdeen AB2 1HY

Tel: 0224 640113/4452

Moray Unemployed &
 Welfare Advice Centre
Elgin Community Centre
Trinity Road
Elgin IV30 1UE

Tel: 0345 48226

HIGHLANDS

Alness Unemployed
 Workers' Centre
Site 8-4 b Industrial Estate
Alness
Wester Ross

Tel: 0349 884435

LANARKSHIRE

Hamilton Centre for Information
Leechlee Road
Hamilton ML3 6AW

LOTHIAN

Regal Resource Centre for
 the Unemployed
24-34 North Bridge Street
Bathgate EH48 4PS

Tel: 0506 630017

Dalkeith Unemployed
 Workers' Centre
10 Woodburn Road
Dalkeith EH22 2AR

Tel: 031 663 0400

Edinburgh Unemployed
 Workers' Centre
103 Broughton Street
Edinburgh EH1 3RZ

Tel: 031 557 0718

Musselburgh Unemployed
 Workers' Centre
12a Pickady Place
Edinburgh EH1

Tel: 031 556 7318

RENFREWSHIRE

Johnstone Unemployed
 Workers' Centre
Dimity Street Hall
Dimity Street
Johnstone

Tel: 0505 29434

STRATHCLYDE

Alloa Unemployed Workers'
 Centre
!Cogwheels! Centre
19 Marr Street
Alloa

Barrhead & Neilston
 Unemployed Workers'
 Centre
Main Street
Barrhead
Glasgow G78 1SW

Cambuslang Unemployed
 Workers' Centre
Morriston Street
Cambuslang
Cambuslang
Glasgow G72 7HZ

Clydebank UB40 Centre
17 Miller Street
Clydebank
Glasgow G81 1UQ

Tel: 041 952 1599

Cumberland Unemployed
 Workers' Centre
Town Centre South
Cumbernauld
Glasgow G67 1XX

Dougrie Unemployed
 Workers' Centre
Dougrie Terrace
Castlemilk
Dougrie
Glasgow G45

Tel: 041 634 7911

Drumchapel Unemployed
 Workers' Centre
6 Hecla Place
Drumchapel
Glasgow G15

East Kilbride Unemployed
 Workers' Centre
Murray Hall
Rotunda
East Kilbride

Falkirk Unemployed
 Advisory Service
Bean Road
Falkirk

Ruchill TUC Unemployed
 Workers' Centre
201 Shuna Street
Glasgow G20 9EY

Tel: 041 946 5675

Rutherglen Unemployed
 Workers' Centre
Victoria Street
Rutherglen
Glasgow G73

Gorbals TUC Unemployed
 Workers' Centre
52 Waddell Street
Gorbals
Glasgow G5 0IU

Tel: 041 429 3905

Govan TUC Unemployed
 Workers' Centre
Pearce Institute
840 Govan Road
Govan
Glasgow G51 3UT

Tel: 041 445 4263

Kilmarnock & District
 Resource Centre
43 Tichfield Street
Kilmarnock

Tel: 0563 41301

Milton Unemployed
 Workers' Centre
460 Ashgill Road
Milton
Glasgow G22 7HJ

Tel: 041 762 4879

Paisley Unemployed
 Workers' Centre
71 George Street
Paisley PA1 2JY

Tel: 041 887 8118

Renfrew Unemployed
 Workers' Centre
St James School Annexe
Albert Road
Renfrew

TAYSIDE

Perth Unemployed Workers'
 Centre
George Inn Lane
Perth

Tel: 0738 20706

South East

BEDFORDSHIRE

Bedford TUC Unemployed
 Workers' Centre
125a High Street
Bedford

Tel: 0234 364558

Luton Unemployed
 Workers' Centre
57 Guildford Street
Luton LU1 2NL

Tel: 0582 453372

BERKSHIRE

Slough Unemployed
 Workers' Centre
29 Church Street
Slough SL1 1PL

Tel: 0753 77621

EAST SUSSEX

Brighton Unemployed
    Workers' Centre
6 Tilbury Place
Brighton BN2 2GY

Tel: 0273 671213

Hastings Unemployed
    Claimants Advice Centre
Upper Central Hall
Bank Building
Hastings

Tel: 0424 428375

ESSEX

Basildon Unemployed
    Workers' Centre
Broadmayne
The Gore
Basildon SS14 2EA

Tel: 0268 289420

Braintree Unemployed
    Workers' Centre
The Annex
Old Town Hall
Braintree

Tel: 0376 465354

Harlow Trade Union
    Resource Centre
2 Wych Elm
Harlow CM20 1QP

Tel: 0279 435000

GREATER LONDON

Catford Centre for the
    Unemployed
20 Holbeach Road
Catford SE6

Tel: 081 690 8427

Hammersmith Unemployed
    Workers' Centre
190 Shepherds Bush Road
Hammersmith W6 7NL

Tel: 071 603 4278

Lambeth TUC Unemployed
    Centre
14 Thornton Street
Lambeth SW9 0BL

Tel: 071 733 51352

HAMPSHIRE

Havant TUC Unemployed
    Workers' Centre
Focus 230
230 Dunsbury Way
Leigh Park
Havant

Tel: 0705 4521134

Southampton Unemployed
    Workers' Centre
11 Porchester Place Road
Woolstone
Southampton

Tel: 0703 431435

OXFORD

Banbury Unemployed Project
Borough House
Marlborough Road
Banbury OX16 8TH

SURREY

Guildford Area Community
    Care Centre
Buryfields House
Buryfields
Guildford GU2 5AZ

Tel: 0482 33942

WEST SUSSEX

Crawley Community
    Resource Centre
17 Spencer Road
West Green
Crawley RH11 7DE

Tel: 0293 547996

Worthing Unemployed
    Centre
The Portakabin
11 North Street
Worthing BN11 1DU

Tel: 0903 231011

South West

DORSET

Advice Centre for the
    Unemployed
27 Lincoln Avenue
Springbourne
Bournemouth
Dorset BH1 4QS

Tel: 0202 309942

GLOUCESTERSHIRE

Cheltenham Centre for
    Unemployed People
Salem Baptist Church
Clarence Parade
Cheltenham

Tel: 0242 584853

Cinderford Unemployed
    Workers' Centre
Forest Road Centre
Forest Road
Cinderford

Tel: 0594 824932

Gloucester Centre for the Unemployed
4 Wellington Street
Gloucester

Tel: 0452 528964

Wales

GWENT

Caldicot Resource Centre
5a Church Road
(Old Post Office) Caldicot
Newport NP6 4BP

Tel: 0291 424704

WEA Centre for the Unemployed
Trosnant House
Trosnant Street
Pontypool NP4 8AT

Tel: 0495 764835

GWYNEDD

Holyhead TUC Unemployed Workers' Centre
Townrow House
Hill Street
Holyhead LL65 1NE

Tel: 0407 766208

MID GLAMORGAN

Treorchy Unemployed Workers' Centre
Horeb Street
Treorchy

Tel: 0443 773763

Voluntary Care for Unemployed
VCU Centre
Green Street Methodist Church
Green Street
Aberdare

Tel: 0685 872670

Community Project
1 Cross Street
Penyclaig
Rhondda CF40 1LD

Tel: 0443 438770

West Midlands

STAFFORDSHIRE

Burton Project for the Unemployed
1 George Street
Burton on Trent

Tel: 0285 515890

Cannock TUC Advice Centre
27 Park Road
Cannock WS11 1JN

Tel: 0543 579611

The Villa
c/o Millward Hall Salisbury Street
Leek ST13 5EE

Tel: 0538 371740

Lichfield Centre for the Unemployed
Well Cottage Street
Chads Road
Lichfield WS13 7ND

Stafford Unemployed Day Centre
24 Lichfield Road
Stafford ST16 2AR

Tel: 0785 223549

Tamworth Unemployed Advice Centre
(Over Sports Centre)
Corporation Street
Tamworth B79 7DN

Tel: 0827 310038

WARWICKSHIRE

Nuneaton Trades Council Unemployed Centre
Bus Station
Newtown Road
Nuneaton CV11 4HR

Tel: 0203 344515

WEST MIDLANDS

Chemsley Wood Advice and Resource Agency
k/pers Lodge
Chemsley Road
Solihull B11 4AE

Tel: 021 771 0871

Coventry Unemployed Workers' Project
Unit 15
The Arches Industrial Estate
Spon End
Coventry CV1 3JQ

Tel: 0203 714082

Halesowen Unemployed Group
181 Furnace Lane
Halesowen B63 3LU

Tel: 021 550 8117

Sandwell Unemployment &
 Community Resource Centre
324 High Street
West Bromwich
Sandwell B70 8DT

Tel: 021 525 5275

WORCESTERSHIRE

Redditch Employment
 Development Initiative
54 South Street
Redditch B98 7DQ

Tel: 0527 68583

Welfare Rights Centre
Angel Centre
Angel Place
Worcester WR1 3QN

Tel: 0905 612774

Yorkshire & Humberside

HUMBERSIDE

Riby Square Resource Centre
Riby Square
Grimsby DN31 3HA

Tel: 0472 242000

Hull Unemployed Advice
 Centre
161 High Street
Kingston on Hull
Humberside HU1 1NQ

Tel: 0482 27368/222434

SOUTH YORKSHIRE

Barnsley Unemployed
 Workers' Centre
1 Pontefract Road
Barnsley S71 1AJ

Tel: 0226 770770

Dearne Centre Against
 Unemployment
1 Barnburgh Lane
Goldthorpe
Barnsley S63 9PG

Tel: 0709 897703

Sheffield Co-ord Centre
 Against Unemployment
73 West Street
Sheffield SE1 4EQ

Tel: 0742 724866

WEST YORKSHIRE

Bradford Centre Against
 Unemployment
108 Sunbridge Road
Bradford BD1 2NF

Tel: 0274 723304

Keighley Access to Training
68b North Street
Keighley BD21 3RY

Leeds Centre for the
 Unemployed
30 York Place
Leeds

Shipley Centre Against
 Unemployment
c/o New Start
16 Otley Road
Shipley

Tel: 0274 757178

Wakefield Centre for the
 Unemployed
25 King Street
Wakefield WF1 3SR

Tel: 0924 295949

NATIONAL CONSULTATION MEETING REPRESENTATIVES

Scotland

Centre Representative

Eamon Monaghan
81-83 Carlton Place
Glasgow G20 9BJ

Tel: 041 429 4845

Organiser

Bill Speirs
Deputy Gen/Sec STUC
Middleton House
16 Woodlands Terrace
Glasgow G3 6DF

Tel: 041 332 4946

Northern

Centre Representative

Kevin Flynn
Centres Against
 Unemployment
4 The Cloth Market
Newcastle
Tyne & Wear

Tel: 091 232 4606

Organiser

Maggie Lang
CIC
Kennilworth Road
Ashington
Northumberland
NE 63 8AH

Tel: 0670 853619

North West

Centre Represenative

Kevin Coyne
MTUCURC
24 Hardman Street
Liverpool
WN8 9HB

Tel: 051 709 3995

Organiser

Les Mawdesley
74 Beech Trees
Digmoor
Skelmersdale

Yorkshire & Humberside

Centre Representative

Doug Low
SCAU
73 West Street
South Yorks SE1 4EQ

Tel: 0742 724866

Organiser

Janet Edgar
25 King Street
Wakefield
West Yorks WF1 3SR

Tel: 0924 295949

West Midlands

Centre Representative

Norman Hendry
Unemployed Centre
Bus Station
Newton Road
Warks CV11 4HR

Tel: 0203 344515

Organiser

Andrew Brown
Welfare Rights Centre
Angel Centre
Angel Place
Worcester WR1 3QN

Tel: 0905 612774

East Midlands

Centre Representative

Colin Hampton
Unemployed Workers' Centre
54 Saltergate
Chesterfield S40 1JR

Tel: 0246 231441

Organiser

Chris Preston12 Emmanuel Avenue
Nottingham NG3 6HF

Tel: 0602 501035

South West

Centre Representative

Graham Thomas
TUC Regional Office
1 Henbury Road
Westbury-on-Trymm
Bristol BS9 3HH

Tel: 0272 506425

Organiser

Diane Martin
Unemployed Centre
4 Wellington Street
Gloucester

Tel: 0452 528964

South East

Centre Representative

Neil Wycherely
Unemployed Centre
The Portakabin
11 North Street
Worthing
West Sussex BN11 1DU

Tel: 0903 231011

Organiser

John Hansford
Unemployed Workers' Centre
Broadmayne
The Gore
Basildon
Essex SS14 2EA

Tel: 0268 289420

East Anglia

Centre Representative

Sarah Sandford
Unemployed Workers' Centre
16 Foundry Road
Ipswich
Suffolk IP1 2DU

Tel: 0473 255652

Organiser

Mike Ward
Honeytop
Clay Lane
Edingthorpe
North Walsham
Norfolk

Tel: 0692 405067

Wales

Brian Maurice
WEAUWC
Trosnant House
Trosnant Street
Pontypool
Gwent NP4 8AT

Tel: 0495 764835

National

Ralph Don
TUC National Devt Officer
(Services for the
  Unemployed)
Congress House
Great Russell Street
London WC1B 3LS

Tel: 071 636 4030

National Consultative Meetings

Take place three times a year to process developments in the work of Unemployed centres, both in the regions and nationally.

Centre Representatives

Nominated by the Regional Co-ordinating Committee of Centres and report regularly to the Regional Council Co-ordinating Committee of Centres. Attends the National Consultative meeting with the Centre representative.

Organiser

Appointed by the Regional Council to co-ordinate Regional Centres and report regularly to the Regional Co-ordinating meeting of Centres. Attends the National Consultative meeting with the Centre Representative.

LIST OF REGIONAL EDUCATION STAFF

Northern

Mr Steve Grinter
Ms Isobel Holmes
Second Office Line
Swinburne House
Swinburne Street
Gateshead NE8 1AX

Tel: 091 490 0048/0054

Yorkshire/Humberside

Mr Malcolm Ball
Ms Caroline McLoughlin
Mr Paul Johnson
30 York Place
Leeds LS1 2ED

Tel: 0532 429296/440992

North Western

Ms Liz Smith
Ms Jean Bryant
Ms Barbara Taylor
Baird House
41 Merton Road
Bootle
Merseyside L20 7AP

Tel: 051 933 4403/4408

East & West Midlands

Mr Tom Cook
Ms Lorraine Reah
Ms Pat Jackson
10 Pershore Street
Birmingham B5 4HU

Tel: 021 666 6179/6184

South Eastern & East Anglia

Mr Barry Bennett
Ms Annette Bradshaw
Ms Cathy Temple
Congress House
Great Russell Street
London WC1B 3LS

Tel: 071 636 4030

Wales & South West England

Ms Julie Crew
Ms Lillian Evans
Ms Pam Hanson
1 Cathedral Road
Cardiff CF1 9SD

Tel: 0222 227449/227290

Scotland

Mr Lary Cairns
Ms Maureen McKenzie
Ms Mary Donnelly
16 Woodlands Terrace
Glasgow G3 6ED

Tel: 041 332 2045/3363

Special Needs

EMPLOYERS' FORUM ON DISABILITY

2nd Floor, Nutmeg House
60 Gainsford Street
London SE1 2NY

Tel: 071 403 3020

The Employers' Forum on Disability is the only employers' organisation exclusively concerned with the training and employment of people with disabilities. The Forum aims to improve the job prospects of people with disabilities by making it easier for employers to recruit, retain and develop them.

In practical terms it does this by:
- providing information on employer best practice, specialist services and legislation;
- promoting working partnerships between employers, service providers and disabled people;
- providing 'help line' services to member companies and encouraging employers to exchange information and examples of good practice;
- working with Government, people with disabilities and voluntary organisations to improve the quality of training and work related services available to both employers and people with disabilities.

The Forum was established because:
- it is difficult to access qualified disabled applicants using traditional methods;
- there was little, if any, business-to-business communication on the issue;
- British industry cannot afford to waste such talent and potential.

The Forum is a non-profit-making organisation, funded by its 50 member companies, and works in association with the Prince of Wales' Advisory Group on Disability.

RADAR: Royal Association for Disability and Rehabilitation

12 City Forum
250 City Road
London EC1V 8AF

Tel: 071 250 3222   Minicom: 071 250 4119

REMPLOY LTD

415 Edgware Road
Cricklewood
London NW2 6LR

Tel: 081 452 8020

Remploy Ltd, a state-funded manufacturing and services company with 9,500 severely disabled employees, provides special needs training, sheltered employment and progression to jobs in open industry and commerce.

SKILL: NATIONAL BUREAU FOR PEOPLE WITH DISABILITIES

336 Brixton Road
London SW9 7AA

Tel: 071 274 0565

Skill provides an information/advice service for people with disabilities or learning difficulties, and the professionals who work with them, on all aspects of post-16 education, training and employment. A range of other help including staff development as well as free information sheets and priced publications is available. Membership fee includes subscription to two newsletters and one journal.

RESIDENTIAL TRAINING COLLEGES

Queen Elizabeth's Training College
Leatherhead
Surrey KT22 0BN

Tel: 0372 842204

St Loye's College Foundation
Topsham Road
Exeter
Devon EX2 6EP

Tel: 0392 55428

Finchale College
Durham DH1 5RX

Tel: 091 386 2634

Portland Training College
Nottingham Road
Mansfield
Notts NG18 4TJ

Tel: 0623 792141

COLLEGES FOR THE BLIND

The Royal National College
College Road
Hereford HR1 1EB

Lincolnshire College of Agriculture and Horticulture
Riseholme Hall
Riseholme
Lincs LN2 2RG

RNIB Vocational College
Radmoor Road
Loughborough
Leics LE11 3BS

Tel: 0509 611077

Queen Alexandra College
Court Oak Road
Harbourne
Birmingham B17 9TG

Dorton College
Seal Drive
Seal
Nr Sevenoaks
Kent TN15 0AH

RNIB Redhill College
Philanthropic Road
Redhill
Surrey RH1 4DZ

COLLEGES FOR THE DEAF

RNID Court Grange Residential Training College
Abbotskerswell
Newton Abbot
Devon TQ12 5NH

Tel: 0626 53401

Doncaster College for the Deaf
Leger Way
Doncaster
South Yorks DN2 6AY

OTHER SPECIALIST ORGANISATIONS

The Fortune Centre of Riding Therapy
Avon Tyrell
Bransgore
Christchurch
Dorset BH23 8EE

Police Dependant's Trust
c/o Peter Cripps BEM
Home Office
Queen Anne's Gate
London SW1

Apex Trust

Apex Trust helps people with criminal records obtain jobs or self-employment, by providing them with the skills they need in the labour market, and by working to break down the barriers to their employment.

The trust offers basic skills and vocational training in a range of areas, tailored to the needs of the local labour markets. Some of the training courses provided include carpentry, business administration, upholstery, photography and forklift truck driving. Through job clubs, Apex Trust offers jobsearch courses, job seminars and correspondence and advice services to ex-offenders and the long-term unemployed. Eleven job clubs are currently operating around the country. Three of these are based in prisons (Manchester, Bristol and Pentonville in London) in order to improve offenders' job prospects on release.

Apex Trust has regional centres in London, Bristol, Birmingham, Coventry and Leeds offering advice and guidance as well as jobsearch support. Other assessment and guidance services are provided in Derbyshire and Northamptonshire and will soon be available in Gloucestershire.

Another aspect of the trust's work is its involvement with employers, working with them to develop their recruitment practices in relation to the recruitment and retention of ex-offender employees. This involves awareness sessions, training and consultancy to provide information and advice on the recruitment of ex-offenders. Apex Trust offers a fidelity bond insurance to employers to protect them against loss of money or property caused through the dishonest acts of employees.

Apex Trust also seeks to influence Government by highlighting the problems of crime and unemployment and the need to develop policies and resources which will promote the resettlement of offenders through employment.

West Midlands

Apex Employment Centre (Birmingham)
Northfield Complex
Tinkers Farm Road
Northfield
Birmingham B31 1RR

Tel: 021 411 2929

Contact: Tony Pearson (Regional Manager)

Sandwell Job Club
Apex Trust
Unit 107-108
Rolfe Street
Smethwick
Birmingham B66 2AR

Tel: 021 565 0433

Contact: Steve Stokes

HMP Birmingham
(Winson Green)

Tel: 021 411 2929

Contact: Marion Parker

East Midlands

Apex Employment Centre (Coventry)
36 Grafton Street
Coventry CV1 2HW

Tel: 0203 226697

Contact: Alex Adams (Regional Manager)

Hillfields Job Club
12 Victoria Street
Coventry CV1 5LZ

Tel: 0203 634544

Contact: Evadne Headley

Onley Young Offenders
  Institute
Onley
Willoughby
Rugby CV23 8AP

Tel: 0788 522022

Contact: Liz Walker

Offenders into Work Project
20 Oxford Street
Wellingborough
Northants NN8 4HY

Tel: 0933 276141
Tel: 0604 28231
  (Northampton)

Contact: Julie Knight

Careers Guidance and
  Employment Service
Apex Trust
Careers Exchange
4-8 Osmaston Road
Derby DE1 2HR

Tel: 0332 200331

Contact: Margaret James

Careers Guidance and
  Employment Service
Apex Trust
Options Centre
63 Low Pavements
Chesterfield S40 1PB

Tel: 0246 200034

Contact: Mark Raven

London

Apex Employment Centre
  (South West London)
168-170 Battersea Park Road
Wandsworth
London SW11 4ND

Tel: 071 627 3882

*Contact: Declan Lowndes
  (Regional Manager) or Sue
  Smith (Area Manager)*

Wandsworth Youth
  Employment Project
168-170 Battersea Park Road
Wandsworth
London SW11 4ND

Tel: 071 498 0235

Contact: Philip Heard

Pentonville Job Club
HMP Pentonville
Caledonian Road
London N7 8TT

Tel: 071 607 5353

Contact: Carol Parker

North

Apex Employment Centre
  (Leeds)
c/o Mount Preston Hostel
63 Clarendon Road
Leeds LS2 9NZ

Tel: 0532 444207

*Contact: Keith Nathan
  (Regional Manager) or Chris
  Gale (Employer Volunteer
  Programme)*

Morley Job Club
Albion Chambers
Albion Street
Morley
Leeds LS27

Tel: 0532 383040

Contact: Christine Mann

Seacroft Job Club
Crown House
310 North Parkway
1st Floor
Job Club Rooms
Seacroft
Leeds LS14 6LU

Tel: 0532 650287

Contact: Donald Craig

South Leeds Job Club
c/o Leeds United Football
  Association
Elland Road
Leeds
LS11 0ES

Tel: 0532 770656

Contact: Ray Thorpe

Manchester Prison Job Club
HMP Manchester
Southall Street
Manchester M60 9AH

Tel: 061 834 8626

Contact: Lorraine Clark

West & South West

Apex Employment Centre (Bristol)
The Coach House
2 Upper York Street
St Pauls
Bristol BS2 8QN

Tel: 0272 45635

Contact: Sue Thomas (Regional Manager)

Bristol Prison Job Club
HMP Bristol
19 Cambridge Road
Bristol BS7 8PS

Tel: 0272 426661

Contact: Ann Dodson

HMP Shepton Malet
HMP Dorchester
HMP The Verne
Guys Marsh Young Offenders Institution

Tel: 0272 426661

Contact: Alan Ashdale (via Bristol Centre)

Head Office

Apex Trust
St Alphage House
2 Fore Street
London EC2Y 5DA

Tel: 071 638 5931

Central Services Unit

Apex Trust
6th Floor, Bridge House
121 Smallbrook Queensway
Birmingham B5 2JP

Tel: 021 643 9266

Offender Employment Consultancy Unit

2-4 Brixton Hill Place
London SW2 1HJ

Tel: 081 671 7633

Contact: Rita O'Hare

National Association for the Care and Resettlement of Offenders (NACRO)

The National Association for the Care and Resettlement of Offenders can provide information concerning criminal offences, the police, the courts and criminal records. In nine areas of England NACRO run Youth Activities Units where young people participate in organising their own activities when previously there were very few. Projects recruit volunteers (including 15-21 year-olds) to help develop new provision. NACRO also has a number of Youth Training and Employment Training Schemes.

CENTRAL UNITS

Prisons Section:
107 Soho Hill
Birmingham B19 1AY

Tel: 021 554 2266

Youth Activities Unit:
2nd Floor
16 Darlington Street
Wolverhampton WV1 4HW

Tel: 0902 715557

New Careers Training:
Ground Floor, Island House
2 Fazeley Street
Birmingham B5 5JP

Tel: 021 643 7475

Crime and Social Policy:
1st Floor
Princess House
105-107 Princess Street
Manchester M1 6DD

Tel: 061 236 5271

Pensions:
1st Floor
16 Darlington Street
Wolverhampton WV1 4HW

Tel: 0902 21141

Units based at NACRO's Head Office:

Housing Press
Youth Crime Section
Administration and Personnel
Information
Mental Health Unit
Research Unit
Training
Development Services
Finance Offices

Head Office

169 Clapham Road
Stockwell
London SW9 0PU

Tel: 071 582 6500

NEW CAREERS TRAINING

North

Outwood Hall
Victoria Street
Outwood
Wakefield WF1 2NN

Tel: 0924 827619

Divisional Head: Jean Sowerby

Midlands & North West

567a Barlow Moor Road
Chorlton-cum-Hardy
Manchester M21 2AE

Tel: 061 861 9737

Divisional Head: Craig Harris

London & East

169 Clapham Road
London SW9 0PU

Tel: 071 582 6500

Divisional Head: Winston Castello

West

2nd Floor
Council House
2 Emlyn Walk
Kingsway Shopping Centre
Newport
Gwent NP9 1EW

Tel: 0633 350349

Divisional Head: Suzanne Fall

EMPLOYMENT POLICY

Ground Floor
Island House
2 Fazeley Street
Birmingham B5 5JP

Tel: 021 643 7475

Programme Development Officer: Anna Hraboweckyj

TRAINING CENTRES

TFW = Training for Work (Adults)
YT = Youth Training

Birmingham NCT
(TFW and YT)
21 Clifton Road
Aston
Birmingham B6 5QJ

Tel: 021 326 7788

Manager: Anne Harman

Cambridgeshire NCT
(TFW and YT)
1 Hill Street
Wisbech
Cambs PE13 1BA

Tel: 0945 587898

Manager: Linda Goult

Central London NCT
(TFW)
55-61 Brewery Road
London N7 9QH

Tel: 071 700 2919

Manager: Richard Shepherdson

Chiltern NCT
(TFW and YT)
Unit D
Cradock Road
Luton
Beds LU4 0JF

Tel: 0582 492444

Manager: Dai Davies

Cleveland NCT
(YT)
123 Marton Road
Middlesbrough
Cleveland TS1 2DU

Tel: 0642 223551

(TFW)
Hutchinson Street
Stockton on Tees
Cleveland TS18 1RW

Tel: 0642 615554

Manager: Brian Rowcroft

Crewe NCT
(TFW and YT)
Cecil House
Hightown
Crewe
Cheshire CW1 3BZ

Tel: 0270 257074

Manager: John Fuller

Croydon NCT
(TFW)
Unit A
Maides Estate
281-329 Davidson Road
Croydon
Surrey CR0 6DP

Tel: 081 656 6699

Dorset NCT
(TFW and YT)
433-437 Wimbourne Road
Winton
Bournemouth BH9 2AN

Tel: 0202 539966

Manager: Ray Glen

Durham NCT
(TFW)
The Old Junior School
Bowman Street
Darlington DL3 0HE

Tel: 0325 485746

Manager: Maurice Robson

East Derbyshire NCT
(TFW)
PO Box 10
Bolsover Enterprise Park
Station Road
Bolsover
Chesterfield S44 7BH

Tel: 0246 240014

Manager: Chris Holloway

East Midlands NCT
(TFW)
Colton House
2-4 Colton Street
Leicester LE1 1QA

Tel: 0533 532150

Manager: Bernadette Hickey

Ellesmere Port NCT
(TFW and YT)
1 Cambridge Road
Ellesmere Port
South Wirral L65 4AE

Tel: 051 355 0163

Manager: Ron Wilkie

Essex NCT
(TFW)
66b Barrack Street
Colchester
Essex CO1 2LS

Tel: 0206 798977

Manager: Vic Vant

Greater Manchester NCT
(TFW)
Onward Industries
Unit 3
Ellesmere Street
Manchester M15 4LZ

Tel: 061 834 4487

Manager: Roger Tanner
Unit Manager: Colin Ryder

Bolton
(TFW and YT)
Unit 7
No 3 Mill Lane
Halliwell Industrial Estate
Wapping Street
Bolton
Lancs BL1 8DL

Tel: 0204 494228

Manager: Roger Tanner
Unit Manager: John Seddon

Gwent NCT
(TFW and YT)
2nd Floor
Council House
2 Emlyn Walk
Kingsway Shopping Centre
Newport
Gwent NP9 1EW

Tel: 0633 256141

Manager: Ron Cole

Hampshire NCT
(TFW)
Eastpoint Community
  Centre
Burgoyne Road
Thornhill
Southampton SO2 6PB

Tel: 0703 405116

Manager: Brian Pratt

Humberside NCT
(TFW and YT)
Eagle Works
49 Cleveland Street
Witham
Hull HU8 7AU

Tel: 0482 26836

Manager: George Baker

Lambeth NCT
(YT)
Unit 16
The Windsor Centre
Windsor Grove
West Norwood
London SE27 9NT

Tel: 081 761 6242

Manager: Sam Sykes

Leeds NCT
(TFW and YT)
Midland Place
167 Water Lane
Holbeck
Leeds LS11 9UD

Tel: 0532 434684

Manager: Sue Scott

Medway NCT
(TFW)
No 1 Workbase
Historic Dockyard
Dock Street
Chatham
Kent NE4 4TE

Tel: 0634 818305

Manager: Deryck Bettridge

Merseyside NCT
(TFW)
St Vincents Training Centre
Greetham Street
Liverpool L1 5BX

Tel: 051 709 2300

Manager: Dave Roberts

Mid Glamorgan NCT
(TFW and YT)
Unit B
Abercanaid Industrial Estate
Abercanaid
Merthyr Tydfil
Mid Glamorgan CF48 1YL

Tel: 0685 370959

Manager: Barbara Corcoran

Norfolk & Waveney NCT
(TFW)
1d Hurricane Way
Airport Industrial Estate
Norwich NR6 6EW

Tel: 0603 415672

Manager: Christa McGrath

NATIONAL ASSOCIATION FOR THE CARE AND RESETTLEMENT OF OFFENDERS

North and Mid Cheshire NCT
(TFW and YT)
Fleming Industrial Estate
5-6 Fennel Street
Warrington
Cheshire WA1 2PA

Tel: 0925 53277

Manager: Fran Jackson

Northumbria NCT
(YT)
Welbeck Road
Byker Village
Newcastle upon Tyne
NE6 2DY

Tel: 091 265 8164

Manager: Mary Coyle

(TFW)
1st Floor
Lambton House
6-8 Lambton Road
Jesmond
Newcastle Upon Tyne
NE2 4RX

Tel: 091 281 5391

Manager: Sid Ramsay

Rotherham NCT
(TFW)
The Crofts Industrial Complex
Quarry Hill
Off Moorgate
Rotherham
South Yorks S60 2DN

Tel: 0709 367630

Manager: Bill Johnson

Sandwell NCT
(YT)
Lower City Road
Tividale
Warley B69 2HF

Tel: 021 520 8161

Manager: Brian Kynaston

Sheffield NCT
(TFW)
Boden House
210-216 Newhall Road
Sheffield S9 2QL

Tel: 0742 610660

Manager: Gess Boothby

(YT)
80 Headford Street
Sheffield S3 7WB

Tel: 0742 722319

Manager: Eileen Lamb

Shropshire and Clwyd NCT
(TFW and YT)
Units 18-19
Burway Trading Estate
Bromfield Road
Ludlow
Shropshire SY8 1EN

Tel: 0584 878375

Manager: Howard Taylor

South East London NCT
(TFW and YT)
Unit 165
Mellish Industrial Estate
Harrington Way
Warspite Road
London SE18 5NU

Tel: 081 854 4198

Manager: Roy Koerner

South Glamorgan NCT
(TFW and YT)
50 Holton Road
Barry
South Glamorgan CF6 6HE

Tel: 0446 745080

Manager: Will Hills

Staffordshire NCT
(TFW and ET)
2nd Floor
EMEB Buildings
59-60 Church Street
Tamworth
Staffs B79 7DF

Tel: 0827 57219

Manager: Ian Threlfall

Suffolk NCT
(TFW and YT)
Hadleigh Road Industrial Estate
Dunlop Road
Ipswich IP2 0UG

Tel: 0473 288838

Manager: Lawrie Budd

Surrey NCT
(TFW)
12 Guildford Street
Chertsey
Surrey KT16 9BQ

Tel: 0932 570888

Manager: Liz Martin

Sussex NCT
(TFW)
7 Rock Place
Brighton BN2 1PF

Tel: 0273 683318

Wakefield Focus
Outwood Hall
Victoria Street
Outwood
Wakefield WF1 2NN

Tel: 0924 821029

Manager: Sue Scott

JOB CLUBS

Central London

55-61 Brewery Road
London N7 9QH

Tel: 071 700 0089

Contact: Richard Sheperdson

Chatham

340 High Street
Rochester ME1 1BT

Tel: 0634 818465

Contact: Sue Pearce

Holloway

55-61 Brewery Road
London N7 9QH

Tel: 071 700 0367

Contact: Richard Sheperdson (Women Only)

Hull

1-7 Thomas Street
Holderness Road
Hull HU9 1EH

Tel: 0482 25287

Contact (acting): George Walker

Sheffield

Cavalry and Lancer Court
Hillsborough Barracks
639-641 Penistone Road
Sheffield S6 2GG

Tel: 0742 853565

Contact: Wendy Ducker

Tyneside

Somervyl Centre
Chesters Avenue
Longbenton
Newcastle Upon Tyne
NE12 8QP

Tel: 091 215 0034

Warrington

Fleming Industrial Estate
5-6 Fennel Street
Warrington
Cheshire WA1 2PA

Tel: 0925 413772

Contact: Barbara Sharp

Widnes

Simms Cross School
Milton Road
Widnes WA8 6NR

Tel: 051 424 9390

Contact: Barbara Wheeler

Wigan

1st Floor
17-19 King Street
Wigan WN1 1BY

Tel: 0942 824852

Contact: Veronica Hudson

Winsford

2nd Floor
Commerce House
Dene Drive
Winsford
Cheshire CW7 1AF

Tel: 0606 861090

Contact: Jack Kerevan

TRAINING AGENTS

Merseyside STA (Specialist Training Agency)
Suite 403, 4th Floor
National Bank Building
24 Fenwick Street
Liverpool L2 7NE

Tel: 051 231 1355

Manager: Val Metcalf

Sheffield Assessment and Referral Service
Boden House
210-216 Newhall Road
Sheffield S9 2QL

Tel: 0742 610660

Manager: Gess Boothby

EDUCATION

National Education Advisory Service
567a Barlow Moor Road
Chorlton-cum-Hardy
Manchester M21 2AE

Tel: 061 681 9737

Contact: Blythe Wood

Knowsley Activities Resource Centre
90 Liverpool Road
Page Moss
Liverpool L36 3RF

Tel: 051 480 3100

Contact: Brenda Burns

North London Education Project (NLEP)
16 Nevill Road N16 8SR

Tel: 071 275 8310

Contact: Monica Marshall

TRAINING & DEVELOPMENT SERVICES

169 Clapham Road
London SW9 0PU

Tel: 071 582 6500

Contact: Leon Roach

107 Soho Hill
Birmingham B19 1AY

Tel: 021 515 4711

Contact: Harlene Dandy

567a Barlow Moor Road
Chorlton-cum-Hardy
Manchester M21 2AE

Tel: 061 861 9737

Contact: Zetta Bear

29a Southgate
Bath BA1 1TP

Tel: 0225 447135

Contact: Maggie Hadley

South West Regional Drugs Training Service
29a Southgate
Bath BA1 1TP

Tel: 0225 336766

Contact: Stewart Gregory

Management Development Service
29a Southgate
Bath BA1 1TP

Tel: 0225 447135

Contact: Charmaine Storer

MENTAL HEALTH

Diversion Project
(Lambeth, Leicestershire, Havering)
169 Clapham Road
London SW9 0PU

Tel: 071 582 6500

Contact: Dermot Boyle, Deryck Browne

(Avon)
Hebron House
Sion Road
Bedminster
Bristol BS3 3BD

Tel: 0272 637634

Contact: Dave Spurgeon

Vocational Qualifications

Careers, Education and Training for Agriculture and the Countryside (CETAC)
c/o Warwickshire Careers Service
10 Northgate Street
Warwick CV34 4SR

Contact CETAC for advice and information on education, training, voluntary work, careers for people with disabilities, careers in agriculture.

Construction Industry Training Board (CITB)
Careers Advisory Service
Bircham Newton
King's Lynn
Norfolk PE31 7RH

Tel: 0553 776677

The CITB can give advice and information on all aspects of the construction industry from traditional trades used to house building and renovation such as bricklaying, scaffolding, plumbing, roofing, joinery, painting and decorating and plastering to the skills required on large construction projects.

National Vocational Qualifications (NVQs)
National Council for Vocational Qualifications
222 Euston Road
London NW1 2BZ

Tel: 071 387 9898

NVQs are work-related qualifications based on national standards set by industry and commerce, designed to reward individuals who can demonstrate competence in their performance at work. Each NVQ is made up of a number of units. Each unit is certificated separately which enables you to choose which units to study and at the pace that suits you best. It is up to you how and where you study, whether at work, at college or at home. More information on NVQs is available from schools careers services and Careers Offices (look in the phone book under 'C').

National Extension College (NEC)
18 Brooklands Avenue
Cambridge CB2 2HN

Tel: 0223 316644

The National Extension College offers a wide range of courses which people of all ages can undertake in their own time, at their own pace, and in their own way. Independent Study courses leading to GCSEs, City and Guilds, BTEC, A-levels, RSA, degrees etc. are available. 'Open Entry' to an independent study course means that you can start a course at any time. Students are given ongoing support by personal tutors – usually by letter or telephone – leading to examinations which can be taken when and if the student chooses. Full courses list available from NEC.

The Open College (OC)
Customer Services
St Paul's
781 Wilmslow Road
Didsbury
Manchester M20 8RW

Tel: 061 434 0007

The Open College offers a range of work skills courses through 'open learning'. This system allows you to study at your own pace using specially designed course books, audio and visual tapes. Open College training materials offer a valuable learning experience in their own right. However, to gain full benefit from studying our materials we recommend that you obtain tutor support from a local college or training centre. This is advisable for all learners, but it is usually essential if you wish to work towards a qualification.

Scottish Vocational Education Council (SCOTVEC)
Hanover House
24 Douglas Street
Glasgow G2 7NQ

Tel: 041 248 7900

SCOTVEC is the broad equivalent in Scotland of BTEC. They approve a wide range of work-related courses and exams suitable for part-time or full-time study depending on the type of course. They can provide information on the large range of vocational courses available throughout Scotland – what you need to get on, how long it will take, what you will gain, and where the courses are held. Information about the range of courses in your area is also available at your local Careers Office. Look in the phone book under 'Careers'.

Government Offices

Government Office for the North East

Stanegate House
2 Groat Market
Newcastle-upon-Tyne
NE1 1YN

Tel: 091 235 7201

Regional Director: Pamela Denham

Employment & Training
Eastgate House
Kings Manor
Newcastle-upon-Tyne
NE1 6PA

Tel: 091 235 7068

Director: Keith Heslop

Government Office for the North West

2010 Sunley Tower
Piccadilly Plaza
Manchester M1 4BA

Tel: 061 8383 5505/5500

Regional Director: Marianne Neville Rolfe

Employment & Training
Washington House
New Bailey Street
Manchester M3 5ER

Tel: 061 837 7038

Director : Paul Keen

Government Office for Merseyside

Room 404
Graeme House
Derby Square
Liverpool L2 7SU

Tel: 051 227 4111

Regional Director: John Stoker

Employment & Training
Floor 3
Washington House
New Bailey Street
Manchester M3 5ER

Tel: 061 837 7037

Director: Peter Houten

Government Office for Yorkshire & Humberside

7th Floor
City House
New Station Street
Leeds LS1 4JD

Tel: 0532 835200

Regional Director: Jeremy Walker

Employment & Training
Room 608
City House
New Station Street
Leeds LS1 4JD

Tel: 0532 835209

Director: Greg Dyche

Government Office for the West Midlands

77 Paradise Circus
Queensway
Birmingham B1 2DT

Tel: 021 212 5055

Regional Director: David Ritchie

Employment & Training
20th Floor
Alpha Tower
Queensway
Birmingham B1 1UR

Tel: 021 631 4203

Director: Liz Eastwood

Government Office for the East Midlands

Level 5
Cranbrook House
Cranbrook Street
Nottingham NG1 1EY

Tel: 0602 352420

Regional Director: Mark Lanyon

Employment & Training
21-33 Castlegate
Nottingham NG1 7AQ

Tel: 0602 454813

Director: Peter Lauener

Government Office for the Eastern Region

Heron House
49-53 Goldington Road
Bedford MK40 3LL

Tel: 0234 276178/276161

Regional Director: John Turner

Employment & Training
Victory House
Vision Park
Histon
Cambridge CB4 1YG

Tel: 0223 202028

Director: Celia Johnson

Government Office for London

Room P2/023
2 Marsham Street
London SW1P 3EB

Tel: 071 276 5825

Regional Director: Robin Young

Employment & Training
Room 402c
236 Grays Inn Road
London WC1X 8HL

Tel: 071 211 4186

Director: Win Harris

Government Office for the South East

Charles House
375 Kensington High Street
London W14 8QH

Tel: 071 605 9095

Regional Director: Gillian Ashmore

Employment & Training
Room 307
Telford House
Hamilton Close
Basingstoke RG21 2UZ

Tel: 0256 799266

Director: David Main

Government Office for the South West

4th Floor
The Pithay
All Saints Street
Bristol BS1 2NQ

Tel: 0272 456670

Regional Director: Brian Leonard

Employment & Training
4th Floor
The Pithay
All Saints Street
Bristol BS1 2NQ

Tel: 0272 456600

Director: Wendy Mauger

Other Useful Addresses

ACTION WORKWISE

Cutbush House
Whitehall Lane
Saham Toney
Thetford
Norfolk IP25 7HP

Tel: 0953 883390 (Helpline))

Action Workwise, initially formed as a voluntary group in 1991, was established as a charity in 1992 by a group of Christians with professional experience in employment, training and counselling. The vision throughout the development of Action Workwise has been to help those and their families who are unemployed, facing redundancy or suffering the effects of serious stress in their current employment.

The overall concern is to care for the person and to do so in a long-term way. Central to this has been the development of services in such a way as to enable people to have local access to the support provided.

Following a successful pilot scheme Action Workwise has set up eight contact points around Norfolk and Waveney. Each meets regularly to enable people to support and encourage one another and also receive practical advice and job search assistance.

Action Workwise has also developed a telephone helpline service which is available to give immediate counselling and job search assistance, and in addition to this meetings can be arranged on a one to one basis as necessary.

Action Workwise believes that each person is a unique combination of gifts, talents, experience and qualities with the potential for further development. Playing a part in encouraging this development is central to the activities of Action Workwise.

CAREER DEVELOPMENT LOANS (CDLs)

Tel: 0800 585505

Career Development Loans are available throughout Great Britain to help individuals aged 18+ pay for vocational training to improve their job prospects. You can apply for a loan of between £300 and £5,000 to cover up to 80 per cent of fees, plus other course support expenses – whether full-time, part-time or distance learning – lasting between one week and a year. The Employment Department, which runs CDLs in conjunction with Barclays, the Co-operative and Clydesdale Banks, offer successful applicants a 'repayment holiday': no repayments are required during training and for up to three months afterwards, during which time the Department pays the interest on the loan. It's then up to you to repay the loan, plus any interest.

For further details and an application form call the above number free of charge.

DRIVE FOR YOUTH (DFY)
Celmi Centre,
Llanegrym
Tywyn
Gwynedd LL36 9SA

Tel: 0654 710454

Drive For Youth specialises in 22-week courses for motivating the young, long-term unemployed, and placing them in jobs or further education. The success rate is among the highest in the country. To qualify for acceptance as a DFY Trainee, you need to have been out of work for at least one year, and have a genuine desire (however small!) to escape from the mess which you feel your life has become. Our intense career and development programme, based at our own residential centre in the Snowdonia National Park, includes: outdoor pursuits with the emphasis on working as a team, personal counselling, community projects in Britain and abroad where you help others, and in-depth careers help and guidance. Completion of the course earns you a DFY Graduate's Diploma and a City and Guilds Certificate.

For information, advice, brochure and regular newsletter, telephone Celmi Training Centre or write Freepost (no stamp necessary) to the Celmi Centre address.

Go for it!
Drive for Youth are also co-sponsors, with the Prince's Trust and the Institute for Citizenship Studies, of *Go for it! Martyn Lewis's Essential Guide to Opportunities for Young People*. This is a handbook compiled by Martyn Lewis, BBC news presenter and chairman of Drive for Youth, which provides, in over 500 pages, information on organisations offering opportunities to people who would like to involve themselves in activites from adventure challenges and volunteer work abroad to cultural exchanges and community projects. Go for it! is revised annually and is available (price £7.99) from Lennard Publishing, Windmill Cottage, Mackerye End, Harpenden, Herts AL5 5DR. Tel: 0582 715866.

FULLEMPLOY TRAINING
91 Brick Lane
London E1 6QN

Tel: 071 377 9536

A training organisation helping young people, mainly from minority ethnic communities, into work. Training is provided in many areas, and particularly in office skills and self-employment. May also be able to provide advice and access to equipment, and can provide ongoing training and counselling for new businesses.

GRANDMET TRUST

64-65 North Road
Brighton
East Sussex BN1 1YD

Tel: 0273 570170

Grand Metropolitan is one of the UK's most successful national companies. GrandMet Trust is the part of the company that gives all kinds of help to people in need. Its special concern is with deprived inner-city areas where young people in particular want jobs and homes. The Trust can boost your job chances at one of its nationwide network of training centres where you can get the very best training in a huge range of skills. But the Trust doesn't stop at occupational training. The training teams offer moral support, expert advice on the sort of job you should be trying for and all the encouragement you need when you are applying for jobs.

other GrandMet addresses:
91 Brick Lane, London E1 6QN   Tel: 071 247 5884

Suite 4, Thrift House, 12-15 Wellington Place, Hastings, East Sussex TN34 1NY
Tel: 0424 718491

Olympic House, 142 Queen Street, Glasgow G1 3BU   Tel: 041 204 4090

INSTANT MUSCLE LTD (IM)

Springside House
84 North End Road
London W14 9ES

Tel: 071 603 2604

Instant Muscle provides a free, intensive, one-to-one business counselling and enterprise training, particularly for unemployed and disadvantaged people. IM will guide you through all the skills you need, such as taxation, marketing, accounting, book-keeping, and market research until your business is fit to be up and running. It also offers a free 24-month aftercare service to all new businesses started at its centres or on board its innovative Mobile Training Units.

Other addresses:
7 Tey Road, Earls Colne, Colchester CO6 1LG   Tel: 0787 222027

Ground Floor, Carmelite House, Posterngate, Hull HU1 2JN   Tel: 0482 588202

OTHER USEFUL ADDRESSES

LIVEWIRE
Hawthorne House
Forth Banks
Newcastle Upon Tyne NE1 3SG

Tel: 091 261 5584

Livewire can provide information, advice and support to young people who are thinking of starting up in business, and to those already established in business. Sponsored by Shell (UK) Limited, there are three key elements to the Livewire service:
- The Enquiry and Link Up Service: young people anywhere in the UK can be linked to appropriate local advice and support on starting up in business.
- The Business Start Up Awards: £175,000 worth of cash awards and help in kind is available through this awards competition in a series of county, regional, national and UK events. It is based on submission of a business plan for a new business and awards are made by independent judging panels.
- Business Growth Challenge: a management development programme for young owner managers of established businesses.

Regional addresses:
Livewire England, The Fishergate Centre, 4 Fishergate, York YO1 4AB
Tel: 0904 613696

Livewire Scotland, Romano House, 43 Station Road, Corstorphine, Edinburgh EH12 7AF
Tel: 031 334 9876

Livewire Northern Ireland, Young Business Centre, 103-107 York Street, Belfast BT15 1AB
Tel: 0232 328000

Livewire Cymru, Greenfield Valley Enterprise Centre, Greenfield Road, Greenfield, Holywell, Clwyd CH8 7QB Tel: 0352 710199

THE PRINCE'S SCOTTISH YOUTH BUSINESS TRUST
6th Floor
Mercantile Chambers
53 Bothwell Street
Glasgow G2 6TS

Tel: 041 248 4999

The aim of the Prince's Scottish Business Trust is to provide seedcorn finance and professional support to young people in Scotland, aged 18–25, whoever they are and wherever they come from, so that they can set up and continue to run their own businesses. The Trust has particular concern for the disadvantaged. Applicants must have a viable business idea, be unable to raise all or part of the finance necessary to set up their own business and be able to work at their business full-time. The Trust offers free professional advice; access to pre-start training; loans of up to £5,000 over a period of up to five years at 4 per cent interest; grants of up to £1,000; assistance from professional advisers for a minimum period of two years.

URBAN DEVELOPMENT CORPORATIONS

An Urban Development Corporation is a public body established to secure the regeneration of its designated inner city area. It is equipped with statutory powers and is primarily funded by Government grant. English UDCs are the development control authorities for their areas. Each UDC is run by a board whose members are appointed for the wide range of talents and experience each can offer. There are 12 UDCs throughout England and one in Wales.

A UDC aims to bring land and buildings into effective use, to encourage the development of existing and new industry and commerce, to create an attractive environment and to ensure that housing and social facilities are available to encourage people to live and work in the area. A UDC has powers to acquire, reclaim, service and dispose of land; it may assist environmental improvement and the restoration of existing buildings; it can help with the provision of health, education, training and community facilities, and may assist the voluntary sector. UDCs administer city grants within their areas, and can also provide grants under the inner urban areas act to assist industry.

Contact Department of the Environment on: 071 276 4603
Contact Welsh Office for Cardiff Bay DC on: 0222 823958

A GLOSSARY OF ABBREVIATIONS

ACCA	Association of Certified and Chartered Accountants
ACE	Action for Community Employment
BEP	Business Enterprise Programme
BES	Business Enterprise Scheme
BITC	Business in the Community
BTEC	Business and Technology Education Council
CDL	Career Development Loan
CETAC	Careers Education and Training for Agriculture and the Countryside
CITB	Construction Industry Training Board
CV	Curriculum Vitae (personal details, eductaion and job history)
DAS	Disablement Advisory Service
DFY	Drive for Youth
DRO	Disablement Resettlement Officer
DSS	Department of Social Security
DTI	Department of Trade and Industry
DTP	Desktop Publishing
EAS	Employment Action Scheme
EBP	Education Business Partnership
ERC	Employment Rehabilitaion Centre
FIN	Friends in Need
GCSE	General Certificate of Secondary Education
HND	Higher National Diploma
IM	Instant Muscle
IiP	Investors in People
IT	Information Technology
LEAP	Linked Accommadation and Employment Project
LEC	Local Enterprise Company
MAPS	Machine Assembly and Processing Skills
NACRO	National Association for the Care and Resettlement of Offenders
NCT	New Careers Training
NEC	National Extension College
OC	The Open College
NVQ	National Vocational Qualification
PYBT	Prince's Youth Business Trust
PSYBT	Prince's Scottish Youth Business Trust
RADAR	Royal Association for Disability and Rehabilitation
RSA	Royal Society of Arts
SCOTVEC	Scottish Vocational Education Council
TEC	Training and Enterprise Council
TFW	Training for Work
TUC	Trades Union Congress
UDC	Urban Development Corporation
YE	Young Enterprise
YT	Youth Training